CAMBRIDGE TEXTS IN THE HISTORY
OF PHILOSOPHY

IMMANUEL KANT
Anthropology from a Pragmatic Point of View

CAMBRIDGE TEXTS IN THE HISTORY OF PHILOSOPHY

Series editors

KARL AMERIKS
Professor of Philosophy at the University of Notre Dame

DESMOND M. CLARKE
Professor of Philosophy at University College Cork

The main objective of Cambridge Texts in the History of Philosophy is to expand the range, variety and quality of texts in the history of philosophy which are available in English. The series includes texts by familiar names (such as Descartes and Kant) and also by less well-known authors. Wherever possible, texts are published in complete and unabridged form, and translations are specially commissioned for the series. Each volume contains a critical introduction together with a guide to further reading and any necessary glossaries and textual apparatus. The volumes are designed for student use at undergraduate and postgraduate level and will be of interest not only to students of philosophy, but also to a wider audience of readers in the history of science, the history of theology and the history of ideas.

For a list of titles published in the series, please see end of book.

IMMANUEL KANT

Anthropology from a Pragmatic Point of View

TRANSLATED AND EDITED BY
ROBERT B. LOUDEN
University of Southern Maine

WITH AN INTRODUCTION BY
MANFRED KUEHN
Boston University

CAMBRIDGE
UNIVERSITY PRESS

CAMBRIDGE UNIVERSITY PRESS
Cambridge, New York, Melbourne, Madrid, Cape Town, Singapore, São Paulo,
Delhi, Dubai, Tokyo

Cambridge Univesity Press
The Edinburgh Building, Cambridge CB2 8RU, UK

Published in the United States of America by Cambridge University Press, New York

www.cambridge.org
Information on this title: www.cambridge.org/9780521671651

© Cambridge University Press 2006

First published 2006
Third printing 2010

Printed in the United Kingdom at the University Press, Cambridge

A catalogue record for this publication is available from the British Library

ISBN-13 978-0-521-85556-3 hardback
ISBN-13 978-0-521-67165-1 paperback

Contents

Introduction

The origins of *Anthropology from a Pragmatic Point of View*

Anthropology as understood today is a discipline concerned with the study of the physical, cultural, social, and linguistic development of human beings from prehistoric times to the present. It is a relatively new phenomenon, which came into its own only during the early nineteenth century. Its roots, however, can be traced back to the last third of the eighteenth century. Voltaire, Montesquieu, and Condorcet in France, Lord Kames, Lord Monboddo, and William Robertson in Scotland, and Immanuel Kant, Georg Forster, Christoph Meiners, and Ernst Platner in Germany were among the most important early contributors to this new field of study. It grew ultimately from a fundamental concern of the European Enlightenment, being conceived as an alternative to the theological understanding of the nature of man and born of the belief that the proper study of mankind is man, not God.

Kant fully subscribed to this Enlightenment conception, even though, as we shall also see, he did not want to deny that theological concerns were very important for the proper understanding of human nature. He was, in any case, one of the first thinkers ever to lecture on anthropology as an independent academic discipline at university level. Though the *Anthropology from a Pragmatic Point of View* was published at the end of the eighteenth century in 1798, he had by then already lectured on it for twenty-five years. Indeed, his first lectures predate Kames's *Sketches of the History of Man* of 1774 by more than a year. And his concern with anthropological topics is already evident in his first course on physical geography, which he offered in the summer of 1756. Kant's *Anthropology* is thus an important document in the history of this discipline. When he first offered a course explicitly dedicated to anthropology in the winter semester of 1772–3, he had already thought about its contents for some time. On the other hand, there was not much precedent for it, and he had every right to feel like a pioneer.

Kant's conception of anthropology was in many ways rather different from the way it is conceived of today. From the very beginning he viewed it not just as an empirical or descriptive discipline, but also as a useful tool for the moral and cultural improvement of his students. Thus he wrote toward the end of 1773 to his former student Marcus Herz – someone who he knew had a great interest in the subject – that he was offering for the second time a *colloquium privatum* on anthropology, and that he was planning to transform this subject into a proper academic discipline. This plan was, he said, "unique," for the main purpose of the new course of studies was to

> introduce the sources of all the sciences that are concerned with morals, with the ability of commerce, and the method of educating and ruling human beings, or all that is practical. In this discipline I will, then, be more concerned to seek out the phenomena and their laws than the first principles of the possibility of *modifying* human nature itself. (10, p. 145)[1]

His goal was twofold: (1) a theoretical investigation of the source of all practical philosophy, its phenomena, and its laws, and (2) a doctrine that was itself practical in teaching the rudiments of prudence, wisdom, or knowledge of the world.

Kant went on to assure Herz that the contents of the course would be enjoyable rather than dry and academic. Drawing an explicit parallel to his lectures on physical geography, he characterized it as an "observational doctrine" (*Beobachtungslehre*) that he intended to develop in such a way that it would serve his students in later life. He also felt it necessary to point out explicitly that he would not address such "subtle" but

---

[1] All references in the text refer to Immanuel Kant, *Gesammelte Schriften*, vols. 1–22, ed. Preussische Akademie der Wissenschaften, vol. 23, Deutsche Akademie der Wissenschaften zu Berlin, from vol. 24, Akademie der Wissenschaften zu Göttingen (Berlin: Walter de Gruyter, 1907–) (AA). Since the Cambridge edition of Kant's works includes the pagination of the Akademie edition, they can also be checked in the English translation.

"eternally futile" questions or philosophical problems as the mind–body relation. The lectures should be "popular" both in the sense that the subject matter was treated "popularly" and in the sense that the lectures should attract many students as (paying) customers.

It should also be obvious that the plan for this new academic discipline, concerned with the sources of all that is practical, moral, or has to do with human interaction, is connected with the attempts of other contemporaries in this direction. Indeed, Herz's review of Ernst Platner's newly published *Anthropology for Physicians and Philosophers* provided the immediate occasion for his remarks in the letter. And there is other evidence which shows how closely he was attuned to the developments having to do with the newly emerging study of anthropological issues, and how he consciously chose a different direction from that taken by his contemporaries.[2]

It appears by all accounts that he was successful in his attempt to be popular. While his lectures on metaphysics were considered very difficult by most of his students, the lectures on anthropology (like the lecture on physical geography) were among the best attended he ever offered, even though they were not free like the lectures on metaphysics.[3] It is therefore not surprising that Kant felt at the end of his teaching career that the notes for these lectures that he had prepared over the years deserved to be published in their own right as a textbook on which other professors could base their lectures, just as he had relied for so many years on Alexander Gottlieb Baumgarten's *Metaphysica* in his lectures on metaphysics and anthropology. He must have taken this decision during the early summer of 1798.[4] Johann Friedrich Abegg, who visited Königsberg in 1798, wrote on June 1 in his travel journal that earlier that morning Kant had corrected his *Anthropology*, as this work would

[2] In the *Allgemeine deutsche Bibliothek* 20 (1773), pp. 25–51. Platner plays some role in Kant's lectures on anthropology as well. See AA25, p. 83 and the index at p. 1082. Kant contrasts his own conception to that of Platner and other "philosophical *medici*," who speculate about things that he is not going to cover. Herz's review constitutes the occasion for Kant's remarks. It also suggests that Kant and Herz had talked about anthropological concerns earlier. For a discussion of the different "programs" for the new discipline of anthropology, see John Zammito, *Kant, Herder, and the Birth of Anthropology* (Chicago: Chicago University Press, 2002), pp. 237–253. Kant was obviously aware of most, if not all, of these developments.

[3] See Manfred Kuehn, *Immanuel Kant: A Biography* (Cambridge: Cambridge University Press, 2001); see also Reinhard Brandt and Werner Stark, "Introduction" to vol. 25 of the Akademie edition.

[4] See also Kuehn, *Immanuel Kant*, pp. 391f.

now be published as well. We do not know whether these "corrections" were revisions of Kant's own manuscript, a version of which is extant in the Library of the University of Rostock, or whether he was working on the proof sheets sent by the printer. It seems likely that it was the former, as Kant was not in the habit of going carefully through the proofs himself.[5]

Two thousand copies of the *Anthropology* were printed – more than any of his other works.[6] The book seems to have sold well, for just two years later a second edition appeared. But it was not a critical success. Apart from Friedrich Schleiermacher's entirely negative review in the *Athenäum*, a journal devoted to the cause of Romanticism and highly critical of many of the ideals of the Enlightenment, there was no discussion.[7] Not surprisingly, Schleiermacher's review was not designed to create a need for such a discussion. It begins as follows: "A summary of this book could not be much more than a collection of trivial matters. If, on the other hand, it were intended to give a sketch of the plan and its execution ... it would necessarily give a distinct picture of the most peculiar confusion."

These claims are not entirely unfair. Kant's *Anthropology from a Pragmatic Point of View* is a difficult book, and it is difficult precisely because it reveals a certain tension between particular factual observations and assertions that seem homely and trivial, if not downright false, and somewhat muted suggestions that the whole enterprise is highly significant without a clear indication of what precisely makes it so significant. On the one hand, it is described by Kant as a "manual" or *Handbuch* concerned with the down-to-earth task of providing the rudiments of "knowledge of the world" to students in their early teens, the implication being that it is not just based on his own lectures but it could and should be used by other university teachers as the basis for their own lectures on this subject. On the other hand, the book ends with the assertion that

---

[5] It is catalogued as "Mss Var. 32." Its contents are, of course, taken into consideration in this translation.

[6] See Friedrich Wilhelm Schubert, *Immanuel Kant's Biographie zum grossen Theil nach handschriftlichen Nachrichten dargestellt* (Leipzig: Leopold Voss, 1842), p. 154. Schubert also claims that this was the largest printing of all of Kant's works.

[7] *Athenäum* 2 (1799), pp. 300–306. See Friedrich Schleiermacher, *Kritische Gesamtausgabe* (Berlin: Walter de Gruyter, 1984), vol. 5.1, pp. 366–369. All other quotations from Schleiermacher are from this review.

> the admission that this race of terrestrial rational beings deserve no honorable place among the (to us unknown) other rational beings . . . [precisely] reveals a moral disposition in us, an innate demand of reason, to also work against this propensity. So it presents the human species not as evil, but as a species of rational being that strives among obstacles to rise out of evil in constant progress toward the good. (6, pp. 332f.)

It thus presents itself as a contribution to the political task of the progressive organization of the *citizens of the earth*, "united by cosmo-political bonds," and aligns itself with the earlier essays on history and the *Religion Within the Limits of Reason Alone*.

It is this peculiar combination of the homely and the sublime that makes for both the charm and the difficulty of the book. And the question is how Kant can hope to perform in one book two tasks that are ultimately quite different. The *Anthropology* clearly belongs among the small group of works which were conceived as textbooks for introductory courses given at university level. In this respect it is similar to the *Logic*, the *Physical Geography*, and the *Pedagogy*, which were edited by Benjamin Jäsche and Friedrich Theodor Rink on the basis of Kant's notes. What makes the *Anthropology* different from those works, however, is that Kant himself edited it; but he clearly had some difficulties in doing so. We may also ask whether a textbook should be measured by the same criteria as an original contribution to philosophical discussion. How precisely can the *Anthropology from a Pragmatic Point of View* be compared with the *Critique of Pure Reason*, the *Critique of Practical Reason*, or the *Metaphysics of Morals*, for instance? Does the published *Anthropology* give the best possible expression of Kant's fundamental intention?

The philosophical nature of the work

Some philosophical scholars have argued not only that the *Anthropology* does not express Kant's deepest philosophical concerns, but that it is irrelevant to them. Some have even argued that it actually contradicts them. But there are also passages in Kant's work that suggest the opposite view, and so it has also been argued that the *Anthropology* is of central importance to the entire Kantian project. Support for this view can be found in a passage from Kant's *Logic* that summarizes "philosophy in the cosmopolitan sense of the word" in four questions:

What can I know?
What should I do?
What may I hope for?
What is a human being?

The first question is answered in *metaphysics*, the second in *morals*, the third in *religion* and the fourth in *anthropology*.   (9, p. 25)

Kant then claims that all this can be included within anthropology because the four questions "relate to anthropology."[8] Since the first three questions also appear in the *Critique of Pure Reason* as a summary of all the "interests of my reason" (no matter whether they are speculative or practical), one may indeed argue that the *Critique of Pure Reason* and the *Critique of Practical Reason* need a foundation in a critical anthropology that uncovers the very essence of humans as finite beings and constitutes a fundamental ontology.[9] This has been argued most famously by Martin Heidegger, who claimed that Kant's philosophical enterprise could be summed up as the attempt to lay the ground of metaphysics by revealing its "inner possibility" in "the subjectivity of the human subject." Kant's "question as to the essence of metaphysics is the question concerning the unity of the basic faculties of the human 'mind.' The Kantian ground-laying yields [this conclusion]: the grounding of metaphysics is a questioning with regard to the human being, i.e., Anthropology."[10] However interesting such a conception of a Kantian anthropology may be in its own right, it is clearly not the one Kant himself envisaged. As we have just seen, his anthropology is an Anthropology from a Pragmatic Point of View, perhaps even an "Anthropology from a Cosmopolitan Point of View," but it is most definitely not an "Anthropology from an Ontological (or Metaphysical) Point of View." Because of this, it does not belong to the very center of Kant's philosophical concerns. It is a "pragmatic" enterprise: peripheral, but important for the application of his thought. We can see this also from the characterization of the three

---

[8] See also *Metaphysik Pölitz*, 28.2.1, pp. 33f., where he makes the same claim about "philosophy *in sensu cosmopolitico*." Compare also the letter to Stäudlin of May 4, 1793 (10, p. 429).

[9] Immanuel Kant, *Critique of Pure Reason*, trans. Paul Guyer and Allen W. Wood (Cambridge: Cambridge University Press, 1998), A 804f./B 833f. (from now on, all references preceded by "A" and/or "B" are to this edition). In this context Kant does not characterize the three questions as anthropological and claims that they exhaust all interests of reason.

[10] Martin Heidegger, *Kant and the Problem of Metaphysics*, 5th, enlarged edition, trans. Richard Taft (Bloomington and Indianapolis: Indiana University Press, 1997), p. 144.

questions that make up the question "What is a human being?" as questions that are asked "in the cosmopolitan sense" of the philosophy, not in a transcendental sense. They are important when we are concerned with the application of philosophical principles, or indeed when we talk about the role or function which philosophical principles can assume in the world. They are not important when we come to talk about the foundation or justification of such philosophical principles.

This is not just an argument against the fundamental importance of anthropology to Kant's enterprise; it is also an argument against anyone who would claim that Kant's anthropological considerations are so peripheral that they would not be missed if they had not survived. I would argue that they would be missed in so far as they add a certain dimension to the "cosmopolitical sense" of Kant's entire philosophy. Even if the published *Anthropology* were to express this dimension only imperfectly, it might give significant clues about how we should or should not conceive of it.

As Schleiermacher pointed out, neither the contents nor the overall plan of the book are easily summarized. Kant defines anthropology as "a doctrine of the knowledge of the human being, systematically formulated," and he claims that such a doctrine can take (only?) two forms. It is either physiological or pragmatic. The first "concerns the investigation of what nature makes of the human being," the second "the investigation of what he as a free acting being makes of himself, or can and should make of himself." Physical anthropology may be observational or speculative. The latter is absolutely useless, or, as Kant puts it, "a pure waste of time." But even the former is not useful because "the observer" must let "nature run its course" without being able to change it (7, p. 119). Added to this, both introspection and the observation of others encounter difficulties that are "inherent in human nature itself" (7, p. 119). We can observe neither ourselves as we "really" are nor others as they "really" are because the very act of observing changes the behavior that is observed. Dissimulation and habit interfere. So it is difficult to grasp what human nature actually is, and it is better to concentrate on what humans as free acting beings make of themselves and what they can and should make of themselves. That is the reason why Kant does not want to discuss issues of physical anthropology in the context of a pragmatic anthropology, even though he was very interested in such issues and wrote articles on topics of race and the physical nature of human beings in learned and popular journals.

The structure of the *Anthropology*

The work itself is divided into two parts, namely the "Anthropological Didactic" and the "Anthropological Characteristic." The first of these parts deals with what Kant would have called "empirical psychology," but it is perhaps better characterized as his "faculty psychology" or his classificatory scheme for mental "phenomena" as more or less static tendencies and faculties. It consists of three "books," the first of which deals with the "cognitive faculty," i.e., with such things as inner sense, the five external senses, the understanding, the voluntary and involuntary imagination, fantasy, and memory, as well as with many things closely connected with it. One might say that he deals in this book with those matters that form the psychological background of the first *Critique*. Book II deals with the "feeling of pleasure and displeasure," or with matters related to taste, while Book III is concerned with the "faculty of desire," or with the psychological background of moral philosophy or ethics. Indeed, paragraphs 73–88 must be carefully read by anyone concerned with Kant's moral philosophy, if only because one finds there clear definitions of the psychological vocabulary which is relevant to his moral theory. This first part of the *Anthropology* seems to be most closely connected with the first origins of the lectures on anthropology, since Kant first conceived of anthropology as a replacement and expansion of his discussion of empirical psychology in the lectures on metaphysics, and this part deals with psychological issues. That the metaphysical origin of the lectures remained important is shown by the fact that Kant continued to use as a basis for his lectures on anthropology the *Psychologia Empirica*, i.e., the third part of Baumgarten's *Metaphysica*. Previously he had used this part in the lectures on metaphysics to introduce psychological issues to his students; now he used it less in his lectures on metaphysics and more in his lectures on anthropology. As late as 1778 he explicitly pointed out to Herz that after having begun lecturing on anthropology he no longer treated empirical psychology extensively in his lectures on metaphysics, which suggests that he thought of anthropology as a replacement for that part of the lectures on metaphysics (10, p. 181).[11]

---

[11] Even the word "anthropology" seems to come from Baumgarten, who speaks in the section on rational psychology of his *Metaphysica* of "*anthropologia philosophica*," "*anthropologia mathematica*," "*anthroponomia*," and "*anthropognosia*" (17, p. 142). Kant himself contrasts "anthropology"

Part II bears the subtitle "On the Way of Cognizing the Interior of the Human Being from the Exterior," but Kant also seems to have considered the subtitle "By What is the Peculiarity of Each Human Being to be Cognized?" and thought that the first part could be described as the doctrine of the elements of anthropology and the second as the doctrine of method (7, 299). A similar division can be found in the *Critique of Pure Reason*, the *Critique of Practical Reason*, the *Critique of Judgment*, and the *Metaphysics of Morals*. If we were to take this seriously, then Part II would amount to an "estimate of the building materials" and the determination of their suitability "for what sort of edifice, with what height and strength" we may build (A707/B735). The second part would have less to do with the materials than with the blueprint for the building (or discipline). And this blueprint is a plan for the future of the human species. Unfortunately, the "Doctrine of Method" is even shorter in the *Anthropology* than it is in the other works mentioned above.

It is the notion of "character" which is of central importance for Kant and which plays a key role in the second part of the *Anthropology*. He deals with the character of individual human beings, the character of the sexes, the character of different peoples or nations and of different races, and ultimately the character of the human species. This part of the book has little to do with Baumgarten's *Psychologia Empirica*, but rather deals with issues relating to the final goal of human beings (*die Bestimmung des Menschen*). As such it belongs in the context of discussions by Thomas Abbt, Moses Mendelssohn, and Johann Joachim Spalding on the one hand, and of Kant's own writings on the philosophy of history and theology on the other. Repeating claims he defended in those writings, Kant says that ultimate moral achievement cannot be expected of any one individual, but only of the species as a whole. Morality and anthropology thus lead to political and historical considerations, to questions about what the ultimate destination of the human race is.

Furthermore, anthropology is for Kant a description not of human beings but of human nature. Even when we speak of the nature of the individual or of the "character" of an individual, we do not speak of his particular choices, but about his principles or maxims. An individual's nature cannot be reduced to that individual's choices. Indeed, the

with "anthroponomy" at one point in his *Metaphysics of Morals* of 1798, saying that the former is merely empirical and cannot count as evidence against the latter, which "is established by the absolute power of the law-giving reason" (6, p. 406).

expression "an individual's human nature" would be an oxymoron for Kant (and for others besides him). But none of this is explicitly argued for or fully developed. Kant seems to want to refer his readers to the earlier essays and books which he had written about these subjects.

The *Anthropology from a Pragmatic Point of View* reads like a work in progress, not like a finished product. And it may just be that old age – Kant had to stop lecturing in 1797, one year before the publication of the *Anthropology* – prevented a development that might have given rise to the "complete anthropology" that he had envisaged in the *Critique of Pure Reason* as being the true home of "empirical psychology" after it had been "banned from metaphysics." This complete anthropology would have been "the pendant to the empirical doctrine of nature." Unfortunately, Kant did not live long enough for this to happen, but we are fortunate to have access to other materials. The intentions and conclusions of these materials can be properly understood only if their background in Kant's teaching is taken into account, which is why it is important to say something about the relation of the published text to the lecture notes by Kant and his students. The notes show how Kant's thoughts on anthropology developed, and how this discipline relates to his philosophical system as a whole.

The relation of the published *Anthropology* to the lectures on anthropology

In the early 1770s Kant began to deliver his lectures on empirical psychology – which until then had formed part of his course on metaphysics – in a new course, entitled "anthropology." The reason for this appears to be quite simple, and has to do with a radical change of his views on metaphysics in the Inaugural Dissertation of 1770. One of the most important new doctrines in this work was the radical distinction between "intellect" on the one hand and "sensation" on the other. Kant argued that these two faculties are independent and irreducible. They constitute sources of entirely different kinds of knowledge, namely the intellectual and the sensible. Because of this, he argued, we must assume two worlds, namely a *mundus intelligibilis* and a *mundus sensibilis*. Each of these worlds obeys its own principles and exhibits forms peculiar to it, and each of them has its own objects: "The object of sensibility is the sensible, that which contains nothing but what is to be cognized through

xvi

the intelligence is intelligible. In the schools of the ancients the former was called a *phenomenon* and the latter a *noumenon*" (2, p. 393). Phenomena are "representations of things *as they appear*," and *noumena* are "representations of things *as they are*" (2, p. 392). It would therefore be a serious mistake in his view if we were to regard sensibility as nothing but confused thinking, or thinking as nothing but distinct sensation (as Leibniz, Wolff, and most other moderns have done). To quote Kant's own words, "the sensitive is poorly defined as that which is *more confusedly* cognized, and that which belongs to the understanding as that of which there is a *distinct* cognition. For these are only logical distinctions which *do not touch* at all the things *given*, which underlie every logical distinction" (2, p. 395). Even if sensitive knowledge presupposes the use of certain concepts of the understanding, this use of the understanding is merely logical or formal. It is of secondary importance compared with the real use of the understanding by means of which "the concepts themselves, whether of things, or relations, *are given*" (2, p. 393).

Eleven years later, in his first *Critique*, Kant accused Leibniz and Locke in particular of having committed this error, saying that the former had "intellectualised appearances," while the latter had "sensualised all concepts of the understanding" (A271/B327). In the Dissertation, however, he singles out for special criticism "the illustrious Wolff," who "has, by this distinction between what is sensitive and what belongs to the understanding, a distinction which for him is only logical, completely abolished, to the great detriment of philosophy, the noblest of the enterprises of antiquity, the determining of the *character of phenomena and noumena . . .*" (2, p. 394).

This implies that "empirical psychology belongs just as little to metaphysics as empirical physics" (28, p. 223). Metaphysics deals with "*conceptus puri* or concepts which are either given purely through reason or whose knowledge has at least its source within human knowledge," whereas anthropology has to do with empirical concepts only. Even if these empirical concepts are to a large extent based on inner sense, they do not afford any rational knowledge of man (25, p. 243). His first lecture course was therefore entitled "Natural Knowledge of Man." Since the sharp division of reason and sensibility that characterizes the first lecture on anthropology and the excision of empirical psychology from metaphysics can be traced back to the changes that characterize the Inaugural Dissertation, we may also claim that these changes lead ultimately to

Kant's conception of anthropology as an empirical discipline of the knowledge of human beings.

It is well known that this new thesis of the radical discontinuity of sensibility and intellect is closely connected with another doctrine that makes its first appearance in this work, namely that of the subjectivity of space and time. What is generally overlooked, however, is that Kant's rejection of the continuity thesis also had immediate consequences for moral philosophy. As Kant himself points out in the Dissertation, the pure principles of the understanding or reason allow us to have the concept of an important "paradigm." This paradigm is "noumenal perfection," and "noumenal perfection" has two senses: it is "perfection either in the theoretical sense or in the practical sense. In the former sense it is the Supreme Being, GOD; in the latter sense it is MORAL PERFECTION. *Moral philosophy*, therefore, in so far as it furnishes the first *principles of judgment*, is cognized by the pure understanding and belongs only to pure philosophy" (2, p. 396). Moral principles are intellectual and therefore cannot be reduced to sensibility. Pure moral metaphysics has just as little place for sensible concepts as has pure speculative metaphysics.

Kant argued from this time on that as well as metaphysics in the theoretical sense and metaphysics in the practical sense, we need an empirical physics, i.e., an empirical discipline concerned with the investigation of material objects, and an empirical psychology or anthropology. In the Inaugural Dissertation he believed that reason could secure the foundation of a universal moral theory in knowledge of things as they are in themselves, and he believed that we could obtain this knowledge through reason. It is thus not surprising that in the letter in which he first told Herz of his new lecture, he also speaks of moral philosophy, saying that the concept of "reality" should not be applied to morals because it

> is so important in the highest abstractions of speculative reason and so empty when applied to the practical. For this concept is transcendental, whereas the highest practical elements are pleasure and displeasure, which are empirical, and their object may thus be anything at all. Now, a mere pure concept of the understanding cannot state the laws or prescriptions for the objects of pleasure and displeasure, since the pure concept is entirely undetermined in regard to objects of sense experience. The highest ground of morality must not simply be inferred from the pleasant; it must itself be

xviii

> pleasing in the highest degree. For it is no mere speculative idea; it must have the power to move. Therefore, though the highest ground of morality is intellectual, it must nevertheless have a direct relation to the primary springs of the will. (10, p. 145)

Even though Kant believed in 1773 that "the highest ground of morality is intellectual," he also thought that it needed "primary springs of the will," which were *not* intellectual. He takes this position also in the lectures on ethics delivered during the summer of 1775. We need both moral motivations and purely intellectual principles to judge whether an action is moral. There must be a *principium diiudicationis* that is objective, and a subjective principle that motivates us, a *principium executionis* that is related to human nature and sensibility.

Kant explicitly argues that the latter is to be found in a moral sense.[12] And this is the domain of empirical psychology and is concerned with the "sources of all the sciences that are concerned with morals, with the ability of commerce, and the method of educating and ruling human beings, or all that is practical" (10, p. 145). Kant's anthropology originates thus from a new conception of the metaphysics of nature and the metaphysics of morals. Both call for an empirical counterpart. Anthropology is to contain moral psychology or the discussion of "the primary springs of the will." Though Kant's faith in the possibility of founding pure morality in purely rational knowledge of things in themselves dissipated as he developed the doctrines put forward in the first *Critique* of 1781, he continued to hold the view that moral philosophy had both a pure and an empirical part. Like the epistemic or metaphysical context, the moral context required both pure rational principles and sensible content.

> The anthropology is pragmatic but provides moral knowledge of man because we must find in it the motives (*Bewegungsgründe*) for morality and without it morality would be scholastic and not applicable to the world at all. It would not be pleasant for it. Anthropology is related to Morality as spatial geometry to geodesics. (25, p. 1211)

and:

> Morality cannot exist without anthropology, for one must first know of the agent whether he is in a position to accomplish what

---

[12] See Manfred Kuehn, "Einleitung" to Immanuel Kant, *Vorlesungen zur Moralphilosophie*, ed. Werner Stark (Berlin: de Gruyter, 2004), pp. vii–xxxv.

is required of him ... One can ... consider practical philosophy even without anthropology, or without knowledge of the agent, only then it is merely speculative; so man must at least be studied accordingly. (27, p. 244)

This is in stark contrast to the view Kant puts forward in the *Groundwork of the Metaphysics of Morals* of 1785, where he argued that the categorical imperative constituted both the *principium diiudicationis* and the *principium executionis* and relegated the moral sense or moral feeling to the periphery of moral philosophy.

This had important consequences for the role of anthropology in his system. While it was central in 1773 and 1775 because it concerned "the primary springs of the will" that he thought were not rational but rather part of our empirical nature, it became peripheral as soon as these primary springs themselves were conceived as rational. In 1775, Kant went so far as to argue that moral philosophy without anthropology was "merely speculative" and "empty"; anthropology was needed in ethics in so far as "ought" must imply "can" and we must therefore first determine whether we *can* meet the demands that a purely rational morality makes on us (19, p. 137 – written around 1772). In 1785, he was convinced that anthropology and metaphysics of morals have nothing in common and should not be mixed. Because "ought" implies "can," we *are* "obligated." "Practical anthropology" is no longer part of morals proper. The task was to work out a "pure moral philosophy, completely cleansed of everything that may be empirical and that belongs to anthropology" (4, pp. 388f.).

We may therefore say that the moral relevance of the lectures on anthropology decreased as Kant's thought on moral issues developed. It may appear that after 1785 anthropology lost all importance for morals proper, because

all moral concepts have their seat and origin completely a priori in reason ... Just in this purity of their origin lies their dignity, so that they can serve us as supreme practical principles, that in adding anything empirical to them one subtracts just as much from their genuine influence and from the unlimited worth of actions ... it is of the greatest practical importance not to make its principles dependent upon the special nature of human reason ... just because moral laws are to hold for every rational being as such.

Morality needs anthropology only "for its application to human beings," not for morality itself (4, pp. 411f.) But "all moral philosophy is based entirely on its pure part; and it does not borrow in the least thing from acquaintance with mankind (from anthropology)" (4, p. 389). Partly as a result of this, the pragmatic dimension of anthropology, which had always been important, now became the most important concern of anthropology, something that is borne out by the very title of the published *Anthropology from a Pragmatic Point of View*.

But what does "pragmatic" mean? While this is not the place to trace the details of the development of the term in Kant's thinking, it is worth pointing out that its meaning also undergoes some change, and that this change roughly corresponds to the change in Kant's conception of moral motivation. First of all, there is a sense of "pragmatic" that concerns a certain way of writing history, namely a non-scholastic way that indicates writing not just for the academy but for a broader public. It is roughly equivalent to "popular" as opposed to "academic" and remains constant in all of Kant's writings. But this is not the sense of "pragmatic" which is primarily relevant in anthropological and moral contexts. More important is the sense that has to do with "motivation." Around 1773 "pragmatic" meant "what moves the will" or is an "incentive" (*Triebfeder*) that "corresponds to a rule" (15, p. 516). Differentiating between "impulse" (*Antrieb*), which is subjective and pathological, on the one hand, and objective, "*motiva*," on the other, Kant characterized the motives as either "pragmatic or moral," and asserted that even the "pragmatic imperatives are categorical" (19, p. 104). "Pragmatic" and "moral" do not exclude one another at this point. This changes in 1785. From then on, "pragmatic" imperatives are for Kant always "conditioned" and "hypothetical," and only moral imperatives are categorical. He now worries about "mistaking the pragmatic for the moral" (19, p. 93). Pragmatic imperatives concern rules of prudence. And rules of prudence concern mainly the use we can make of other people to achieve our own ends, or the means of obtaining our own happiness. They are thus in Kant's mature philosophy essentially at cross-purposes with the fundamental duties of virtue. Given the sharp contrast between anything that is prudential and what is truly moral in Kant's mature ethics, pragmatic considerations are *per se* non-moral.

To sum up, in 1773 "pragmatic" meant for Kant "everything that pertains to the practical," but at least since 1785 it indicated everything that pertains to the practical, *except* what is purely moral. This can also be seen from Kant's description of the relationship between pure morals and moral anthropology in the *Metaphysics of Morals*, the only passage in all of his published works in which he uses the expression "moral anthropology":

> The counterpart of a metaphysics of morals, the other member of the division of practical philosophy ... would be moral anthropology, which, however, would deal only with the subjective conditions in human nature that hinder or help us in fulfilling the laws of the metaphysics of morals. It would deal with the development, spreading, and strengthening of moral principles (in education through schools and popular instruction), and with other similar teachings and precepts based on experience. It cannot be dispensed with, but it must neither precede it nor be mixed with it, for one would then run the risk of bringing forth false or at least indulgent moral laws that would misrepresent as unattainable what is not attained just because the law has not been presented in all its purity (which constitutes its very strength) or because false and impure incentives were used in addition to it in itself in accordance with duty and good. This would leave no certain moral principles as a guide for judging or disciplining the mind in the observance of duty, the precepts of which must be given a priori by pure reason alone.   (6, p. 217)

"Pragmatic" in the title of the published *Anthropology* cannot include the strictly "moral" dimension. Kant says that

> Just as there must be principles in a metaphysics of nature for applying those highest universal principles of nature in general to objects of experience, a metaphysics of morals cannot dispense with principles of application, and we shall often have to take as our object the particular *nature* of the human being, which is known only through experience in order to *indicate* the inferences from the universal moral principles [relevant] for it. But this will in no way detract from the purity of these principles or cast doubt on their a priori origin. – In other words: a metaphysics of morals cannot be based upon anthropology, but it may be applied to it.   (6, p. 217)

And at the beginning of the *Groundwork*, he further claims that the "empirical part" of morality will treat "the will of human beings in so far as it is affected by nature" (4, p. 387).

Anthropological questions are therefore not morally irrelevant, and for this reason the published *Anthropology* is not irrelevant either. "Pragmatic" is defined by Kant here as "what the human being as a free acting being can and should make of himself." It primarily concerns what is open to observation or what we can be observed to make of ourselves (i.e., what we *can* do), but at least secondarily it also concerns moral rules (or what we *ought* to make of ourselves). We must now ask what the precise relevance of the published *Anthropology* for Kant's mature moral theory is. How far does or can it extend? The *Groundwork* does not seem to leave much room for it.

Anthropology and moral philosophy: the mature view

Kant claims in *The Metaphysics of Morals* that anthropology cannot be dispensed with, but it cannot precede morality. And mixing anthropology in any way with the discussion of the pure principles of morals is for him one of the most serious mistakes of moral theory. Thus moral anthropology is a secondary concern. Moral anthropology would have to deal with what empirical agents do, i.e., with the observation of what they actually do in contexts that we call "moral." If only for this reason, he must have thought that he could not dispense with anthropological concerns in a full discussion of morality.

This is not all that can be said, however. In so far as a specifically moral anthropology has to deal with the conditions that hinder or further the execution of the moral laws "in human nature" and the "spread and strengthening of moral principles through the education" in schools and in public, and also with the personal and public contexts of morality that are open to empirical observation, it is even more important. Anthropology must be concerned with the sociological and even historical developments which are relevant to morality. In so far as pragmatic anthropology also deals with these questions, it is also relevant here. Furthermore, in so far as it also addresses the question of the relationship between "can" and "ought," it necessarily raises (or leads up to) questions that belong to moral anthropology. Nevertheless, as should be clear from Kant's claims in the *Groundwork* and *The Metaphysics of Morals*, these do not seem to be questions that can be answered within the context of a pragmatic anthropology itself. A specifically moral anthropology can cover at best only a very small part of what Kant intends to deal with in the *Anthropology from a Pragmatic Point of View*. Even if there is perhaps some overlap between the pragmatic anthropology and the projected moral anthropology, this overlap is not very great. So where is the moral anthropology Kant envisaged?

The answer to *this* question is easy, for, strictly speaking, it does not exist. Kant clearly never completed it. There is no book or article in which he explicitly sets himself that task and tackles it directly. Still, there are beginnings. We might look for hints in the place where Kant talks most explicitly about both the moral law and human nature, namely the "Doctrine of Virtue" in the *Metaphysics of Morals*, where he claims that "virtue" is the point at which morality makes contact with *human nature*. This is interesting, as "virtue" or *Tugend* does not play a significant role in Kant's *Groundwork*, and while it is important in the discussion of the postulates in the *Critique of Practical Reason*, even there it is not an explicit topic of discussion. Even though Kant claims that "virtue is the greatest that finite practical reason can achieve" (5, p. 33), he does not pursue the topic any further.

This is no accident, since virtue is for Kant not a topic of pure moral philosophy, which is concerned with reason in general. Virtue is of the greatest importance for a specific kind of reason, namely our *own* reason. It concerns morality "applied" to human beings. Kant makes this very clear in the early lectures on moral philosophy, where he argues that a doctrine of virtue cannot capture moral philosophy as a whole:

> Ethics explained by a *doctrine of virtue* is good inasmuch as virtue belongs solely to the inner tribunal; but since virtue entails not just *morally good* actions, but at the same time the possibility of the opposite, and thus incorporates an inner struggle, this is therefore too narrow a concept, since we can also ascribe *ethics*, but not virtue (properly speaking) to the angels and to God, for in them there is assuredly holiness but not virtue. (27, p. 13)

Virtue cannot express "quite accurately the notion of moral goodness" precisely because it has to do with the "strength in mastering and overcoming" ourselves, i.e., with our moral disposition (27, p. 300). It is important, however, because it is the ability to overcome the inclination of evil "on moral principles" (27, p. 463) and is "the moral perfection of man. To virtue we attach power, strength and authority. It is a victory over inclination" (27, p. 465). For this reason it is also "the greatest worth of the person" (29, pp. 599f.).

"Holy beings are not virtuous" (27, p. 215). In this respect, virtue is similar to piety. Both concern internal matters and consist in dispositions. They differ "not in actions, but in their motivating grounds." In virtue the motivating ground is morality or the "good disposition" alone. In piety there are other reasons. Piety not only does not exclude virtue; it actually demands it (27, pp. 308f.), but just as God and the angels are not pious, so they are not virtuous. Virtue is something essentially human, and for this reason it cannot serve as a central concept in a "pure moral philosophy that is completely cleared of everything which can only be empirical and anthropological." To argue that virtue is impossible would be misanthropic and would amount to what Kant calls "moral unbelief" (27, p. 316). The doctrine of the virtues is important in describing the common moral praxis, but it is not part of the science of morals. Only beings like us can be or need to be virtuous. This is a position that Kant never gave up. Thus he defines virtue in the *Metaphysics of Morals* as "the ability and the considered purpose to resist . . . the enemy of the moral disposition (*Gesinnung*) within ourselves" (6, p. 380). In his more technical terminology, he says that virtue is "the strength of man's maxim in fulfilling his duty" (6, p. 394).

To sum up: virtue is something human, perhaps even all-too-human. It is a notion that gives us a preliminary idea of morality, and it must be discussed in anthropological contexts. Already in his announcement of his lectures of 1765, Kant said as much when he proclaimed that he intended to make clear what his method is by first considering "what actually takes place before indicating what should happen." And as late as 1785 he says that "morality" may not be the best word to indicate what he is after, but he is sure that "we cannot take virtue to do so" (27, p. 300). Still, virtue must form the beginning of Kant's moral anthropology or his "morality applied to man."

The discussion of virtue is embedded in a more general discussion of human ends or goals. Kant argues there that there is at least one end that is "in itself" or "at the same time" a duty, and he calls this a "duty of virtue" or *Tugendpflicht*, in specific contrast to general "ethical obligation." While ethical obligation is singular and concerns the "merely formal" aspect of moral obligation, there are many duties of virtue (6, p. 383). Actually, there are, according to Kant, two basic or fundamental duties of virtue (which give rise to many others), namely the duty to perfect oneself and the duty to further the happiness of others. To perfect oneself, for him, means among other things to raise oneself "from the crude state" of our nature or animality "more and more to humanity" (6, p. 387). And to promote the happiness of others depends also on their own conception of happiness. For both these duties anthropological considerations are not only relevant but even necessary. We need to know others and ourselves, for without such knowledge we are likely to go wrong in the application of moral principles. Only if we know the nature of human beings can we hope to become virtuous. And it is for this reason that anthropology from a pragmatic point of view is important. Just because it is concerned with "what the human being as a free acting being can and should make of himself," it is also important for the discussion of those virtues that are also duties. It is also relevant for a better understanding of the concept of "virtue," for if virtue is "the strength of a maxim" in the actual fulfillment of duty, and if this strength can be measured only "by the obstacles it can overcome," then we must know these "obstacles." And because they are "in the case of virtue . . . natural inclinations which can come into conflict with the human being's resolution, and since it is man himself who puts these obstacles in the way of his maxims," the kind of self-knowledge that pragmatic anthropology provides is very important for the discussion of virtue (6, p. 393).

Now, virtue or the virtues as discussed by Kant in the *Metaphysics of Morals* correspond very closely to the notion of character in anthropological contexts. "Virtue" is the moral and ideal concept; "character" refers to the empirical reality (6, p. 47). A person who is virtuous must also have a good character, even if someone with a good character need not necessarily be virtuous. More importantly, perhaps, someone without character cannot possibly be virtuous in Kant's view. Indeed, one might say that a good character is a necessary condition for virtue and that virtue would be a necessary and sufficient condition for a good character. Therefore, questions about virtue in moral contexts become questions about character in anthropological contexts.

Thus, when Kant talks in anthropological contexts of a good character, he is indirectly talking also about a virtuous person. In his *Religion* he distinguishes between the firm ability that allows us to fulfill our duty in a legal sense and goodness in the eyes of God, calling the former *virtus phaenomenon* and the latter *virtus noumenon*. If the "practical" or "moral anthropology" and pure moral philosophy require an *Übergang* or a connecting link, then this link must be the one between "virtue" and "character." It is clear that Kant's discussion of character in the second part of the *Anthropology* (and in the lectures on anthropology) is very important for his moral anthropology and his applied ethics. According to Kant, "the character of any human being is based on the rule of the maxims. Character could therefore also be defined as the determination of the free will of man by lasting and firm maxims" (25, p. 1385). For this reason he identifies character with our "way of thinking" (*Denkungsart*), which is opposed to the way of sensing (*Sinnesart*).

The close relation of character to virtue should be almost immediately apparent. Even though they are not identical and the phrase "moral character" is for the mature Kant almost an oxymoron, he frequently uses it in the early lectures on anthropology and sometimes also in his critical writings. But the concept of "character" is more deeply embedded than "virtue" in anthropological concerns. Indeed, Kant's moral psychology is a psychology of character: in applied morality the question is not "What shall I do?" but "What kind of person should I be?" It has to do with leading a certain kind of life, or being a certain kind of person. But character is not fundamental. Indeed, as he says in his *Anthropology*,

> The sole proof a man's consciousness affords him that he has character is his having made it his supreme maxim to be truthful, both in his admission to himself and in his conduct toward every other man. And since having character is both the minimum that can be required of a reasonable man and the maximum of inner worth (of human dignity), it must be possible for the most ordinary human reason to be a man of principles (to have determinate character) and yet, according to its dignity, surpass the greatest talent. (7, p. 295)

Ultimately it comes down again to the question of the morality of the supreme maxim, not to a question about empirical character. Still, the discussion of the nature of character in the second half of the *Anthropology* is highly relevant for any understanding of Kant's view of the nature of morality and its relation to virtue.

Given the preceding discussion, it might be thought that Kant's moral theory must ultimately be understood as some sort of virtue ethics. But this is not so. Kant's published texts do not offer a theory that can usefully be described as "virtue ethics," and were not intended to do so. They were intended to offer something much more general, namely the beginnings of a "metaphysics of morals" or a fundamental discussion of what Kant took to be the general framework of morals. Contemporary discussions of Kant's virtue ethics often confuse different levels of discourse that, as we have seen, Kant meant to keep separate. For this reason, they distort his view of the virtues. On the other hand, Kant's published texts do presuppose or start out from a particular kind of virtue ethics. His general discussion of the framework of morals is based on a certain conception of morals in which virtues played a fundamental role. Therefore we may expect on the one hand that Kant's theory has some relevance for the virtues, and on the other hand that his conception of the framework of morals is not independent of the conception of the virtues from which he started out.

It is sometimes suggested that this virtue theory is close to that of Aristotle, but the *Anthropology* suggests that this is a mistaken view. The virtue ethics presupposed by Kant is definitely not Aristotelian in character; rather, it is an example of the kind of ethics prevalent in Europe and North America during the eighteenth century. It possessed (almost inevitably) some Aristotelian features, but it was much more influenced by Christian and Stoic doctrines and imbued with local Prussian convictions. Also in the *Anthropology*, however, are the beginnings of a universalist virtue ethics that would be appropriate for a cosmopolitan or a citizen of the world, and that is further developed in Kant's writings on history. It would not be entirely inappropriate to call these "virtues of the Enlightenment," although Kant himself did not develop them because he was convinced that the progress of human individuals was insignificant compared with the progress of the human race as a whole. But even that latter point is for Kant an anthropological question, and the discussion of this problem must therefore be informed to some extent by the *Anthropology from a Pragmatic Point of View*. So, while the "moral anthropology" described by Kant is obviously not identical with what we find in the lectures on anthropology or the published *Anthropology*, the views presented there may have some relevance for it. This means that there is at least the possibility that this work includes considerations and materials that would also form part of a genuinely moral anthropology, but it also means that it should not be straightforwardly identified with it. The approach to Kant's moral anthropology must ultimately be "multi-textual."[13]

Kant intended in his mature works to offer an ethical theory which was "carefully cleansed of everything empirical." The *Anthropology* shows us what an empirical morality looks like, and which concepts in such an empirical morality correspond to the pure concepts of will and maxim. The *Anthropology* also discusses the implications which Kant's doctrine of the relation between the empirical and the pure part has for the virtues. In doing both of these things it helps us to develop a Kantian ethics in a direction that Kant himself would have recognized as Kantian – something that is not true of all contemporary positions that are purportedly "Kantian." Kant's rigorous moral theory emphasizes that "rational beings" need not necessarily be human, and that we ought nevertheless to be motivated by pure rational principles. Some critics regard this as a departure from the Enlightenment motto that the proper study of mankind is man. Kant's *Anthropology from a Pragmatic Point of View* provides an answer to these critics, because it contains the kernel of a cosmopolitan virtue theory in the Enlightenment tradition. The task of the contemporary Kantian should be to develop the suggestions contained in this profound text.

Finally, at a time in which there is an increasing tendency to "naturalize" Kant, it is advisable to take a very close look at what Kant does and does not say about "human nature." A new translation and edition of Kant's *Anthropology* is therefore timely and important, and a discussion of the relevance of this work in the context of Kant's philosophy is long overdue.

---

[13] Robert B. Louden's *Kant's Impure Ethics* (Oxford: Oxford University Press, 2000) argues most persuasively for the importance of this "impure ethics."

Chronology

1724   Immanuel Kant born April 22 in Königsberg, East Prussia

1730–1732   Attended Vorstädter Hospitalschule (elementary school)

1732–1740   Attends the Collegium Fridericianum (parochial – Pietist – school)

1740–1746   Attends the University of Königsberg

1747   *Thoughts on the True Estimation of Living Forces*

1747–1754   Serves as private tutor for families in the vicinity of Königsberg

1755   Completes dissertation entitled "Succinct Exposition of Some Meditations on Fire" and receives his doctoral degree from the Faculty of Philosophy at the University of Königsberg

      Universal Natural History and Theory of the Heavens, in which Kant proposes an astronomical theory now known as the Kant–Laplace hypothesis

      New Elucidation of the First Principles of Metaphysical Cognition, paper presented to the Philosophy Faculty

1756   Three treatises on an earthquake in Lisbon

      Physical Monadology

1762   *The False Subtlety of the Four Syllogistic Figures*

1763   *The Only Possible Argument in Support of a Demonstration of the Existence of God*

1764   *Observations on the Feeling of the Beautiful and the Sublime*

1764	*Inquiry Concerning the Distinctiveness of the Principles of Natural Theology and Morals*
1766	*Dreams of a Spirit-Seer Elucidated by Dreams of Metaphysics*
1770	Appointed Professor of Logic and Metaphysics at the University of Königsberg; inaugural dissertation entitled *Concerning the Form and Principles of the Sensible and the Intelligible World*
1781	*Critique of Pure Reason*, first (A) edition
1783	*Prolegomena to Any Future Metaphysics*
1784	*Ideas Towards a Universal History from a Cosmopolitan Point of View*
	An Answer to the Question: What is Enlightenment?
1785	Review of Herder's *Ideas for a Philosophy of the History of Mankind*
	Groundwork of the Metaphysics of Morals
1786	Elected to the Academy of Sciences in Berlin
	Conjectural Beginning of Human History
	Metaphysical Foundations of Natural Science
	What is Orientation in Thinking?
1787	*Critique of Pure Reason*, second (B) edition
1788	*Critique of Practical Reason*
	Concerning the Use of Teleological Principles in Philosophy
1790	*Critique of Judgment*, first edition
1793	*On the Proverb: That May be True in Theory but is of No Practical Use*
	Critique of Judgment, second edition
	Religion within the Limits of Reason Alone
1794	Censured by the Imperial Censor; elected to the Academy of Sciences, St. Petersburg
	The End of All Things
1795	*On Perpetual Peace*
1796	July: Kant's last lecture
1797	*Metaphysics of Morals*
	On the Supposed Right to Tell Lies from Benevolent Motives
1798	*Anthropology from a Pragmatic Point of View*
	The Conflict of the Faculties (Part II: "An Old Question Raised Again: Is the Human Race Constantly Progressing?")

1800	*Logic*
1803	Kant becomes ill
	Education (*Pedagogy*)
1804	Kant dies on February 12, buried February 28

Further reading

The *Anthropology from a Pragmatic Point of View* was first published under the title *Anthropologie in pragmatischer Hinsicht abgefaßt von Immanuel Kant* (Königsberg bey Friedrich Nicolovius, 1798). A second editon appeared two years later: *Anthropologie in pragmatischer Hinsicht abgefaßt von Immanuel Kant. Zweyte verbesserte Auflage* (Königsberg bey Friedrich Nicolovius, 1800). There was also another printing with the same title and an index in 1799: *Anthropologie in pragmatischer Hinsicht abgefaßt von Immanuel Kant. Mit einem zu diesem Buch notwendigen Register versehen* (Frankfurt u. Leipzig, 1799). The most widely used German edition of this work is found in Immanuel Kant, *Gesammelte Schriften*, vols. 1–22, ed. Preussische Akademie der Wissenschaften, vol. 23, Deutsche Akademie der Wissenschaften zu Berlin, from vol. 24, Akademie der Wissenschaften zu Göttingen (Berlin: Walter de Gruyter, 1907–), vol. 7, pp. 117–333. It is based on the second edition of the *Anthropologie*.

The contents of the published work should be compared with Kant's reflections on anthropology as contained in volume 15 of his *Gesammelte Schriften*, which contains both reflections on Baumgarten's *Psychologia Empirica* and independent drafts for the lecture course from the 1770s and 1780s. These reflections and drafts complement the material found in the published *Anthropology*. They show not only how his thought on different matters developed, but also how it remained in its overall structure relatively constant over the years.

There are also transcripts of notes taken by students, which appear to have received a fairly wide distribution in hand-written form during Kant's lifetime. They are collected in vol. 25, 1 and 2 of the

Gesammelte Schriften, edited by Reinhard Brandt and Werner Stark (Berlin: de Gruyter, 1997). These large volumes contain texts from 1772/ 1773 (Collins), 1772/1773 (Parow), 1775/1776 (Friedländer), 1777/1778 (Pillau 1781/1782), *Menschenkunde*, 1784/1785 (Mrongovius), and 1788/ 1789 (Busolt). For the exact description of these texts and the students to whom they are attributed, see the Introduction by Werner Stark and Reinhard Brandt. Werner Stark, "Historical Notes and Interpretative Questions," in *Essays on Kant's Anthropology*, ed. Brian Jacobs and Patrick Kain (Cambridge: Cambridge University Press, 2003), pp. 15–37, is also very helpful in this regard. An annotated translation of the Friedländer lectures is being prepared by G. Felicitas Munzel.

It cannot be emphasized enough that a thorough study of Kant's anthropology must be based on all three of these sources – that is, on his texts, his reflections, and student notes of his lectures. Since most of these materials should soon be available within the context of the Cambridge Edition of the Works of Immanuel Kant, such a study will be possible even for those who don't read German easily.

The first complete translation of the *Anthropology* into English was pre-pared by Mary Gregor (The Hague: Martinus Nijhoff, 1974). There is another translation by Victor Lyle Dowdell, with an introduction by Frederick P. Van De Pitte (Carbondale/Edwardsville: University of Southern Illinois Press, 1978; paperback edition, 1996). Of some interest also is the translation of Part I by A. E. Kroeger in the *Journal of Speculative Philosophy* 9, pp. 16–27, 239–245, 406–416; 10, pp. 319–323, 11, pp. 310–317, 353–363; 13, pp. 281–299; 14, pp. 154–169, and 15, pp. 62–63.

Frederick Van De Pitte, *Kant as Philosophical Anthropologist* (The Hague: Martinus Nijhoff, 1971), and "Kant as a Philosophical Anthropologist," in *Proceedings of the 3rd International Kant Congress*, ed. L. W. Beck (Dordrecht: Reidel, 1972), pp. 574–581, argues that the anthropology is absolutely fundamental for Kant's philosophy as a whole. For more recent views on this problem, see the contributions in Patrick R. Frierson, *Freedom and Anthropology in Kant's Moral Philosophy* (Cambridge: Cambridge University Press, 2003).

A nice discussion of the different senses of "pragmatic" in Kant's writings can be found in Allen Wood, "Kant and the Problem of Human Nature," in *Essays on Kant's Anthropology*, pp. 38–59.

For a discussion of the role and status of empirical psychology in Kant's work, see Thomas Sturm, "Kant on Empirical Psychology: How

Not to Investigate the Human Mind," in *Kant and the Sciences*, ed. Eric Watkins (Oxford: Oxford University Press, 2001), pp. 163–184, and Rudolf Makkreel, "Kant on the Scientific Status of Psychology, Anthropology, and History," in the same volume, pp. 185–204.

Paul Guyer's investigation of the relationship between anthropology and aesthetics, "Beauty, Freedom, and Morality: Kant's *Lectures on Anthropology* and the Development of his Aesthetic Theory," in *Essays on Kant's Anthropology*, pp. 135–163, concentrates less on the published version of the *Anthropology* than on the actual lectures and shows how ideas that appear in the third *Critique* were prepared in the lectures.

The important connections between Kant's anthropology and his writings on history are explored by Sharon Anderson-Gold, "Kant's Ethical Anthropology and the Critical Foundation of the Philosophy of History," *History of Philosophy Quarterly* 11 (1994), pp. 405–441; Sidney Axinn, "Ambivalence: Kant's View of Human Nature," *Kant-Studien* 72 (1981), pp. 169–174; Roger Sullivan, "The Influence of Kant's Anthropology on his Moral Theory," *Review of Metaphysics* 49 (1995), pp. 77–94; Holly L. Wilson, "Kant's Integration of Morality and Anthropology," *Kant-Studien* 88 (1997), pp. 87–10; and Allen W. Wood, "Unsocial Sociability: The Anthropological Basis for Kant's Ethics," *Philosophical Topics* 19 (1991), pp. 325–351.

The relation of Kant's anthropology to his ethics is discussed by David G. Sussman, *The Idea of Humanity: Anthropology and Anthroponomy in Kant's Ethics* (London and New York: Routledge, 2001), Patrick R. Frierson, *Freedom and Anthropology in Kant's Moral Philosophy* (Cambridge: Cambridge University Press, 2003), and most importantly by Robert B. Louden in *Kant's Impure Ethics* (Oxford: Oxford University Press, 2000). Finally, those who would like to find out more about the historical context of Kant's anthropology might want to consult John H. Zammito, *Kant, Herder, and the Birth of Anthropology* (Chicago: Chicago University Press, 2002). Relevant too in this context is G. Felicitas Munzel's *Kant's Conception of Character: The "Critical" Link of Morality, Anthropology and Reflective Judgment* (Chicago: Chicago University Press, 1999).

Note on the text and translation

Two editions of *Anthropology from a Pragmatic Point of View* were published during Kant's lifetime – the first in 1798, two years after he had retired from teaching at the University of Königsberg; the second in 1800, four years before his death. The present translation is based on Oswald Külpe's edition of the text in volume 7 (1907; 2nd ed., 1917) of the Prussian Academy of the Sciences edition of Kant's works. Külpe's edition is based on the second edition of 1800.

The *Anthropology* is unique among Kant's published books in that it is the only one for which a virtually complete hand-written manuscript (prepared by Kant) still exists. This *Handschrift*, which was given to the University of Rostock Library in 1840 by the son of a former student of Kant's who himself had bought the manuscript at an auction in 1808, occasionally differs substantially from both the first and second editions of the *Anthropology*, and in the judgment of many scholars gives us a closer indication of Kant's original intentions. The changes between the first and second editions (abbreviated as "A1" and "A2" in my notes), though numerous, are mostly stylistic, and were probably made not by Kant himself but by Christian Gottfried Schütz. For instance, in a letter to Kant of May 22, 1800, Schütz refers to "the pleasant business, which I had taken on, of attending to the final proofreading of the second edition of your *Anthropology*" (12: 307). The differences between the *Handschrift* (abbreviated as "*H*" in the footnotes) and the first edition of 1798 are more substantial, but even here it is not clear how big a role Kant played in preparing the manuscript for publication. (He was by now seventy-four years old, retired, and not in good health, and seems even in earlier years often to have allowed others to handle proofreading details for him.) How many of the changes between the *Handschrift* and the first edition were approved by Kant himself? We do not know.

In preparing this edition of the *Anthropology* for Cambridge Texts in the History of Philosophy, an edition designed for students, it has not proved feasible to note most of the many variant readings of specific words and phrases that exist between the *Handschrift*, the first edition, and the second edition. (All of these variant readings will be noted in the edition of the text that is to appear in a forthcoming volume of The Cambridge Edition of the Works of Immanuel Kant – *Anthropology, History, and Education*, ed. Günter Zöller and Robert B. Louden.) However, I have included all of the longer supplementary texts (*Ergänzungen*) from the *Handschrift*. These additional texts are of two types: (1) remarks written in the margins of the *Handschrift*, and (2) passages that are crossed out (but by whom?) in the *Handschrift*. Both are printed as footnotes in the present text, and are always prefaced either by "*Marginal note in H:*" or "*Crossed out in H:*".

This supplementary material from the *Handschrift* presents multiple challenges to the translator. Kant's remarks here sometimes have a rough "notes to oneself" feel, do not always follow grammatical conventions, and sometimes lack end punctuation. I have tried to render the *Ergänzungen* literally, and so my translations of them also occasionally have these same characteristics. Again, the main rationale for printing them is the hypothesis that at least in some cases they take us closer to Kant's own considered views. Words and phrases within the *Ergänzungen* footnotes enclosed by "<>" have been crossed out in the *Handschrift*; "[?]" indicates that the preceding word in the *Handschrift* is illegible. In translating this supplementary material from the *Handschrift*, I have relied primarily on Külpe's printed version, which is located in the back of Academy volume 7. However, I would also like to thank Heike Tröger of the Special Collections Division of the University of Rostock Library for providing me with a photocopy of the *Handschrift* as well as for help and advice in deciphering the *Handschrift* during an exciting visit to Rostock in June 2003.

Kant's own footnotes from the first two printed editions of the *Anthropology* are indicated by lower-case letters. All other footnotes – my own as well as the supplementary material from the *Handschrift* and occasional notes on variant readings – are indicated by Arabic numerals. In preparing notes dealing with the content of the text, I have often followed Külpe's own extensive notes, though in some places (where indicated), I have also borrowed from other German- as well as English-language editions of the text. Readers who find themselves pursuing issues and questions not addressed in my footnotes are encouraged to consult Reinhard Brandt's extensive and detailed commentary on the text (*Kritische Kommentar zu Kants Anthropologie in pragmatischer Hinsicht* (*1798*) [Hamburg: Felix Meiner, 1999]).

The *Anthropology* is essentially Kant's last set of lecture notes for his annual anthropology course, which he began teaching in 1772. In a footnote at the end of the Preface, he describes the work simply as "the present manual for my anthropology course" (7: 122n.). As noted in the Introduction and Further Reading sections, earlier versions of these lectures – in the form of notes taken by students and auditors – also exist. Seven different versions of these latter lectures, dating from 1772 to 1789, along with short selections from still other versions, are collected in volume 25 of the Academy Edition (1997), edited by Reinhard Brandt and Werner Stark. An English translation of some of this material is also forthcoming in a volume of The Cambridge Edition of the Works of Immanuel Kant (*Lectures on Anthropology*, ed. Robert B. Louden and Allen W. Wood). By comparing Kant's own final set of anthropology notes with earlier transcriptions made by students and auditors, one gains a sense of how his conception of anthropology developed and changed over the years.

Kant's *Anthropology* has been translated into English twice before – by Mary J. Gregor (The Hague: Martinus Nijhoff, 1974), and by Victor Lyle Dowdell (revised and edited by Hans H. Rudnick, with an Introduction by Frederick P. Van De Pitte [Carbondale: Southern Illinois University Press, 1978]). Both translations are good, and the present translation owes a debt to each. In preparing this new translation, I have tried to adhere strictly to the translation principles summarized in the General Editors' Preface printed at the beginning of each volume in The Cambridge Edition, with one notable exception: Kant's own division of sentences has not always been followed. I have shortened some of them.

I would like to thank the Board of Trustees of the University of Maine System for awarding me a 2001–2002 Trustee Professorship, as well as Francis C. McGrath, Interim Dean of the College of Arts and Sciences at the University of Southern Maine, for awarding me a reduced teaching schedule in fall 2000. Most of the translation work was done during this period. I would also like to thank the Alexander von Humboldt Foundation for its support via a research fellowship that enabled me to work in Germany during 1991–1992 and again in 1996–1997, during which time my interest in both Kant's philosophy and the German language increased greatly. Thanks also to the following individuals, who provided helpful comments, suggestions, and advice on earlier drafts of the translation: Karl Ameriks, Alix Cohen, Patrick Frierson, Hilary Gaskin, Patrick Kain, Manfred Kuehn, David Bruce Louden, Pauline Marsh, Frederick Rauscher, Judith Schlick, Claudia Schmidt, Niko Strobauch, and Allen Wood.

Robert Louden

Anthropology from a Pragmatic Point of View

Preface[1]

All cultural progress, by means of which the human being advances his [7:119] education,[2] has the goal of applying this acquired knowledge and skill for the world's use. But the most important object in the world to which he can apply them is the human being: because the human being is his own final end. – Therefore to know the human being according to his species as an earthly being endowed with reason especially deserves to be called *knowledge of the world*, even though he constitutes only one part of the creatures on earth.

A doctrine of knowledge of the human being, systematically formulated (anthropology), can exist either in a physiological or in a pragmatic point of view. – Physiological knowledge of the human being concerns the investigation of what *nature* makes of the human being; pragmatic, the investigation of what *he* as a free-acting being makes of himself, or can and should make of himself. – He who ponders natural phenomena, for example, what the causes of the faculty of memory may rest on, can speculate back and forth (like Descartes)[3] over the traces of impressions remaining in the brain, but in doing so he must admit that in this play of his representations he is a mere observer and must let nature run its course, for he does not know the cranial nerves and fibers, nor does he understand how to put them to use for his purposes. Therefore all theoretical speculation about this is a pure waste of time. – – But if he uses perceptions concerning what has been found to hinder or stimulate memory in order to enlarge it or make it agile, and if he requires knowledge of the human being

---

[1] The Preface and contents are missing in the *Handschrift* (*H*).   [2] *seine Schule macht.*
[3] See, e.g., Descartes's *Passions of the Soul* (1649), Art. 42.

3

for this, then this would be a part of anthropology with a *pragmatic* purpose, and this is precisely what concerns us here.

[120] Such an anthropology, considered as *knowledge of the world*, which must come after our *schooling*, is actually not yet called *pragmatic* when it contains an extensive knowledge of *things* in the world, for example, animals, plants, and minerals from various lands and climates, but only when it contains knowledge of the human being as a *citizen of the world*. – Therefore, even knowledge of the races of human beings as products belonging to the play of nature is not yet counted as pragmatic knowledge of the world, but only as theoretical knowledge of the world.

In addition, the expressions "to *know* the world" and "to *have* the world"[4] are rather far from each other in their meaning, since one only *understands* the play that one has watched, while the other has *participated* in it. – But the anthropologist is in a very unfavorable position for judging so-called *high* society, the estate of the nobles,[5] because they are too close to one another, but too far from others.

Travel belongs to the means of broadening the range of anthropology, even if it is only the reading of travel books. But if one wants to know what to look for abroad, in order to broaden the range of anthropology, first one must have acquired knowledge of human beings at home, through social intercourse with one's townsmen or countrymen.[a] Without such a plan (which already presupposes knowledge of human beings) the citizen of the world remains very limited with regard to his anthropology. *General* knowledge always precedes *local* knowledge here, if the latter is to be ordered and directed through philosophy: in the absence of which all acquired knowledge can yield nothing more than fragmentary groping around and no science.

***

However, all such attempts to arrive at such a science with thoroughness [121] encounter considerable difficulties that are inherent in human nature itself.

---

[4] *die Welt kennen und Welt haben.*   [5] *die sogenannte große Welt aber, den Stand der Vornehmen.*

[a] A large city such as Königsberg on the river Pregel, which is the center of a kingdom, in which the provincial councils of the government are located, which has a university (for cultivation of the sciences) and which has also the right location for maritime commerce – a city which, by way of rivers, has the advantages of commerce both with the interior of the country and with neighboring and distant lands of different languages and customs, can well be taken as an appropriate place for broadening one's knowledge of human beings as well as of the world, where this knowledge can be acquired without even traveling.

1. If a human being notices that someone is observing him and trying to study him, he will either appear embarrassed (self-conscious) and *cannot* show himself as he really is; or he dissembles, and does not *want* to be known as he is.
2. Even if he only wants to study himself, he will reach a critical point, particularly as concerns his condition in affect,[6] which normally does not allow *dissimulation*: that is to say, when the incentives are active, he does not observe himself, and when he does observe himself, the incentives are at rest.
3. Circumstances of place and time, when they are constant, produce *habits* which, as is said, are second nature, and make it difficult for the human being to judge how to consider himself, but even more difficult to judge how he should form an idea of others with whom he is in contact; for the variation of conditions in which the human being is placed by his fate or, if he is an adventurer, places himself, make it very difficult for anthropology to rise to the rank of a formal science.

Finally, while not exactly sources for anthropology, these are nevertheless aids: world history, biographies, even plays and novels. For although the latter two are not actually based on experience and truth, but only on invention, and while here the exaggeration of characters and situations in which human beings are placed is allowed, as if in a dream, thus appearing to show us nothing concerning knowledge of human beings – yet even so, in such characters as are sketched by a Richardson or a Molière,[7] the *main features* must have been taken from the observation of the real actions of human beings: for while they are exaggerated in degree, they must nevertheless correspond to human nature in kind.

An anthropology written from a pragmatic point of view that is systematically designed and yet popular (through reference to examples which can be found by every reader) yields an advantage for the reading public: the completeness of the headings under which this or that observed human quality of practical relevance can be subsumed offers [122]

---

[6] *seinen Zustand im Affekt* (or, "his emotional condition").

[7] Samuel Richardson, 1689–1761: English writer whose epistolary novels include *Pamela; or Virtue Rewarded* (1740) and *Clarissa, or, the History of a Young Lady* (7 vols., 1747–1748). Jean-Baptiste Poquelin Molière, 1622–1673: French playwright, author of the comedies *Tartuffe* (1664) and *The Misanthrope* (1666).

readers many occasions and invitations to make each particular into a theme of its own, so as to place it in the appropriate category. Through this means the details of the work are naturally divided among the connoisseurs of this study, and they are gradually united into a whole through the unity of the plan. As a result, the growth of science for the common good is promoted and accelerated.[b]

[b] In my work with *pure philosophy*, at first freely undertaken, later included as part of my teaching duties, I have for some thirty years given lectures twice a year aimed at *knowledge of the world* – namely (in the winter semester) *anthropology* and (in summer) *physical geography*, which, because they were popular lectures, were also attended by people of different estates (*andere Stände*). This is the present manual for my anthropology course. As for physical geography, it is scarcely possible at my age to produce a manuscript from my text, which is hardly legible to anyone but myself. [Kant first offered his geography course in 1757. The anthropology course, which to a certain extent grew out of the geography course, was first offered in the winter semester of 1772–1773. A poorly edited version of Kant's physical geography lectures was eventually published by Friedrich Theodor Rink in 1802 (9: 151–436).]

Contents

Anthropology [125]

Part I

Anthropological Didactic. On the way of cognizing the interior as well as the exterior of the human being

Book I On the cognitive faculty

On consciousness of oneself

§1

The fact that the human being can have the "I" in his representations raises him infinitely above all other living beings on earth. Because of this he is a *person*, and by virtue of the unity of consciousness through all changes that happen to him, one and the same person – i.e., through rank and dignity an entirely different being from *things*, such as irrational animals, with which one can do as one likes. This holds even when he cannot yet say "I," because he still has it in thoughts, just as all languages must think it when they speak in the first person, even if they do not have a special word to express this concept of "I." For this faculty (namely to think) is *understanding*.

But it is noteworthy that the child who can already speak fairly fluently nevertheless first begins to talk by means of "I" fairly late (perhaps a year later); in the meantime speaking of himself in the third person (Karl wants to eat, to walk, etc.). When he starts to speak by means of "I" a light seems to dawn on him, as it were, and from that day on he never again returns to his former way of speaking. – Before he merely *felt* himself; now he *thinks* himself. – The explanation of this phenomenon might be rather difficult for the anthropologist.

The observation that a child neither expresses tears nor laughs until three months after his birth appears to be based on the development of certain ideas of offense and injustice,[1] which point to reason. – In this period of time he begins to follow with his eyes shining objects held [128] before him, and this is the crude beginning of the progress[2] of *perception* (apprehension of the ideas of sense), which enlarges to *knowledge* of objects of sense, that is, of *experience*.

Furthermore, when the child tries to speak, the mangling of words is so charming for the mother and nurse, and this inclines them to hug and kiss him constantly, and they thoroughly spoil the tiny dictator by fulfilling his every wish and desire. On the one hand, this creature's charm in the time period of his development toward humanity must be credited to the innocence and openness of all of his still faulty utterances, during which no dissimulation and no malice are present. But on the other hand, the child's charm must also be credited to the natural tendency of the nurses to comfort a creature that ingratiatingly entrusts himself entirely to the will of another.[3] This permits him a playtime, the happiest time of all, during which the teacher once more enjoys the charm of childhood, and practically makes himself a child.

However, the memory of the teacher's childhood does not reach back to that time; for it was not the time of experiences, but merely of scattered perceptions not yet united under the concept of an object.

On egoism

§2

From the day that the human being begins to speak by means of "I," he brings his beloved self to light wherever he is permitted to, and egoism progresses unchecked. If he does not do so openly (for then the egoism of others opposes him), nevertheless he does so covertly and with seeming self-abnegation and pretended modesty, in order all the more reliably to give himself a superior worth in the judgment of others.

Egoism can contain three kinds of presumption: the presumption of understanding, of taste, and of practical interest; that is, it can be logical, aesthetic, or practical.

---

[1] A1 and A2: injustice; *H*: kindness.   [2] of the progress not in *H*.

[3] *Marginal note in H*: Cognition consists of two parts, intuition and thought. To be aware of both in one's consciousness is not to perceive oneself, but the representation of the I in thought. In order to know oneself, one must perceive oneself. *perceptio.* and also added to this *apperceptio.*

The *logical egoist* considers it unnecessary to test his judgment also by the understanding of others; as if he had no need at all for this touchstone (*criterium veritatis externum*).[4] But it is so certain that we cannot dispense with this means of assuring ourselves of the truth of our judgment that this may be the most important reason why learned people cry out so urgently for *freedom of the press*. For if this freedom is denied, we are [129] deprived at the same time of a great means of testing the correctness of our own judgments, and we are exposed to error. One must not even say that *mathematics* is at least privileged to judge from its complete authority, for if the perceived general agreement of the surveyor's judgment did not follow from the judgment of all others who with talent and industry dedicated themselves to this discipline, then even mathematics itself would not be free from fear of somewhere falling into error. – There are also many cases where we do not even trust the judgment of our own senses alone, for example, whether a ringing is merely in our ears or whether it is the hearing of bells actually being rung, but find it necessary to ask others whether it seemed the same to them. And while in philosophizing we may not call up the judgments of others to confirm our own, as jurists do in calling up the judgments of those versed in the law, nevertheless each writer[5] who finds no followers with his publicly avowed opinion on an important topic is suspected of being in error.

For this very reason it is a *hazardous enterprise*, even for intelligent people, to entertain an assertion that contradicts generally accepted opinion. This semblance of egoism is called *paradox*. It is not boldness to run the risk that what one says might be untrue, but rather that only a few people might accept it. – The predilection for paradox is in fact *logical obstinacy*, in which someone does not want to be an imitator of others, but to appear as a rare human being. Instead, a person like this often appears only *strange*. But because every person must have and assert his own thoughts (*Si omnes patres sic, at ego non sic. Abelard*),[6] the reproach of paradox, when it is not based on vanity, or simply wanting to be different, carries no bad connotations. – The opposite of paradox is

---

[4] Trans.: an external criterion for truth.

[5] *Crossed out in H*: writer [When the writer deprived of general public acclamation by others who freely admit not to understand such investigations nevertheless remains in suspicion, this must be because what he has taught is in error; for one cannot so casually overlook the judgment of others as a touchstone of truth].

[6] Trans.: Even if all fathers are this way, I am not this way. Peter Abelard (1079–1144), French philosopher, logician, and theologian.

17

banality, which has common opinion on its side. But with this there is just as little guarantee, if not less, because it lulls one to sleep; whereas paradox arouses the mind to attention and investigation, which often leads to discoveries.

The *aesthetic egoist* is satisfied with his own taste, even if others find his verses, paintings, music, and similar things ever so bad, and criticize or even laugh at them. He deprives himself of progress toward that which is [130] better when he isolates himself with his own judgment; he applauds himself and seeks the touchstone of artistic beauty only in himself.

Finally, the *moral egoist* limits all ends to himself, sees no use in anything except that which is useful to himself, and as a eudaemonist[7] puts the supreme determining ground of his will simply in utility and his own happiness, not in the thought of duty. For, since every other human being also forms his own different concept of what he counts as happiness, it is precisely egoism which drives him to have no touchstone at all of the genuine concept of duty, which absolutely must be a universally valid principle.[8] – That is why all eudaemonists are practical egoists.

The opposite of egoism can only be *pluralism*, that is, the way of thinking in which one is not concerned with oneself as the whole world, but rather regards and conducts oneself as a mere citizen of the world. – This much belongs to anthropology. As for what concerns this distinction according to metaphysical concepts, it lies entirely beyond the field of the science treated here. That is to say, if the question were merely whether I as a thinking being have reason to assume, in addition to my own existence, the existence of a whole of other beings existing in community with me (called the world), then the question is not anthropological but merely metaphysical.

Remark. On the formality of egoistic language

In our time, the language of the head of state is normally in the plural when addressing the people (We ..., by the grace of God, etc.). The question arises, whether the meaning of this is not rather egoistic; that is, indicative of the speaker's own complete power, and means exactly the

---

[7] *H*: eudaemonist <instructed quite incorrectly in his principle>.
[8] A1 and A2: which ... principle. *H*: which <can only be found with respect to the end, in the determining grounds of the free will which must be valid for everyone.>

same as what the King of Spain says with his *Io, el Rey* ("I, the King")? However, it appears that this formality of the highest authority was originally supposed to indicate condescension (We, the King and his council, or estates). – But how did it happen that the reciprocal form of address, which in the ancient classical languages was expressed through *thou*, hence in the singular, came to be indicated by different people (particularly Germanic peoples) in the plural through *you*? In order to indicate more precisely the person being addressed, the Germans have even invented two expressions; namely *he* and *they* (as if it were [131] not a form of address at all, but rather an account of someone absent, and indeed, either one or more than one person). Finally, to complete all the absurdity of professed abasement before the person being addressed and exalting him, expressions have come into use by means of which we address not the person but the abstract quality of his estate (Your Grace, Right Honorable, Right Noble, High and Noble, and so on). – All of this is probably a result of the feudal system, which took care that the degree of respect due to the nobility was not missing,[9] from the royal dignity on through all gradations up to the point where even human dignity stops and only the human being remains – that is, to the estate of the serf, who alone is addressed by his superiors by means of *thou*, or of a child, who is not yet permitted to have his own way.

On the voluntary consciousness of one's representations

§3

The endeavor to become conscious of one's representations is either the *paying attention to* (*attentio*) or the *turning away from* an idea of which I am conscious (*abstractio*). – The latter is not the mere failure and omission of the former (for that would be distraction, *distractio*), but rather a real act of the cognitive faculty of stopping a representation of which I am conscious from being in connection with other representations in one consciousness. That is why one does not say "to abstract (isolate) *something*," but rather "to abstract (isolate) *from something*;" that is, to abstract a determination[10] from the object of my representation, whereby this

---

[9] "Degree of respect ... missing" not in *H*. [10] *eine Bestimmung*.

19

determination obtains the universality of a concept, and is thus taken into the understanding.

To be able to abstract from a representation, even when the senses force it on a person, is a far greater faculty than that of paying attention to a representation, because it demonstrates a freedom of the faculty of thought and the authority of the mind, *in having the object of one's representations under one's control* (*animus sui compos*). – In this respect, the faculty of *abstraction* is much more difficult than that of attention, but also more important, when it concerns sense representations.

[132] Many human beings are unhappy because they cannot abstract. The suitor could make a good marriage if only he could overlook a wart on his beloved's face, or a gap between her teeth. But it is an especially bad habit of our faculty of attention to fix itself directly, even involuntarily, on what is faulty in others: to fix one's eyes on a button missing from the coat of someone who is directly in front of us, or on gaps between his teeth, or to direct attention to a habitual speech defect, thereby confusing the other person and ruining the game not only for him but also for conversation. If the essentials are good, then it is not only fair, but also prudent, to *look away from* the misfortune of others, yes, even from our own good fortune. But this faculty of abstraction is a strength of mind[11] that can only be acquired through practice.

On self-observation

§4

Noticing oneself (*animadvertere*) is not yet *observing* oneself (*observare*). The latter is a methodical compilation of the perceptions formed in us, which deliver material for a diary of an *observer of oneself*, and easily lead to enthusiasm and madness.[12]

---

[11] *H*: strength of soul.

[12] *Schwärmerei und Wahnsinn*. "Enthusiasm" is the traditional rendering for *Schwärmerei*. However, throughout the Enlightenment, "enthusiasm" often was meant in a sense closer to our "fanaticism." As Locke wrote: "This I take to be properly enthusiasm, which, though founded neither on reason nor divine revelation, but rising from the conceits of a warmed or over-weening brain, works yet, where it once gets footing, more powerfully on the persuasions and actions of men, than either of those two, or both together" (*An Essay Concerning Human Understanding* [1689], IV.xix.7).

Paying attention (*attentio*) to oneself is necessary, to be sure, when one is dealing with others. But in social intercourse it must not become visible; for then it makes conversation either *embarrassed* (self-conscious) or *affected* (stilted). The opposite of both is *ease* (an *air dégagé*): a self-confidence that one's behavior will not be judged unfavorably by others. He who pretends as if he would like to judge[13] himself in front of the mirror to see how the pose suits him, or who speaks as if he were listening to himself speak (not merely as if someone else were listening to him), is a kind of actor. He wants to *represent*[14] and to feign an illusion of his own person whereby, when others observe this effort of his, he suffers in their judgment, because it arouses the suspicion of an intention to deceive them. – – Candor in the manners by which one shows oneself externally (which gives rise to no such suspicion) is called *natural* behavior (which nevertheless does not exclude all fine art and formation of taste), and it pleases as a result of simple *veracity* in expression. But where at the same time open-heartedness peeks through speech from *simple-mindedness*, that is, from the lack of an art of dissimulation that has already become the rule, then it is called *naïveté*.

The plain manner of expressing oneself, as a result of innocence and [133] simple-mindedness (ignorance in the art of pretence), as evidenced in an adolescent girl who is approached or a peasant unfamiliar with urban manners, arouses a cheerful laugh among those who are already practiced and wise in this art. Their laughter is not a jeering with contempt, for in their hearts they still honor purity and sincerity; but rather a good-humored, affectionate smiling at inexperience in the *art of pretence*, which is evil, even though it is grounded in our already corrupted human nature. But one should sigh for this naïve manner rather than laugh at it, when one compares it to the idea of a still uncorrupted human nature.[a] It is a momentary cheerfulness, as if from a cloudy sky that opens up just once in a single spot to let a sunbeam through, but then immediately closes up again in order to spare the weak mole's eyes of selfishness.

---

[13] *H*: <admire>.
[14] *repräsentieren*. *H*: represent <that is, draw preferable attention to himself and he appears foolish (vain in a silly way)>.

[a] In regard to this one could parody the famous verse of Persius as follows: *Naturam videant ingemiscantque relicta* [Trans.: that they may look on nature, and sigh because they have lost her – Ed.].

But the real purpose of this section concerns the *warning* mentioned above, namely not to concern oneself in the least with spying and, as it were, the affected composition of an inner history of the *involuntary* course of one's thoughts and feelings. The warning is given because this is the most direct path to illuminism or even terrorism, by way of a confusion in the mind of supposed higher inspirations and powers flowing into us, without our help, who knows from where. For without noticing it, we make supposed discoveries of what we ourselves have carried into ourselves, like a Bourignon with his flattering ideas, or a Pascal with his terrifying and fearful ones.[15] Even an otherwise splendid mind, Albrecht Haller, fell into a situation of this kind. While occupied with the long-worked-on but also often-interrupted diary of his spiritual condition, he finally reached the point of asking a famous theologian, his former academic colleague Dr. Less, whether in his vast treasury of theology he could not find consolation for his anguished soul.[16]

To observe the various acts of representative power in myself, *when I summon them*, is indeed worth reflection; it is necessary and useful for logic and metaphysics. – But to wish to eavesdrop on oneself when they come into the mind *unbidden* and on their own (this happens through the play of the power of imagination when it is unintentionally meditating) constitutes a reversal of the natural order in the faculty of knowledge, because then the principles of thought do not lead the way (as they should), but rather follow behind. This eavesdropping on oneself is either already a disease of the mind (melancholy), or leads to one and to the madhouse. He who knows how to describe a great deal about his *inner experiences* (of grace, of temptations) may, with his voyage of discovery in the exploration of himself, land only in Anticyra.[17] For the situation with these inner experiences is not as it is with *external*

[134]

---

[15] Antoinette Bourignon (1616–1680), Flemish Christian mystic, adherent of Quietism. Blaise Pascal (1623–1662), noted French scientist-mathematician and religious philosopher. Pascal's primary philosophical work is the *Pensées* (1670), in which he presents his famous "wager" for God's existence (fragment 418).

[16] Albrecht von Haller (1708–1777), Swiss scientist and writer, appointed professor of anatomy, medicine, and botany at the University of Göttingen in 1736. See Haller's *Tagebuch seiner Beobachtungen über Schriftsteller und über sich selbst*, ed. J. G. Heinzmann (Bern, 1787), vol. 2, pp. 219ff. Gottfried Leß (1736–1797), professor of theology at Göttingen.

[17] Anticyra was an ancient coastal city on the Gulf of Corinth, in Phocis. The medicinal plant hellebore – alleged to cure madness – grew there. See Horace, *Satires* 2.3.166; *De Arte Poetica* 360. Külpe surmises that Kant borrowed the allusion from an article in the *Teutsche Merkur* 2 (1784) entitled "Über das Reisen und jemand, der nach Anticyra reisen sollte" (p. 151).

experiences of objects in space, where the objects appear next to each other and[18] *permanently* fixed.[19] Inner sense sees the relations of its determinations only in time, hence in flux, where the stability of observation necessary for experience does not occur.[b]

On the representations that we have without being conscious of them

§5

A contradiction appears to lie in the claim *to have representations and still not be conscious of them*; for how could we know that we have them if we

---

[18] *Crossed out in H*: and [can be presented persistently to the senses, but where, namely in time, the phenomena (of the mind) are in permanent flux, and in different moments always give different views of exactly the same objects, which here the soul (of the subject himself) is <always new to the faculty of cognition> and can be justified, in order to ground an *experience*, rather the inner perceptions, which are coordinated with each other according to their relation *in time*, <place their object as it were> are themselves conceived in *flux* <with and in continuous change> by the passing by of some and the coming into being of others, whereby it easily happens that imaginings instead of perceptions are inserted and, what we <even unexpectedly> *invent* in addition, is taken falsely for inner experience, and ascribed by us to ourselves].

[19] *Marginal note in H*: Concerning intuiting and *reflecting* consciousness. The former can be empirical or *a priori*. The other is never empirical, but always intellectual.

The latter is either *attending or abstracting*. Importance in pragmatic use.

Reflection is the comparison of representation with consciousness, by which a concept (of the object) becomes possible. Reflection therefore precedes the concept, but presupposes representation in general

Consciousness of oneself (*appercept*:) is not empirical But consciousness of the *apprehension* of a given (*a posteriori*) representation is empirical

Double I.

[b] If we consciously represent two acts: inner activity (spontaneity), by means of which a *concept* (a thought) becomes possible, or *reflection*; and receptiveness (receptivity), by means of which a *perception* (*perception*), i.e., empirical *intuition*, becomes possible, or *apprehension*; then consciousness of oneself (*apperception*) can be divided into that of reflection and that of apprehension. The first is a consciousness of understanding, *pure* apperception; the second a consciousness of inner sense, *empirical* apperception. In this case, the former is falsely named *inner* sense. – In psychology we investigate ourselves according to our ideas of inner sense; in logic, according to what intellectual consciousness suggests. Now here the "I" appears to us to be double (which would be contradictory): 1) the "I" as *subject* of thinking (in logic), which means pure apperception (the merely reflecting "I"), and of which there is nothing more to say except that it is a very simple idea; 2) the "I" as *object* of perception, therefore of inner sense, which contains a manifold of determinations that make an inner *experience* possible.

To ask, given the various inner changes within a man's mind (of his memory or of principles adopted by him), when a person is conscious of these changes, whether he can still say that he remains *the very same* (according to his soul), is an absurd question. For it is only because he represents himself as one and the same *subject* in the different states that he can be conscious of these changes. The human "I" is indeed twofold according to form (manner of representation), but not according to matter (content). [*Marginal note in H*:] Concerning voluntary *ignoring* and not taking notice.

are not conscious of them? Locke already raised this objection, and this is why he also rejected the existence of representations of this nature.[20] – However, we can still be *indirectly* conscious of having a representation, even if we are not directly conscious of it. – Such representations are then called *obscure*; the others are *clear*, and when their clarity also extends to the partial representations that make up a whole together with their connection, they are then called *distinct representations*, whether of thought or intuition.

When I am conscious of seeing a human being far from me in a meadow, even though I am not conscious of seeing his eyes, nose, mouth, etc., I properly *conclude* only that this thing is a human being. For if I wanted to maintain that I do not at all have the representation of him in my intuition because I am not conscious of perceiving these parts of his head (and so also the remaining parts of this human being), then I would also not be able to say that I see a human being, since the representation of the whole (of the head or of the human being) is composed of these partial ideas.

The field of sensuous intuitions and sensations of which we are not conscious, even though we can undoubtedly conclude that we have them; that is, *obscure* representations in the human being (and thus also in animals), is immense. Clear representations, on the other hand, contain only infinitely few points of this field which lie open to consciousness; so that as it were only a few places on the vast *map* of our mind are *illuminated*. This can inspire us with wonder over our own being, for a higher being need only call "Let there be light!" and then, without the slightest cooperation on our part (for instance, if we take an author with all that he has in his memory), as it were set half a world before his eyes. Everything the assisted eye discovers by means of the telescope (perhaps directed toward the moon) or microscope (directed toward infusoria) is seen by means of our naked eyes. For these optical aids do not bring [136] more rays of light and thereby more created images into the eye than would have been reflected in the retina without such artificial tools, rather they only spread the images out more, so that we become conscious of them. – Exactly the same holds for sensations of hearing, when a musician plays a fantasy on the organ with ten fingers and both feet and also speaks with someone standing next to him. In a few moments a host

[20] See Locke, *An Essay Concerning Human Understanding*, II.i.9, 18–19. Note: *Vorstellung* is translated as "representation." But Locke, of course, uses the term "idea."

24

of ideas is awakened in his soul, each of which for its selection stands in need of a special judgment as to its appropriateness, since a single stroke of the finger not in accordance with the harmony would immediately be heard as discordant sound. And yet the whole turns out so well that the freely improvising musician often wishes that he would have preserved in written notation many parts of his happily performed piece, which he perhaps otherwise with all diligence and care could never hope to bring off so well.

Thus the field of *obscure* representations is the largest in the human being. – But because this field can only be perceived in his passive side as a play of sensations, the theory of obscure representations belongs only to physiological anthropology, not to pragmatic anthropology, and so it is properly disregarded here.

We often play with obscure representations, and have an interest in throwing them in the shade before the power of the imagination, when they are liked or disliked. However, more often we ourselves are a play of obscure representations, and our understanding is unable to save itself from the absurdities into which they have placed it, even though it recognizes them as illusions.

Such is the case with sexual love, in so far as its actual aim is not benevolence but rather enjoyment of its object. How much wit has been wasted in throwing a delicate veil over that which, while indeed liked, nevertheless still shows such a close relationship with the common species of animals that it calls for modesty? And in polite society the expressions are not blunt, even though they are transparent enough to bring out a smile. – Here the power of imagination enjoys walking in the dark, and it takes uncommon skill if, in order to avoid *cynicism*, one does not want to run the risk of falling into ridiculous *purism*.

On the other hand, we are often enough the play of obscure representations that are reluctant to vanish even when understanding illuminates [137] them. To arrange for a grave in his garden or under a shady tree, in the field or in dry ground, is often an important matter for a dying man; although in the first case he has no reason to hope for a beautiful view, and in the latter no reason to fear catching a cold from the dampness.

The saying "clothes make the man" holds to a certain extent even for intelligent people. To be sure, the Russian proverb says: "One receives the guest according to his clothes, and sees him to the door according to his understanding." But understanding still cannot prevent the impression

25

that a well-dressed person makes of obscure representations of a certain importance. Rather, at best it can only have the resolution afterwards to correct the pleasing, preliminary judgment.

Even studied obscurity is often used with desired success in order to feign profundity and thoroughness, perhaps in the way that objects seen at *dusk* or through a fog always appear larger than they are.[c] [The Greek motto] "skotison" (make it dark) is the decree of all mystics, in order to lure treasure hunters of wisdom by means of an affected obscurity. – But in general a certain degree of mystery in a book is not unwelcome to the reader, because by means of it his own acumen to resolve the obscure into clear concepts becomes palpable.

On distinctness and indistinctness in consciousness of one's representations

§6

[138] Consciousness of one's representations that suffices for the *distinction* of one object from another is *clarity*. But that consciousness by means of which the *composition* of representations also becomes clear is called **distinctness**. Distinctness alone makes it possible that an aggregate of representations becomes *knowledge*, in which *order* is thought in this manifold, because every conscious combination presupposes unity of consciousness, and consequently a rule for the combination. – One cannot contrast the distinct representation with the *confused* representation (*perceptio confusa*); rather it must simply be contrasted with the *indistinct* representation (*mere clara*). What is confused must be composite, for in what is simple there is neither order nor confusion. Confusion is thus the *cause* of indistinctness, not the *definition* of it. – In every complex representation (*perceptio complexa*), and thus in every cognition

---

[c] Viewed by *daylight*, however, that which is brighter than the surrounding objects also appears to be larger, for example, white stockings present fuller calves than do black ones, a fire started in the night on a high mountain appears to be larger than one finds it to be upon measurement. – Perhaps this also explains the apparent size of the moon as well as the apparently greater distance of stars from each other near the horizon; for in both cases shining objects appear to us which are seen near the horizon through a rather darkened air layer; and what is dark is also judged to be smaller, because of the surrounding light. Thus in target practice a black target with a white circle in the middle would be easier to hit than a white target with the opposite arrangement. [*Marginal note in H*:] Clarity of concepts (clarity of understanding) and of the presentation of concepts. This is brightness of the mind.

(since intuition and concept are always required for it), distinctness rests on the *order* according to which the partial representations are combined, and this prompts either a *merely logical* division (concerning the mere form) into higher and subordinate representations (*perceptio primaria et secundaria*), or a *real* division into principal and accessory representations (*perceptio principalis et adhaerens*). It is through this order that cognition becomes distinct. – One readily sees that if[21] the faculty of *cognition* in general is to be called *understanding* (in the most general meaning of the word), then this must contain the *faculty of apprehending* (*attentio*) given representations in order to produce *intuition*, the *faculty of abstracting* what is common to several of these intuitions (*abstractio*) in order to produce the *concept*, and the *faculty of reflecting* (*reflexio*) in order to produce *cognition* of the object.

He who possesses these faculties to a preeminent degree is called a *brain*, he to whom they are distributed in a very small measure a *blockhead* (because he always needs to be led by others), but he who conducts himself with *originality* in the use of these faculties (in virtue of his bringing forth from himself what must normally be learned under the guidance of others) is called a *genius*.

He who has learned nothing of what one must nevertheless be taught in order to know something is called an *ignoramus*, provided that he claims to be a scholar and so *should* have known it; without this claim he can be a great genius. He who cannot *think for himself*, even though he can learn a great deal, is called a *narrow mind* (limited). – A man can be a *great* scholar (a machine for instructing others, as he himself was instructed) and still be very *limited* with respect to the rational use of his historical knowledge. – [139] He whose way of acting with that which he has learned reveals, in public communication, the constraint of the school (thus a want of freedom in thinking for oneself) is a *pedant*, whether he is a scholar, a soldier, or even a courtier. The scholarly pedant is actually the most tolerable of all of these, because one can still learn from him. On the other hand, with the latter two scrupulousness in formalities (pedantry) is not merely useless but also, on account of the pride to which the pedant unavoidably clings, ridiculous as well, since it is the pride of an *ignoramus*.

---

[21] *Crossed out in H*: if [this cognition is to be *experience* 1) *Apprehension* of the given <objects (*apprehensio*)> representation. 2) *Consciousness* of the manifold of its contents (*apperception*). 3) *Reflection* on the manner of combining the latter in a consciousness (*reflexio*) belonging to such a cognition].

27

However, the art, or rather the facility, of speaking in a sociable *tone* and in general of appearing fashionable is falsely named *popularity* – particularly when it concerns science. It should rather be called polished superficiality, because it frequently cloaks the paltriness of a limited mind. But only children can be misled by it. As the Quaker with Addison said to the chattering officer sitting next to him in the carriage, "Your drum is a symbol of yourself: it resounds because it is empty."[22]

In order to judge human beings according to their cognitive faculty (understanding in general), we divide them into those who must be granted *common sense* (*sensus communis*), which certainly is not *common* (*sensus vulgaris*), and people of *science*. The former are knowledgeable in the application of rules to cases (*in concreto*); the latter, in the rules themselves before their application (*in abstracto*). – The understanding that belongs to the first cognitive faculty is called *sound* human understanding (*bon sens*); that belonging to the second, a *clear mind* (*ingenium perspicax*). – It is strange that sound human understanding, which is usually regarded only as a practical cognitive faculty, is not only presented as something that can manage without culture, but also something for which culture is even disadvantageous, if it is not pursued enough. Some praise it highly to the point of enthusiasm and represent it as a rich source of treasure lying hidden in the mind, and sometimes its pronouncement as an oracle (Socrates' genius) is said to be more reliable than anything academic science offers for sale. – This much is certain, that if the solution to a problem is based on general and innate rules of understanding (possession of which is called mother wit), it is more dangerous to look around for academic and artificially drawn-up princi-

[140] ples (school wit) and thereafter to come to their conclusion than to take a chance on the outburst from the determining grounds of masses of judgment that lie in the obscurity of the mind. One could call this logical *tact*, where reflection on the object is presented from many different sides and comes out with a correct result, without being conscious of the acts that are going on inside the mind during this process.

But sound understanding can demonstrate its superiority only in regard to an object of experience, which consists not only in increasing knowledge *through* experience but also in enlarging experience itself; not,

---

[22] Joseph Addison (1672–1719), English essayist, poet, and statesman. See *The Spectator* 132 (August 1, 1711), p. 198.

28

however, in a speculative, but merely in an empirical-practical respect. For in the speculative employment of the understanding, scientific principles *a priori* are required; however, in the empirical-practical employment of understanding there can also be experiences, that is, judgments which are continually confirmed by trial and outcome.

On sensibility in contrast to understanding

§7

In regard to the state of its representations, my mind is either *active* and exhibits a faculty (*facultas*), or it is *passive* and consists in *receptivity* (*receptivitas*). A *cognition* contains both joined together, and the possibility of having such a cognition bears the name of *cognitive faculty* – from the most distinguished part of this faculty, namely the activity of mind in combining or separating representations from one another.

Representations in regard to which the mind behaves passively, and by means of which the subject is therefore *affected* (whether it *affects* itself or is *affected* by an object), belong to the *sensuous* (*sinnliche*) cognitive faculty. But ideas that comprise a sheer *activity* (thinking) belong to the *intellectual* cognitive faculty. The former is also called the *lower*; the latter, the *higher* cognitive faculty.[d] The lower cognitive faculty has the character [141] of *passivity* of the inner sense of sensations; the higher, of spontaneity of apperception, that is, of pure consciousness of the activity that constitutes thinking. It belongs to logic (a system of rules of the understanding), as

---

[d] To posit *sensibility* merely in the indistinctness of representations, and *intellectuality* by comparison in the distinctness of representations, and thereby in a merely *formal* (logical) distinction of consciousness instead of a *real* (psychological) one, which concerns not merely the form but also the content of thought, was a great error of the Leibniz-Wolffian school. Their error was, namely, to posit sensibility in a lack (of clarity in our partial ideas), and consequently in indistinctness, and to posit the character of ideas of understanding in distinctness; whereas in fact sensibility is something very positive and an indispensable addition to ideas of understanding, in order to bring forth a cognition. – But Leibniz was actually to blame. For he, adhering to the Platonic school, assumed innate, pure intellectual intuitions, called ideas, which are encountered in the human mind, though now only obscurely; and to whose analysis and illumination by means of attention alone we owe the cognition of objects, as they are in themselves. [*Marginal note in H:*] Sensibility is a subject's faculty of representation, in so far as it is affected.
As lack and as supplementary state for cognition.
A representation recollected or made abstract.

29

the former belongs to psychology (a sum of all inner perceptions under laws of nature) and establishes[23] inner experience.

Remark.[24] The object of a representation, which comprises only the way I am affected by it, can only be cognized by me as it appears to me;

[23] *Crossed out in H*: establishes [Now, since with the former, cognition of objects depends merely on the subjective property of being affected by impressions which come from the object (representing it in a certain way), which cannot be exactly the same with all subjects, thus <one can> say: this presents objects of the *senses* to us only as they *appear* to us, not according to what they *are* in themselves. (But since these appearances are closely connected with the law of understanding, cognition (of the objects of the senses), which is called experience, is therefore not less certain, as if it concerned objects in themselves. And because for us there can be no knowledge other than of things which can be presented to our senses, therefore there may always be concepts in the idea of reason which go beyond their limits, but only have objective reality in a practical respect (of the idea of freedom), we are here concerned only with those things that can be given to our senses).

[24] *Crossed out in H*: Remark [Second Section.

On Sensibility

That this proposition applies even to the inner self and the human being, who observes his inner self according to certain impressions from whatever source they may arise, and through this can only recognize himself as he appears to himself, not as he absolutely is: this is a bold *metaphysical proposition* (*paradoxon*), which cannot be dealt with in anthropology. – But if <he> obtains inner experience <from> himself, and if he pursues this investigation as far as he can, he will have to confess that self-knowledge would lead to an unfathomable depth, to an abyss in the exploration of his nature. [Human being, you are such a difficult problem in your own eyes/No I am not able to grasp you. Pope according to Brock's translation. – Külpe notes that the quotation is from B. H. Brockes, *Versuch vom Menschen des Herrn Alexander Pope* (Hamburg, 1740), but more precisely from a French poem contained in this book: *Les contradictions de l'homme*. – Ed.] And this belongs to anthropology.

All cognition presupposes understanding. The irrational animal <perhaps> has something similar to what we call representations (because it has effects that are <very> similar to the representations in the human being), but which may perhaps be entirely different – but no cognition of things; for this requires *understanding*, a faculty of representation with consciousness of action whereby the representations relate to a given object and this relation may be thought. – However, we do not understand anything correctly <according to form> except that which we can make at the same time when the material for it would be given to us. Consequently, understanding is a faculty of spontaneity in our cognition, a higher faculty of cognition, because it submits representations to certain *a priori* rules and itself makes experience possible.

In the self-cognition of the human being through inner experience he does not *make* what he has perceived in himself, for this depends on impressions (the subject matter of representations) that he *receives*. Therefore he is so far enduring, that is, he has a representation of himself as he is affected by himself, which according to its form depends merely on the subjective property of his nature, which should not be interpreted as belonging to the object, even though he still also has the right to attribute it to the object (here his own person), but with the qualification that he can only recognize himself as an object through this representation in experience as he *appears* to himself, not as he, the observed, is in himself. – If he wished to cognize in the latter way, he would have to rely on a consciousness of pure spontaneity (the concept of freedom), (which is also possible), but it would still not be perception of inner sense and the empirical cognition of his inner self (inner experience) which is based on it. Rather, it can only be consciousness of the rule of his actions and omissions, without thereby acquiring a theoretical (physiological) cognition of his nature, which is what psychology actually aims at. – Empirical self-cognition therefore

footnote 24 (continued)

presents to inner sense the human being as he appears to it, not as he is in himself, because every cognition explains merely the *affectability* of the subject, not the inner characteristic of the subject as object.

How then is the great difficulty to be removed, in which consciousness of oneself still presents only the appearance of oneself, and not the human being in himself? And why does it not present a double I, but nevertheless a doubled consciousness of this I, first that of mere *thinking* but then also that of inner *perception* (rational and empirical); that is, discursive and intuitive apperception, of which the first belongs to logic and the other to anthropology (as physiology)? The former is without content (matter of cognition), while the latter is provided with a content by inner sense.

An object of the (external or inner) sense, in so far as it is perceived, is called *appearance* (*phaenomenon*). Cognition of an object in appearance (that is, as phenomenon) is *experience*. Therefore appearance is that representation through which an object of the sense is given (an object of perception, that is, of empirical intuition), but experience or empirical *cognition* is that representation through which the object as such at the same time is *thought*. – Therefore appearance is that representation through which an object of the sense is given (an object of perception, that is, of empirical intuition), but experience or empirical *cognition* is that representation through which the object as such at the same time is *thought*. – Therefore experience is the activity (of the power of imagination) through which appearances are brought under the concept of one object of experience, and experiences are made by *employing* observations (intentional perceptions) and through reflecting (*reflectirt*) about how to unify them under one concept. – We acquire and broaden our cognition through experience by supplying the understanding with appearances of external or even inner sense as material. And no one doubts that we could not equally make inner observations of ourselves and make experiences in this way, but if we dare now to speak of objects of inner sense (which as sense always provides appearances only) it is because we are able to reach only cognition of ourselves, not as we are, but as we appear (internally) to ourselves. There is something shocking in this proposition, which we must consider more carefully. – We allow a judgment of this kind regarding objects outside us, but it looks quite absurd to apply it to what we perceive within ourselves. – That some word-twisters take appearance and *semblance* (*Erscheinung und Schein*) for one and the same thing and say that their statements mean as much as: "it seems (*scheint*) to me that I exist and have this or that representation" is a falsification unworthy of any refutation.

This difficulty rests entirely on the confusion of *inner sense* with *apperception* (intellectual self-consciousness), which are usually taken to be one and the same. The I in every judgment is neither an intuition nor a concept, and not at all a determination of an object, but an act of understanding by the determining subject as such, and the consciousness of oneself; pure apperception itself therefore belongs merely to logic (without any matter and content). On the other hand, the I of inner sense, that is, of the perception and observation of oneself, is not the subject of judgment, but an object. Consciousness of the one who *observes* himself is an entirely simple representation of the subject in judgment as such, of which one knows everything if one merely thinks it. But the I which has been observed by itself is a sum total of so many objects of inner perception that psychology has plenty to do in tracing everything that lies hidden in it. And psychology may not ever hope to complete this task and answer satisfactorily the question: "What is the human being?"

One must therefore distinguish pure apperception (of the understanding) from empirical apperception (of sensibility). The latter, when the subject attends to himself, is also at the same time affected and so calls out sensations in himself, that is, brings representations to consciousness. These representations are in conformity with each other according to the form of their relation, the subjective and formal condition of sensibility; namely intuition in <space and> time (simultaneously or in succession), and not merely according to rules of the understanding. Now since this form cannot be assumed to be valid for every being as such that is conscious of itself, therefore the cognition which has the inner sense of the human being as its ground cannot represent by inner experience how he himself is (because the condition is not valid for all thinking

31

and all experience (empirical cognition), inner no less than outer, is only the cognition of objects as they *appear* to us, not as they *are* (considered in themselves alone). For what kind of sensible intuition there will be depends not merely on the constitution of the object of the representation, but also on the constitution of the subject and its receptivity, after which thinking (the concept of the object) follows. – Now the formal constitution of this receptivity cannot in turn be borrowed from the senses, but rather must (as intuition) be given *a priori*; that is, it must be a sensible intuition which remains even after everything empirical (comprising sense experience) is omitted, and in inner experiences this formal element of intuition is *time*.

Experience is empirical cognition, but cognition (since it rests on judgments) requires reflection (*reflexio*), and consequently consciousness of activity in combining the manifold of ideas according to a rule of the unity of the manifold; that is, it requires concepts and thought in general (as distinct from intuition). Thus consciousness is divided into *discursive* consciousness (which as logical consciousness must lead the way, since it gives the rule), and *intuitive* consciousness. Discursive consciousness (pure apperception of one's mental activity) is simple. The "I" of reflection contains no manifold in itself and is always one and the same in every judgment, because it is merely the formal element of consciousness. On the other hand, *inner experience* contains the mate-

[142] rial of consciousness and a manifold of empirical inner intuition, the "I" of *apprehension* (consequently an empirical apperception).

footnote 24 *(continued)*

beings, for then it would be a representation of the understanding). Rather, it is merely a consciousness of the way that the human being appears to himself in his inner observation.

Cognition of oneself according to the constitution of what one is in oneself cannot be acquired through inner *experience* and does not spring from knowledge of the nature of the human being, but is simply and solely the consciousness of one's freedom, which is known to him through the categorical imperative of duty, therefore only through the highest practical reason.
B
Of the field of sensibility in relation to the field of understanding
§8
Division
The mind (*animus*) of the human being, as the sum total of all representations that have a place within it, has a domain (*sphaera*) which concerns three parts: the faculty of cognition, the feeling of pleasure and displeasure, and the faculty of desire. Each of these has two divisions, the field of *sensibility* and the field of *intellectuality*. (the field of sensible or intellectual cognition, pleasure or displeasure, and desire or abhorrence).

Sensibility can be considered as a weakness or also as a strength.]

It is true that I as a thinking being am one and the same subject with myself as a sensing being. However, as the object of inner empirical intuition; that is, in so far as I am affected inwardly by experiences in time, simultaneous as well as successive, I nevertheless cognize myself only as I appear to myself, not as a thing in itself. For this cognition still depends on the temporal condition, which is not a concept of the understanding (consequently not mere spontaneity); as a result it depends on a condition with regard to which my faculty of ideas is passive (and belongs to receptivity). – Therefore I always cognize myself only through inner experience, as I *appear* to myself; which proposition is then often so maliciously twisted as if it said: it only *seems* to me (*mihi videri*) that I have certain ideas and sensations, indeed it only seems that I exist at all. – The semblance[25] is the ground for an erroneous judgment from subjective causes, which are falsely regarded as objective; however, appearance is not a judgment at all, but merely an empirical intuition which, through reflection and the concept of understanding arising from it, becomes inner experience and consequently truth.

The cause of these errors is that the terms *inner sense* and *apperception* are normally taken by psychologists to be synonymous, despite the fact that the first alone should indicate a psychological (applied) consciousness, and the second merely a logical (pure) consciousness. However, that we only cognize ourselves through inner sense as we *appear* to ourselves is clear from this: apprehension (*apprehensio*) of the impressions of inner sense presupposes a formal condition of inner intuition of the subject, namely time, which is not a concept of understanding and is therefore valid merely as a subjective condition according to which inner sensations are given to us by virtue of the constitution of the human soul. Therefore, apprehension does not give us cognition of how the object is in itself.

✳✳✳

This note does not really belong to anthropology. In anthropology, experiences are appearances united according to laws of understanding, and in taking into consideration our way of representing things, the question of how they are apart from their relation to the *senses* (consequently as they are in themselves) is not pursued at all; for this belongs to [143] metaphysics, which has to do with the possibility of *a priori* cognition.

---

[25] *Der Schein.*

33

But it was nevertheless necessary to go back so far simply in order to stop the offenses of the speculative mind in regard to this question. As for the rest, knowledge of the human being through inner experience, because to a large extent one also judges others according to it, is more important than correct judgment of others, but nevertheless at the same time perhaps more difficult. For he who investigates his interior easily *carries* many things into self-consciousness instead of merely observing. So it is advisable and even necessary to begin with observed *appearances* in oneself, and then to progress above all to the assertion of certain propositions that concern human nature; that is, to *inner experience*.

Apology for sensibility

§8

Everyone shows the greatest respect for understanding, as is already indicated by the very name *higher* cognitive faculty. Anyone who wanted to praise it would be dismissed with the same scorn earned by an orator exalting virtue (*stulte! quis unquam vituperavit*).[26] Sensibility, on the other hand, is in bad repute. Many evil things are said about it: e.g., 1) that it *confuses* the power of representation, 2) that it monopolizes conversation and is like an *autocrat*, stubborn and hard to restrain, when it should be merely the *servant* of the understanding, 3) that it even *deceives* us, and that we cannot be sufficiently on guard where it is concerned. – On the other hand sensibility is not at a loss for eulogists, especially among poets and people of taste, who not only extol the merits of *sensualizing* the concepts of the understanding, but also assign the *fertility* (wealth of ideas) and *emphasis* (vigor) of language and the *evidence* of ideas (their lucidity in consciousness) directly to this sensualizing of concepts and to the view that concepts must not be analyzed into their constituent parts with meticulous care. The bareness[27] of the understanding, however, they declare to be sheer poverty.[e] We do not need any panegyrists here, but only an advocate against the accuser.

---

[26] Trans.: Fool! Who has ever criticized virtue?　　[27] *Nacktheit.*

[e] Since we are speaking here only of the cognitive faculty and therefore of representations (not of the feeling of pleasure or displeasure), *sensation* will mean nothing more than sense representation (empirical intuition) in distinction from concepts (thoughts) as well as from pure intuition

The *passive* element in sensibility, which we after all cannot get rid of, [144] is actually the cause of all the evil said about it. The inner perfection of the human being consists in having in his power the use of all of his faculties, in order to subject them to his *free choice*. For this, it is required that *understanding* should rule without weakening sensibility (which in itself is like a mob, because it does not think), for without sensibility there would be no material that could be processed for the use of legislative understanding.

Defense of sensibility against the first accusation

§9

The senses do not confuse. He who has *grasped* a given manifold, but *not yet ordered* it, cannot be said to have *confused* it. Sense perceptions (empirical representations accompanied by consciousness) can only be called inner *appearances.* The understanding, which comes in and connects appearances under a rule of thought (brings *order* into the manifold), first makes empirical cognition out of them; that is, *experience.* The *understanding* is therefore neglecting its obligation if it judges rashly without first having ordered the sense representations according to concepts, and then later complains about their confusion, which it blames on the particular sensual nature of the human being. This reproach applies to the ungrounded complaint over the confusion of outer as well as inner representations through sensibility.[28]

Certainly, sense representations come before those of the understanding and present themselves *en masse.* But the fruits are all the more plentiful

(representations of space and time). [*Marginal note in H*: Consciousness of oneself is either discursive in concept or intuitive in the inner intuition of time. – The I of apperception is simple and binding; however, the I of apprehension is a matter of a manifold with representations joined to one another in the I as object of intuition. This manifold in one's intuition is given ... [smudged] an *a priori* form in which it can be ordered ...]

[28] *Marginal note in H*: Perception (empirical intuition with consciousness) could be called merely appearance of inner sense. However, in order for it to become inner experience the law must be known which determines the form of this connection in a consciousness of the object.

The human being cannot observe himself internally if he is not led by means of a rule, under which perceptions alone must be united, if they are to furnish him with an experience. Therefore they are together only appearances of himself. To cognize himself from them he must take a principle of appearance (in space and time) as a basis, in order to know what the human being is.

Sensibility as strength or weakness.

35

when understanding comes in with its order and intellectual form and brings into consciousness, e.g., *concise* expressions for the concept, *emphatic* expressions for the feeling, and *interesting* ideas for determining the will. – When the *riches* that the mind produces in rhetoric and poetry [145] are placed before the understanding all at once (*en masse*), the understanding is often embarrassed on account of its rational employment. It often falls into confusion, when it ought to make clear and set forth all the acts of reflection that it actually employs, although obscurely. But sensibility is not at fault here, rather it is much more to its credit that it has presented abundant material to understanding, whereas the abstract concepts of understanding are often only glittering poverty.

Defense of sensibility against the second accusation

§10

The senses do not have command over understanding. Rather, they offer themselves to understanding merely in order to be at its disposal. That the senses do not wish to have their importance misjudged, an importance that is due to them especially in what is called common sense (*sensus communis*), cannot be credited to them because of the presumption of wanting to rule over understanding. It is true that there are judgments which one does not bring *formally* before the tribunal of understanding in order to pronounce sentence on them, and which therefore seem to be directly dictated by sense. They are embodied in so-called aphorisms or oracular outbursts (such as those to whose utterance Socrates attributed his genius). That is to say, it is thereby assumed that the *first* judgment about the right and wise thing to do in a given case is normally also the *correct* one, and that pondering over it will only spoil it. But in fact these judgments do not come from the senses; they come from real, though obscure, reflections of understanding. – The senses make no claim in this matter; they are like the common people who, if they are not a mob (*ignobile vulgus*), gladly submit to their superior understanding, but still want to be heard. But if certain judgments and insights are assumed to spring directly from inner sense (without the help of understanding), and if they are further assumed to command themselves, so that sensations count as judgments, then this is sheer *enthusiasm*, which stands in close relation to derangement of the senses.

36

Defense of sensibility against the third accusation [146]

§11

The senses do not deceive. This proposition is the rejection of the most important but also, on careful consideration, the emptiest reproach made against the senses; not because they always judge correctly, but rather because they do not judge at all. Error is thus a burden only to the understanding. – Still, *sensory appearances* (*species, apparentia*) serve to excuse, if not exactly to justify, understanding. Thus the human being often mistakes what is subjective in his way of representation for objective (the distant tower, on which he sees no corners, seems to be round; the sea, whose distant part strikes his eyes through higher light rays, seems to be higher than the shore (*altum mare*); the full moon, which he sees ascending near the horizon through a hazy air, seems to be further away, and also larger, than when it is high in the heavens, although he catches sight of it from the same visual angle). And so one takes *appearance* for *experience*; thereby falling into error, but it is an error of the understanding, not of the senses.

***

A reproach which logic throws against sensibility is that in so far as cognition is promoted by sensibility, one reproaches it with *superficiality* (individuality, limitation to the particular), whereas understanding, which goes up to the universal and for that reason has to trouble itself with abstractions, encounters the reproach of *dryness*. However, aesthetic treatment, whose first requirement is popularity, adopts a method by which both errors can be avoided.

On ability with regard to the cognitive faculty in general

§12

The preceding paragraph, which dealt with the faculty of appearance, which no human being can control, leads us to a discussion of the concepts of the *easy* and the *difficult* (*leve et grave*), which literally in German signify only physical conditions and powers. But in Latin, according to a certain analogy, they should signify the *practicable* (*facile*) [147] and the *comparatively impracticable* (*difficile*); for the barely practicable is

37

regarded as *subjectively impracticable* by a subject who is doubtful of the degree of his requisite capacity in certain situations and conditions.

Facility in doing something (*promptitudo*) must not be confused with *skill* in such actions (*habitus*). The former signifies a certain degree of mechanical capacity: "I can if I want to," and designates subjective *possibility*. The latter signifies subjective-practical *necessity*, that is, *habit*, and so designates a certain degree of will, acquired through the frequently repeated use of one's faculty: "I choose this, because duty commands it." Therefore one cannot explain *virtue* as *skill* in free lawful actions, for then it would be a mere mechanism of applying power. Rather, virtue is *moral strength* in adherence to one's duty, which never should become habit but should always emerge entirely new and original from one's way of thinking.

The easy is contrasted to the *difficult*, but often it is contrasted to the *onerous* as well. A subject regards something as *easy* whenever he encounters a large surplus in his capacity for applying the requisite power to an action. What is easier than observing the formalities of visits, congratulations, and condolences? But what is also more arduous for a busy man? They are friendship's *vexations* (drudgeries), from which everyone heartily wishes to be free, and yet still carries scruples about offending against custom.

What vexations there are in external customs that are attributed to religion but which actually collect around ecclesiastical form! The merit of piety is set up exactly in such a way that it serves no purpose other than the mere submission of believers to let themselves patiently be tormented by ceremonies and observances, atonements and mortifications of the flesh (the more the better). To be sure, this compulsory service is *mechanically easy* (because no vicious inclination need be sacrificed as a result), but to the reasonable person it must come as *morally very arduous* and onerous. – So when the great moral teacher of the people said, "My commands are not difficult,"[29] he did not mean by this that they require only a limited expenditure of power in order to be fulfilled; for in fact as commands that require pure dispositions of the heart they are the most [148] difficult ones of all that can be commanded. But for a reasonable person they are still infinitely easier than commands of busy inactivity (*gratis*

---

[29] 1 John 5:3. See also Kant's *Religion Within the Boundaries of Mere Reason* 6: 179n.

38

anhelare, multa agendo, nihil agere),[30] such as those which Judaism established. For to a reasonable man the mechanically easy feels like a heavy burden, when he sees that all the effort connected to it still serves no purpose.

To *make* something difficult easy is *meritorious*; to *depict* it to someone as easy, even though one is not able to accomplish it oneself, is *deception*. To do that which is easy is *meritless*. Methods and machines, and among these the division of labor among different craftsmen (manufactured goods), make many things easy which would be difficult to do with one's own hands without other tools.

To *point out* difficulties before one gives instruction for an undertaking (as, e.g., in metaphysical investigations) may admittedly discourage others, but this is still better than *concealing* difficulties from them. He who regards everything that he undertakes as easy is *thoughtless*. He who performs everything that he does with ease is *adept*; just as he whose actions reveal effort is *awkward*. – Social entertainment (conversation) is merely a game in which everything must be easy and must allow easiness. Thus ceremony (stiffness) in conversation, e.g., the solemn good-bye after a banquet, has been gotten rid of as something outmoded.

People's state of mind in a business undertaking varies according to the difference of temperaments. Some begin with difficulties and concerns (the melancholic temperament), with others (the sanguine) hope and the presumed easiness of carrying out the undertaking are the first thoughts that come into their minds.

But how to regard the vainglorious claim of powerful men, which is not based on mere temperament: "What the human being *wills*, he *can* do"? It is nothing more than a high-sounding tautology: namely what he wills *at the order of his morally commanding reason*, he *ought* to do and consequently *can* also do (for the impossible is not commanded to him by reason). However, some years ago there were fools like this who also prided themselves on taking the dictum in a physical sense, announcing themselves as world-assailants; but their breed has long since vanished.

Finally, *becoming accustomed* (*consuetudo*) in fact makes the endurance of misfortune *easy* (which is then falsely honored with the name of a virtue, namely patience), for when sensations of exactly the same kind

---

[30] Trans.: gasping in vain; occupied with many things, but accomplishing nothing. Phaedrus, *Fabulae* 2.5.

[149] persist for a long time without change and draw one's attention away from the senses, one is barely conscious of them any more. But this also makes consciousness and memory of the good that one has received *more difficult*, which then usually leads to ingratitude (a real vice).

Habit (*assuetudo*), however, is a physical inner necessitation to proceed in the same manner that one has proceeded until now. It deprives even good actions of their moral worth because it impairs the freedom of the mind and, moreover, leads to thoughtless repetition of the very same act (*monotony*), and so becomes ridiculous. – Habitual fillers[31] (*phrases* used for the mere filling up of the emptiness of thoughts) make the listener constantly worried that he will have to hear the little sayings yet again, and they turn the speaker into a talking machine. The reason why the habits of another stimulate the arousal of disgust in us is that here the animal in the human being jumps out far too much, and that here one is led *instinctively* by the rule of habituation, exactly like another (non-human) nature, and so runs the risk of falling into one and the same class with the beast. – Nevertheless, certain habits can be started intentionally and put in order when nature refuses free choice her help; for example, accustoming oneself in old age to eating and drinking times, to the quality and quantity of food and drink, or also with sleep, and so gradually becoming mechanical. But this holds only as an exception and in cases of necessity. As a rule all habits are reprehensible.

On artificial play with sensory illusion[32]

§13

Delusion, which is produced in the understanding by means of sense representations (*praestigiae*), can be either natural or artificial, and is either *illusion*[33] (*illusio*) or *deception* (*fraus*). – The delusion by which one

---

[31] *Flickwörter.*

[32] *Sinnenschein.* Throughout this section and the next, the word *Schein* is used a great deal. I have translated it consistently as "illusion," in part because Kant uses other terms such as *Täuschung* and *Illusion* as stand-ins for it that translate unambiguously into "illusion," and also because other translators in the Cambridge Kant Edition render the term this way. However, *Schein* can also mean "semblance, appearance, pretense, show." These multiple meanings should be kept in mind, particularly in §14, where Kant discusses moral *Schein*. His point there is that although moral *Schein* should not be confused with true virtue, it is an external semblance of it that will eventually become the real thing.

[33] *Täuschung.*

is compelled to regard something as real on the testimony of his eyes, though the very same subject declares it to be impossible on the basis of his understanding, is called *optical delusion (praestigiae)*.

Illusion[34] is that delusion which persists even though one knows that the supposed object is not real. – This mental game with sensory illusion [150] is very pleasant and entertaining, as in, for example, the perspective drawing of the interior of a temple, or the painting of the school of Peripatetics (by Correggio, I think), of which Raphael Mengs[35] says: "if one looks at them for long, they seem to walk"; or the painted steps with a half-opened door in the town hall of Amsterdam, where one is induced to climb up them, and so forth.

However, *deception* of the senses exists when, as soon as one knows how the object is constituted, the illusion[36] also immediately ceases. All types of sleights of hand are things like that. Clothing whose color sets off the face to advantage is illusion; but makeup is deception. One is seduced by the first, but mocked by the second. – This is why *statues* of human beings or animals painted with natural colors are not liked: each time they unexpectedly come into sight, one is momentarily deceived into regarding them as living.

Bewitchment (fascinatio) in an otherwise sound state of mind is a delusion of the senses, of which it is said that the senses are not dealing with natural things; for the judgment that an object (or a characteristic of it) *exists* is irresistibly changed after closer attention to the judgment that it does *not exist* (or has a different shape). – So the senses seem to contradict each other; like a bird that flutters against a mirror in which he sees himself and at one moment takes the reflection for a real bird, at another, not. With human beings this game, in which they *do not trust their own senses*, occurs especially in those who are seized by strong passion. When the lover (according to Helvétius)[37] saw his beloved in the arms of another, she could simply deny it to him, saying: "Faithless one! You do not love me any more. You believe what you see more than

---

[34] *Illusion.*
[35] Anton Raphael Mengs (1728–1779), German historical and portrait painter, author of *Gedanken über die Schönheit und über den Geschmack in der Malerei* (Zurich, 1774). The painting referred to is most likely Raphael's *School of Athens*. Külpe, in his note on Mengs, remarks that he was unable to locate Kant's citation in any of Mengs's writings.
[36] *Schein.*
[37] Claude Adrien Helvétius (1715–1771), French materialist philosopher. See his *De l'esprit* (1759), Essay I, Ch. 2.

41

what I say to you." – Cruder, or at least more harmful, was the deception practiced by ventriloquists, Gassnerists, mesmerists,[38] and other alleged necromancers. In former times poor ignorant women who imagined that they could do something supernatural were called *witches*, and even in this century belief in witches has not been rooted out completely.[f] It [151] seems that the feeling of wonder over something outrageous has in itself much that is alluring for the weak man: not merely because new prospects are suddenly opened to him, but also because he is thereby absolved from the burdensome use of reason, while others are induced to make themselves equal to him in ignorance.

On permissible moral illusion

§14

On the whole, the more civilized human beings are, the more they are actors. They adopt the illusion of affection, of respect for others, of modesty, and of unselfishness without deceiving anyone at all, because it is understood by everyone that nothing is meant sincerely by this. And it is also very good that this happens in the world. For when human beings play these roles, eventually the virtues, whose illusion they have merely affected for a considerable length of time, will gradually really be aroused and merge into the disposition. – But to deceive the deceiver in

---

[38] The Gassnerists were followers of Johann J. Gassner (1727–1779), a Catholic priest in Switzerland who allegedly healed diseases by exorcism of the devil. The mesmerists were named after Franz Mesmer (1734–1815), an Austrian physician who sought to treat disease through animal magnetism, an early therapeutic application of hypnotism.

[f] Even in this century a Protestant clergyman in Scotland serving as a witness at a trial about such a case said to the judge: "Your Honor, I assure you on my honor as a minister that this woman is a *witch* (*Hexe*)"; to which the judge replied: "And I assure you on my honor as a judge that you are no sorcerer (*Hexenmeister*)." The word *Hexe*, which has now become a German word, comes from the first words of the formula of the mass used at the Consecration of the Host, which the faithful see with *bodily* eyes as a small disc of bread but which, after the formula has been pronounced, they are obliged to see with *spiritual* eyes as the body of a human being. For the words *hoc est* were initially added to the word *corpus*, and in speaking *hoc est corpus* was changed to *hocuspocus*, presumably from pious timidity at saying and profaning the correct phrase. This is what superstitious people are in the habit of doing with unnatural objects, in order not to profane them. [Kant's etymology is incorrect. At present it is believed that *Hexe* derives from *Hag* (hedge, grove, little forest); a *Hexe* being a demonic woman inhabiting such an area. Kant's interpretation is based on Christoph Adelung's *Versuch eines vollständigen grammatisch-kritisches Wörterbuch der Hochdeutschen Mundart*, 2nd ed. (Leipzig, 1793) –Ed.].

ourselves, the inclinations, is a return again to obedience under the law of virtue and is not a deception, but rather an innocent illusion of ourselves.

An example of this is the *disgust* with one's own existence, which arises when the mind is empty of the sensations toward which it incessantly strives. This is *boredom*, in which one nevertheless at the same time feels a weight of inertia, that is, of weariness with regard to all occupation that could be called work and could drive away disgust because it is associated with hardships, and it is a highly contrary feeling whose cause is none other than the natural inclination toward *ease* (toward rest, before weariness even precedes). – But this inclination is deceptive, even with regard to the ends that reason makes into a law for the human being,[39] it makes [152] him content with himself *when he is doing nothing at all* (vegetating aimlessly), because he *at least is not doing anything bad*. To deceive it in return (which can be done by playing with the fine arts, but most of all through social conversation) is called *passing time* (*tempus fallere*), where the expression already indicates the intention, namely to deceive even the inclination toward idle rest. We are passing time when we keep the mind at play by the fine arts, and even in a game that is aimless in itself within a peaceful rivalry at least the culture of the mind is brought about – otherwise it would be called *killing time*. – – Nothing is accomplished by using force against sensibility in the inclinations; one must outwit them and, as Swift says,[40] surrender a barrel for the whale to play with, in order to save the ship.

In order to save virtue, or at least lead the human being to it, nature has wisely implanted in him the tendency to allow himself willingly to be deceived. Good, honorable *decorum* is an external illusion that instills *respect* in others (so that they do not behave over familiarly with others). It is true that woman[41] would not be content if the male sex did not appear to pay homage to her charms. But *modesty* (*pudicitia*), a self-constraint that conceals passion, is nevertheless very beneficial as an

---

[39] Gregor suggests that Kant has in mind here the duty to cultivate one's natural talents. See, e.g., *The Metaphysics of Morals* 6: 444ff., where Kant discusses "A human being's duty to himself to develop and increase his *natural perfection*, that is, for a pragmatic purpose."

[40] Jonathan Swift (1667–1745), English writer, author of *Gulliver's Travels* (1726). See his *A Tale of a Tub* (1704), ed. A. C. Guthkelch and D. Nichol Smith (Oxford: Clarendon Press, 1958), Preface, p. 40.

[41] *Marginal note in H*: Of a pair who received guests who had not previously announced themselves. Qualification of the claim of sensibility and of the faculty of cognition. – NB. it must ultimately come before the title of the understanding.

illusion that brings about distance between one sex and the other, which is necessary in order that one is not degraded into a mere tool for the other's enjoyment. – In general, everything that is called *propriety* (*decorum*) is of this same sort – namely nothing but *beautiful illusion*.

Politeness (*politesse*) is an illusion of affability that inspires love. *Bowing* (compliments) and all *courtly* gallantry together with the warmest verbal assurances of friendship are to be sure not exactly always truthful ("My dear friends: there is no such thing as a friend." *Aristotle*);[42] but this is precisely why they do not *deceive*, because everyone knows how they should be taken, and especially because these signs of benevolence and respect, though empty at first, gradually lead to real dispositions of this sort.

All human virtue in circulation is small change – it is a child who takes it for real gold. – But it is still better to have small change in circulation than no funds at all, and eventually they can be converted into genuine [153] gold, though at considerable loss. It is committing high treason against humanity to pass them off as *mere tokens* that have no worth at all, to say with the sarcastic Swift:[43] "Honor is a pair of shoes that have been worn out in the manure," etc., or with the preacher Hofstede[44] in his attack on Marmontel's *Belisar* to slander even a Socrates, in order to prevent anyone from believing in virtue. Even the illusion of good in others must have worth for us, for out of this play with pretenses, which acquires respect without perhaps earning it, something quite serious can finally develop. – It is only the illusion of good *in ourselves* that must be wiped out without exemption, and the veil by which self-love conceals our moral defects must be torn away. For illusion does *deceive*, if one deludes oneself that one's debt is cancelled or even thrown away by that which is without any moral content, or persuades oneself that one

---

[42] See *Nicomachean Ethics* IX.10 1171a15–17 and *Eudemian Ethics* VII.12 1145b20 ("He who has many friends has no friend"). See also Diogenes Laertius 5.1.21. Kant repeats this (mis)quotation in several other versions of his anthropology lectures – e.g., *Collins* 25: 106, *Parow* 25:330, *Menschenkunde* 25:933.

[43] Swift, *Tale of a Tub*, Sec. 2, p. 78. Külpe, in his note, refers to the following German translation: *Satyrische und ernsthafte Schriften von Dr. Swift*, trans. Heinrich Waser, vol. 3, 2nd ed. (Hamburg and Leipzig, 1759), p. 86.

[44] Johann Peter Hofstede (1716–1803), Dutch theologian. See his book *Des Herrns Marmontels herausgegebener Belisar beurtheilt . . .* (Leipzig, 1769), Ch. 23, which provoked a lively controversy. E.g., Külpe, in his note, also refers to a response by Kant's later opponent Johann August Eberhard (1738–1809) – *Neue Apologie des Sokrates* (Berlin and Stettin, 1772).

is not guilty – e.g., when repentance for misdeeds at the end of one's life is depicted as real improvement, or intentional transgressions as human weakness.[45]

On the five senses

§15

Sensibility in the cognitive faculty (the faculty of intuitive representations) contains two parts: *sense* and the *power of imagination.* – The first is the faculty of intuition in the presence of an object, the second is intuition even *without* the presence of an object. But the senses, on the other hand, are divided into *outer* and *inner* sense (*sensus internus*). Outer sense is where the human body is affected by physical things; inner sense, where it is affected by the mind. It should be noted that the latter, as a mere faculty of perception (of empirical intuition), is to be thought of differently than the feeling of pleasure and displeasure; that is, from the receptivity of the subject to be determined by certain ideas for the preservation or rejection of the condition of these ideas, which one could call *interior sense* (*sensus interior*). – A representation through sense of which one is conscious as such is called *sensation*,[46] especially when the sensation at the same time arouses the subject's attention to his own state.

§16

To begin with, one can divide the senses of physical sensation into those of *vital sensation* (*sensus vagus*) and those of *organic sensation* (*sensus fixus*); [154] and, since they are met with on the whole only where there are nerves, into those which affect the whole system of nerves, and those that affect only those nerves that belong to a certain part of the body. – Sensations of warm and cold, even those that are aroused by the mind (for example, by quickly rising hope or fear), belong to *vital sensation.* The *shudder* that

---

[45] *Marginal note in H*: To exist without the senses is to proceed thoughtlessly. On the *easiness* of doing something (*promitudo*). On the subjective *necessity* of doing something with *facility* (*habitus*). Distinguish mechanical easiness, which is dependent on practice, from dynamic easiness, which is objective. Virtue is not facility but strength.

[46] *Sensation. Empfindung*, also translated as "sensation," is used four words later.

45

seizes the human being himself at the representation of the sublime, and the *horror* with which nurses' tales drive children to bed late at night, belong to organic sensation; they penetrate the body as far as there is life in it.

The organic senses, however, in so far as they refer to external sensation, can rightly be enumerated as not more or less than five.

Three of them are more objective than subjective, that is, as empirical *intuitions* they contribute more to the *cognition* of the external object than they stir up the consciousness of the affected organ. *Two*, however, are more subjective than objective, that is,[47] the idea obtained from them is more a representation of *enjoyment* than of cognition of the external object. Therefore one can easily come to an agreement with others regarding the objective senses; but with respect to the subjective sense, with one and the same external empirical intuition and name of the object, the way that the subject feels affected by it can be entirely different.[48]

The senses of the first class are 1) *touch* (*tactus*), 2) *sight* (*visus*), 3) *hearing* (*auditus*). – Of the latter class are a) *taste* (*gustus*), b) *smell* (*olfactus*); taken together they are nothing but senses of organic sensation, as it were like so many external entrances prepared by nature so that the animal can distinguish objects.

On the sense of touch

§17

The sense of touch lies in the fingertips and their nerve papillae, so that through touching the surface of a solid body one can inquire after its shape. – Nature appears to have allotted this organ only to the human being, so that he could form a concept from the shape of a body by [155] touching it on all sides; for the antennae of insects seem merely to have the intention of inquiring after the presence of a body, not its shape. – This sense is also the only one of *immediate* external perception; and for

---

[47] *Crossed out in H*: that is [they prompt more the subject's mere feeling of life (an organ affected to know) than they contribute something to the cognition of the affecting object and its constitution. With regard to the first human beings they could therefore very well reach agreement <and as>, but they are usually very far apart from each other regarding the sensation of the latter].

[48] *Marginal note in H*: On the sense of sight without color and of the sense of hearing without music.

this very reason it is also the most important and most reliably instructive, but nevertheless it is the coarsest, because the matter whose surface is to inform us about the shape of the object through touching must be solid. (As concerns vital sensation, whether the surface is soft or rough, much less whether it feels warm or cold, this is not in question here.) – Without this sense organ we would be unable to form any concept at all of a bodily shape, and so the two other senses of the first class must originally be referred to its perception in order to provide cognition of experience.

On hearing

§18

The sense of hearing is one of the senses of merely *mediate* perception. – Through and by means of the air that surrounds us a distant object to a large extent is cognized. And it is by means of just this medium, which is set in motion by the vocal organ, the mouth, that human beings are able most easily and completely to share thoughts and feelings with others, especially when the sounds which each allows the other to hear are articulated and, in their lawful combination by means of the understanding, form a language. – The shape of the object is not given through hearing, and the sounds of language do not lead immediately to the idea of it, but just because of this, and because they are nothing in themselves or at least not objects, but at most signify only inner feelings, they are the best means of designating concepts. And people born deaf, who for this very reason must remain mute (without speech), can never arrive at anything more than an *analogue* of reason.

But with regard to vital sense, *music*, which is a regular play of aural sensations, not only moves sense in a way that is indescribably vivacious and varied, but also strengthens it; for music is as it were a language of sheer sensations (without any concepts). Sounds here are *tones*, and they are for hearing what colors are for seeing; a communication of feelings at a distance to all present within the surrounding space, and a social pleasure that is not diminished by the fact that many participate in it.[49]

---

[49] *Marginal note in H*: On the feeling of the muscles of the mouth at the voice.

On the sense of sight[50]

§19

Sight is also a sense of *mediate* sensation, appearing only to a certain organ (the eyes) that is sensitive to moving matter; and it takes place by means of *light*, which is not, like sound, merely a wave-like motion of a fluid element that spreads itself through space in all directions, but rather a radiation that determines a point for the object in space. By means of sight the cosmos becomes known to us to an extent so immeasurable that, especially with the self-luminous celestial bodies, when we check their distance with our measures here on earth, we become fatigued over the long number sequence. And this almost gives us more reason to be astonished at the delicate sensitivity of this organ in respect to its perception of such weakened impressions than at the magnitude of the object (the cosmos), especially when we take in the world in detail, as presented to our eyes through the mediation of the microscope, e.g., infusoria. – The sense of sight, even if it is not more indispensable than that of hearing, is still the noblest, because among all the senses, it is furthest removed from the sense of touch, the most limited condition of perception: it not only has the widest sphere of perception in space, but also its organ feels least affected (because otherwise it would not be merely sight). Thus sight comes nearer to being a *pure intuition* (the immediate representation of the given object, without admixture of noticeable sensation).

***

These three outer senses lead the subject through reflection to cognition of the object as a thing outside ourselves. – But if the sensation becomes so strong that the consciousness of the movement of the organ becomes stronger than the consciousness of the relation to an external object, then external representations are changed into internal ones. – To notice smoothness or roughness in what can be touched is something entirely different from inquiring about the figure of the external body through touching. So too, when the speech of another is so loud that, as we say, the ears hurt from it, or when someone who steps from a dark room into [157] bright sunshine blinks his eyes. The latter will be blind for a few

---

[50] *Sehen. Gesicht*, also translated as "sight," is the next word.

48

moments because of the too strong or too sudden light, the former will be deaf for a few moments because of the shrieking voice. That is, both persons are unable to find a concept of the object because of the intensity of the sensations; their attention is fixed merely on the subjective representation, namely the change of the organ.[51]

On the senses of taste and smell

§20

The senses of taste and smell are both more subjective than objective. In the former, the organs of the *tongue*, the *throat*, and the *palate* come into contact with the external object; in the latter, we inhale air that is mixed with foreign vapors, and the body itself from which they stream forth can be far away from the organ. Both senses are closely related to each other, and he who lacks a sense of smell always has only a dull sense of taste. – One can say that both senses are affected by *salts* (stable and volatile), one of which must be dissolved by fluid in the mouth, the other by air, which has to penetrate the organ in order to have its specific sensation sent to it.

General remark about the outer senses

§21

One can divide the outer senses into those of *mechanical* and *chemical* influence. The three highest senses belong to the mechanical, the two lower to the chemical. The three highest senses are senses of *perception* (of the surface), the latter two are senses of *pleasure* (of the most intimate taking into ourselves). – Thus it happens that *nausea*, an impulse to free oneself of food through the shortest way out of the esophagus (to vomit), has been allotted to the human being as such a strong vital sensation, for this intimate taking in can be dangerous to the animal.

---

[51] *Marginal note in H*: Thoughtless, he who establishes something without investigating. Gullible, he who trusts on the basis of another witness without investigation.
Skeptical, he who places faith in no witness.
A creditor (*creditor*), he who places trust in the promise of another. The faithful are those who trust an actual or putative promise of a being that cannot deceive.
Superstitious (*superstitios.*) he who keeps that which he mistakes for the gift [?] of another.

However, there is also a *mental pleasure*, which consists in the communication of thoughts. But if it is forced on us and still as mental nutrition is not beneficial to us, the mind finds it repulsive (as in, e.g., the constant repetition of would-be flashes of wit or humor, whose sameness can be [158] unwholesome to us), and thus the natural instinct to be free of it is also called nausea by analogy, although it belongs to inner sense.

Smell is taste at a distance, so to speak, and others are forced to share the pleasure of it, whether they want to or not. And thus smell is contrary to freedom and less sociable than taste, where among many dishes or bottles a guest can choose one according to his liking, without others being forced to share the pleasure of it. – Filth seems to arouse nausea not so much through what is repugnant to the eyes and tongue as through the stench that we presume it has. For taking something in through smell (in the lungs) is even more intimate than taking something in through the absorptive vessels of the mouth or throat.

Given the same degree of influence taking place on them, the senses *teach* less the more strongly they feel themselves being *affected*. Inversely, if they are expected to teach a great deal, they must be affected moderately. In the strongest light we *see* (distinguish) nothing, and a stentorian, strained voice *stuns* us (stifles thought).

The more susceptible to impressions the vital sense is (the more tender and sensitive), the more unfortunate the human being is; on the other hand, the more susceptible he is toward the organic sense (sensitive) and the more inured to the vital sense, the more fortunate he is – I say more fortunate, not exactly morally better – for he has the feeling of his own well-being more under his control. One can call the capacity for sensation that comes from *strength* delicate *sensitivity* (*sensibilitas sthenica*); that coming from the subject's *weakness* – his inability to withstand satisfactorily the penetration of influences on the senses into consciousness, that is, attending to them against his will, can be called *tender sensitivity* (*sensibilitas asthenica*).

Questions

§22

Which organic sense is the most ungrateful and also seems to be the most dispensable? The sense of *smell*. It does not pay to cultivate it or refine it at all in order to enjoy; for there are more disgusting objects than pleasant

50

ones (especially in crowded places), and even when we come across something fragrant, the pleasure coming from the sense of smell is always fleeting and transient. – But as a negative condition of well-being, this sense is not unimportant, in order not to breathe in bad air (oven fumes, the [159] stench of swamps and animal carcasses), or also not to need rotten things for nourishment.[52] – The second sense of pleasure, namely the sense of *taste*, has exactly the same importance, though it also has the specific advantage of promoting sociability in eating and drinking, something the sense of smell does not do. Moreover, taste is superior because it judges the wholesomeness of food beforehand, at the gate of entrance to the intestinal canal; for as long as luxury and indulgence have not over-refined the sense, the agreeableness of the sense of taste is connected to the wholesomeness of food, as a fairly certain prediction of it. – In the case of people who are ill the appetite, which usually takes care of them and is of benefit to them like a medicine, fails. – The smell of food is so to speak a foretaste, and by means of the smell of his favorite food the hungry person is invited to pleasure, just as the satiated person is repelled by the same smell.[53]

Can the senses be used vicariously, that is, can one sense be used as a substitute for another? Through gestures one can coax the usual speech from a deaf person, granted that he has once been able to hear, thus by means of his eyes. Observing the movement of one's lips also belongs here; indeed, exactly the same thing can take place by means of the feeling of touching moving lips in the dark. However, if the person is born deaf, the sense of *seeing* the movement of the speech organs must convert the sounds, which have been coaxed from him by instruction, into a feeling of the movement of his own speech muscles. But he never arrives at real concepts in this way, because the signs that he needs are not

[52] *Marginal note in H*: Smell does not allow itself to be described, but only compared through similarity with another sense (like music with the play of colors), for example, of taste, to compare, e.g., that which smells sour, sweet, rotten – faint odor of slate.

[53] *Marginal note in H*: Division – Anthropological Doctrine of Elements. Exposition and Doctrine of Method. Characteristic. Element. Doctrine. On the Faculty of Cognition., the Feeling of Pleasure and Displeasure, and the Faculty of Desire. – All of this is sensible or intellectual. On the Sensible Faculty of Cognition. 1. On the Senses 2. On the Power of Imagination. Agreeableness which it presses on a – music b. odor. *Curiosus* is he who desires to experience rare things or also to possess them for curiosity.

Overly strong light or shouting makes one blind and deaf; that is, one cannot receive concepts of objects.

Whether there is not really a 6th sense to acquire (*papagey*), namely with regard to sex, the kiss is an enjoyment between both sexes. The embrace of those of the same sex or of small and still stammering children is a mere outburst of love. Analogy.

51

capable of universality. – The lack of a musical ear, although the mere physical organ is uninjured, since it can hear sounds but not tones, and such a human being can speak but not sing, is a deformity difficult to explain. So too there are people who *see* well but cannot distinguish any colors, and to whom all objects seem as though they are in a copper engraving.

Which lack or loss of a sense is more serious, that of hearing or sight? – When it is inborn, the first is the least replaceable of all the senses; however, if it occurs later after the use of the eyes has been cultivated, whether by observation of gestures or more indirectly by means of read-[160] ing of a text, then such a loss can be compensated by sight, especially in one who is well-to-do,[54] though not satisfactorily. But a person who becomes deaf in old age misses this means of social intercourse very much, and while one sees many blind people who are talkative, sociable, and cheerful at the dinner table, it is difficult to find someone who has lost his hearing and who is not annoyed, distrustful, and dissatisfied in a social gathering. In the faces of his table companions he sees all kinds of expressions of affect, or at least of interest, but he wears himself out in vain guessing at their meaning, and thus in the midst of a social gathering he is condemned to solitude.

***

§23

In addition, a receptivity for certain objects of external sensation of a special kind belongs to both of the last two senses (which are more subjective than objective). This receptivity is merely subjective, and acts upon the organs of smell and taste by means of a stimulus that is neither odor nor flavor but is felt like the effect of certain stable salts that incite the organs to specific *evacuations*. That is why these objects are not really enjoyed and taken *intimately* into the organs, but merely come into contact with them in order to be promptly eliminated. But just because of this they can be used throughout the day without satiation (except during mealtime and sleep). – The most common substance for this sensation is *tobacco*, be it in *snuffing*, or in placing it in the mouth between the cheek and the gums to stimulate the flow of saliva, or in *smoking* it through

---

[54] *Crossed out in H*: well-to-do [Very much replaceable. tolerable to replace. A person who is born blind or who in the course of time has at last become blind does not particularly regret his loss,].

52

pipes, just as the Spanish women of Lima smoke a lighted cigar.[55] Instead of tobacco the Malayans, as a last resort, make use of the areca nut rolled up in a betel leaf (betel nut), which has exactly the same effect. – This *craving* (*Pica*), apart from the medical benefit or harm that may result from the secretion of fluids in both organs, is, as a mere excitation of sensuous feeling in general, so to speak a frequently repeated impulse recollecting attention to the state of one's own thoughts, which would otherwise be soporific or boring owing to uniformity and monotony. Instead, these means of stimulation always jerk our attention awake again. This kind of conversation of the human being with himself takes the place of a social [161] gathering, because in place of conversation it fills the emptiness of time with continuous newly excited sensations and with stimuli that are quickly passing, but always renewed.

On inner sense

§24

Inner sense is not pure apperception, a consciousness of what the human being *does*, since this belongs to the faculty of thinking. Rather, it is a consciousness of what he *undergoes*, in so far as he is affected by the play of his own thoughts. It rests on inner intuition, and consequently on the relations of ideas in time (whether they are simultaneous or successive). Its perceptions and the inner experience (true or illusory) composed by means of their connections are not merely *anthropological*, where we abstract from the question of whether the human being has a soul or not (as a special incorporeal substance); but *psychological*, where we believe that we perceive such a thing within ourselves, and the mind, which is represented as a mere faculty of feeling and thinking, is regarded as a special substance dwelling in the human being. – There is then only *one* inner sense, because the human being does not have different organs for sensing himself inwardly, and one could say that the soul is the organ of inner sense. It is said that inner sense is subject to *illusions*, which

---

[55] Tobacco smoking was only mildly popular in Kant's day. The first German cigar factory was founded in Hamburg in 1788, but it had only modest sales at first (Vorländer). However, Kant himself smoked a daily pipe of tobacco with his breakfast tea, and "it is reported that the bowls of his pipes increased considerably in size as the years went on" [Manfred Kuehn, *Kant: A Biography* (New York: Cambridge University Press, 2001), p. 222].

consist either in taking the appearances of inner sense for external appearances, that is, taking imaginings for sensations, or in regarding them as inspirations caused by another being that is not an object of external sense. So the illusion here is either *enthusiasm* or *spiritualism*, and both are *deceptions* of inner sense. In both cases it is *mental illness*: the tendency to accept the play of ideas of inner sense as experiential cognition, although it is only a fiction; and also the tendency to keep oneself in an artificial frame of mind, perhaps because one considers it beneficial and superior to the vulgarity of ideas of sense, and accordingly to trick oneself with the intuitions thus formed (dreaming when awake). – For gradually the human being comes to regard that which he has intentionally put in his mind as [162] something that already must have been there, and he believes that he has merely discovered in the depths of his soul what in reality he has forced on himself.

This is how it was with the fanatically exciting inner sensations of a *Bourignon*, or the fanatically frightening ones of a *Pascal*. This mental depression cannot be conveniently cleared away by rational ideas (for what are they able to do against supposed intuitions?). The tendency to retire into oneself, together with the resulting illusions of inner sense, can only be set right when the human being is led back into the external world and by means of this to the order of things present to the outer senses.[56]

On the causes that increase or decrease sense impressions according to degree

§25

Sense impressions are increased according to degree by means of (1) contrast, (2) novelty, (3) change, (4) intensification.

a Contrast

Dissimilarity (contrast) is the juxtaposition, arousing our attention, of mutually contrary *sense representations* under one and the same concept.

---

[56] *Marginal note in H*: NB Above the *animus sui compos*, who has all mental changes in his power.
On dull, weak, delicate senses – feeling of exhaustion and strength *sagacitaet*, of dogs on the lookout. – The old one believes he will be fine, while the *vital* feeling becomes weak. – The blind distinguish the colors of feeling. Strong senses for perceiving, delicate ones for distinguishing.

It is different from *contradiction*, which consists in the linking of mutually antagonistic *concepts.* A well-cultivated piece of land in a sandy desert, like the alleged paradisaical region in the area of Damascus in Syria, *elevates* the idea of the cultivation by means of mere contrast. – The bustle and glitter of an estate or even of a great city near the quiet, simple, and yet contented life of the farmer; or a house with a thatched roof in which one finds tasteful and comfortable rooms inside, enlivens our representations, and one gladly lingers nearby because the senses are thereby strengthened. – – On the other hand, poverty and ostentatious-ness, the luxurious finery of a lady who glitters with diamonds and whose clothes are dirty; – or, as once with a Polish magnate, extravagantly laden tables and numerous waiters at hand, but in crude footwear – these things [163] do not stand in contrast but in contradiction, and one sense representa-tion destroys or weakens the other because it wants to unite what is opposite under one and the same concept, which is impossible. – – But one can also make a *comical* contrast and express an apparent contra-diction in the *tone* of truth, or express something obviously contemptible in the language of praise, in order to make the absurdity still more palpable – like *Fielding* in his *Jonathan Wild the Great*, or *Blumauer* in his travesty of Virgil; and, for example, one can parody a heart-rending romance, like *Clarissa*,[57] merrily and with profit, and thus strengthen the senses by freeing them from the conflict that false and harmful concepts have mixed into them.

b Novelty

Through the *new*, to which the rare and that which has been kept hidden also belong, attention is enlivened. For it is an acquisition; the sense representation thereby wins more power. *Everyday life* or the *familiar* extinguishes it. But by this are not to be understood[58] the discovery, contact with, or public exhibition of a work of *antiquity*, whereby a thing

---

[57] Henry Fielding (1707–1754), English novelist and dramatist, author of *Tom Thumb* (1730). *Jonathan Wild* (1743 – Kant misquotes the title), the history of a superman of crime, has been called the most sustained piece of irony in English. Johann Aloys Blumauer (1755–98), author of *Die Abenteuer des frommen Helden Äneas* (Vienna, 1783–1786). "*Clarissa*" refers to a book by English novelist Samuel Richardson (1689–1761) – i.e., *Clarissa, or, the History of a Young Lady* (7 vols., 1747–1748).

[58] *Crossed out in H*: understood [for it can be new enough, and because of the rarity and likewise seclusion that lies within it. The attention].

is brought to mind that one would have supposed was destroyed long ago by the force of time according to the natural course of events. To sit on a piece of the wall of an ancient Roman theater (in Verona or Nîmes); to have in one's hands a household utensil of that ancient people, discovered after many centuries under the lava in Herculaneum; to be able to show a coin of the Macedonian kings or a gem of ancient sculpture, and so on, rouses the keenest attention of the expert's senses.[59] The tendency to acquire knowledge merely for the sake of its novelty, rarity, and hiddenness is called *curiosity*. Although this inclination only plays with ideas and is otherwise without interest in their objects, it is not to be criticized, except when it is a matter of spying on that which really is of interest to others alone. – But as concerns sheer sense impressions, each morning, through the mere *novelty* of its sensations, makes all sense representations clearer and livelier (as long as they are not diseased) than they generally are toward evening.

[164] *c Change*

Monotony (complete uniformity in one's sensations) ultimately causes *atony* (lack of attention to one's condition), and the sense impressions grow weak. Change refreshes them, just as a sermon read in the same tone, whether it be shouted out or delivered with a measured yet uniform voice, puts the whole congregation to sleep. – Work and rest, city and country life, social conversation and play, entertainment in solitude, now with stories, then with poems, sometimes with philosophy, and then with mathematics, strengthen the mind. – It is one and the same vital energy that stirs up the consciousness of sensations; but its various organs relieve one another in their activity. Thus it is easier to enjoy oneself in *walking* for a considerable length of time, since one muscle (of the leg) *alternates* at rest with the other, than it is to remain standing rigid in one and the same spot, where one muscle must work for a while without relaxing. – This is why travel is so attractive; the only pity is that with idle people it

---

[59] *Marginal note in H*: Monotony, disharmony, and atony of the faculty of sensation. They increase with the dosage.

Habit makes them necessary. *Crossed out in H*: attention [One calls the inclination to see such rarities *curiosity*; although that which is concealed merely because it is regarded as secret and will be found out is also designated by this name, but then it serves to name an inattentive person.]

leaves behind a *void* (atony), as the consequence of the monotony of domestic life.

Nature itself has arranged things so that pain creeps in, uninvited, between pleasant sensations that entertain the senses, and so makes life interesting. But it is absurd to mix in pain intentionally and to hurt oneself for the sake of variety, to allow oneself to be awakened in order to properly feel oneself falling asleep again; or, as with Fielding's novel (*The Foundling*),[60] where an editor of this book added a final part after the author's death, in order to introduce jealousy that could provide variety in the marriage (with which the story ends). For the deterioration of a state does not increase the interest our senses take in it; not even in a tragedy. And the conclusion is not a variation.

d Intensification extending to perfection

A continuous series of successive sense representations, which *differ* according to degree, has, if each of the following representations is always stronger than the one preceding it, an *outer limit* of *tension* (*intensio*); to [165] approach this limit is *arousing*, on the other hand to exceed it is *relaxing* (*remissio*). But in the point that separates both states lies the *perfection* (*maximum*) of the sensation, which brings about insensitivity and, consequently, lifelessness.

If one wants to keep the faculty of sensing lively, then one must not begin with strong sensations (because they make us insensitive toward those that follow); rather it is better to deny them to oneself at the beginning and apportion them sparingly to oneself, so that one can always climb higher. In the introduction the preacher begins with a cold instruction of the understanding that points to reflection on a concept of duty, then he introduces a moral interest into his analysis of the text, and then he concludes in the application with an appeal to all incentives of the human soul through sensations that can give energy to the moral interest.

Young man! Deny yourself gratifications (of amusement, indulgence, love, and so forth), if not with the Stoic intention of wanting to do without them completely, then with the refined Epicurean intention of having in view an ever-increasing enjoyment. This stinginess with the

---

[60] Kant is referring to Henry Fielding's book, *The History of Tom Jones, A Foundling* (1749).

assets of your enjoyment of life[61] actually makes you richer through the *postponement* of enjoyment, even if, at the end of life, you have had to give up most of the profit from it. Like everything ideal, the consciousness of having enjoyment in your control is more fruitful and comprehensive than anything that gratifies through sense, because by this means it is simultaneously consumed and thus deducted from the total quantity.

On the inhibition, weakening, and total loss of the sense faculties

§26

The sense faculties can be weakened, inhibited, or lost completely. Thus there exist the conditions of drunkenness, sleep, unconsciousness, apparent death (asphyxia), and actual death.

Drunkenness is the unnatural condition of inability to order one's sense representations according to laws of experience, provided that the condition is the effect of an excessive consumption of drink.

[166] According to its verbal definition, sleep is a condition in which a healthy human being is unable to become conscious of representations through the external senses. To find the real definition of this is entirely up to the physiologists, who, if they are able, may explain this relaxation, which is nevertheless at the same time a gathering of power for renewed external sensations (through which the human being sees himself as a newborn in the world, and by which probably a third of our lifetime passes away unconscious and unregretted).[62]

---

[61] *Lebensgefühl.*

[62] *Crossed out in H*: unregretted. [If one feels tired when one goes to bed, but for some unknown reason nevertheless cannot fall asleep, by calm attentiveness to one's physical sensations one may perceive something spastic in the muscles of the foot as well as in the brain, and at the moment of falling asleep feel a fatigue which is also a very agreeable sensation. – That waking is a condition of strain and contraction of all fibers is also observable in the phenomenon that recruits, who, after they have just been woken from sleep and are measured standing up, are found to be about half an inch longer than the still shorter height which they would have been found in if they had been lying awake in their bed for a while.

Sleep is not merely a *need* for relaxation of exhausted powers but also an enjoyment of comfort at the beginning (at the moment of falling asleep) as well as at the end (at the moment of waking up). However, with this, as with all enjoyments, it is necessary to be thrifty, because it exhausts the capacity for sensation and along with this also <weakens> the vital force. – It is the same with this as with the Mohammedan's manner of representing food proportion, where it is said that weighing every single human being at birth shows how much he should eat. If he eats a lot, then he

The unnatural condition of dazed sense organs, which results in a lesser degree of attention to oneself than would normally be the case, is an analogue of drunkenness; that is why he who is suddenly awakened from a firm sleep is called drunk with sleep. – He does not yet have his full consciousness. – But even when awake one can suddenly be seized by confusion while deliberating about what to do in an unforeseen case, an inhibition of the orderly and ordinary use of one's faculty of reflection, which brings the play of sense representations to a standstill. In such a case we say that he is disconcerted, beside himself (with joy or fear), *perplexed, bewildered, astonished*, he has lost his *Tramontano*[g] and so on, and this condition is to be regarded as like a momentary sleep that seizes one and that requires a *collecting* of one's sensations. In a violent, suddenly aroused affect (of fear, anger, or even joy), the human being is, as we say, *beside himself* (in an *ecstasy*, if he believes that he is gripped by an intuition which is not of the senses); he has no control over himself, and is temporarily paralyzed, so to speak, in using his outer senses.

§27

Unconsciousness, which usually follows dizziness (a fast spinning circle of many different sensations that is beyond comprehension), is a foretaste of death. The complete inhibition of all sensation is asphyxia or *apparent death*, which, as far as one can perceive externally, is to be distinguished from actual death only through the result (as in persons drowned, hanged, or suffocated by fumes).

No human being can experience his own *death* (for to constitute an [167] experience requires life), he can only observe it in others. Whether it is painful cannot be judged from the death rattle or convulsions of the dying person; it seems much more to be a purely mechanical reaction of the vital force,[63] and perhaps a gentle sensation of the gradual release

---

will have consumed his portion soon and will die early; if he eats moderately, then he has a long time to eat, and therefore also to live. – One could also say just the same about sleep: he who sleeps a lot in the younger but still manly years will have little sleep in old age, which is a sad fate. – The Kalmucks regard sleeping during the day as shameful, and the Spaniards' *siesta* does not shed a favorable light on their vigor.

[g] The North Star is called *Tramontano* or *Tramontona*, and *perdere la tramontana*, to lose the North Star (as the sailor's guiding star), means to lose one's composure, not to know how to find one's way about.

[63] *Lebenskraft.*

59

from all pain. – The fear of death that is natural to all human beings, even the unhappiest or the wisest, is therefore not a horror of *dying* but, as Montaigne[64] rightly says, horror at the thought of *having died* (that is, of being dead), which the candidate for death thinks he will still have after his death, since he thinks of his corpse, which is no longer himself, as still being himself in a dark grave or somewhere else. – This illusion cannot be pushed aside, for it lies in the nature of thought as a way of speaking to and of oneself. The thought *I am not* simply cannot *exist*; because if I am not then I cannot be conscious that I am not. I can indeed say: "I am not healthy," and think such *predicates* of myself negatively (as is the case with all *verba*); but to *negate* the subject itself when *speaking* in the first person, so that the subject destroys itself, is a contradiction.

On the power of imagination

§28

The power of imagination (*facultas imaginandi*), as a faculty of intuition without the presence of the object, is either *productive*, that is, a faculty of the original presentation of the object (*exhibitio originaria*), which thus precedes experience; or *reproductive*, a faculty of the derivative present-ation of the object (*exhibitio derivativa*), which brings back to the mind an empirical intuition that it had previously. – Pure intuitions of space and time belong to the productive faculty; all others presuppose empirical intuition, which, when it is connected with the concept of the object and thus becomes empirical cognition, is called *experience*. – The power of imagination, in so far as it also produces images involuntarily, is called *fantasy*. He who is accustomed to regarding these images as (inner or outer) experiences is a *visionary*. – An involuntary play of one's images in *sleep* (a state of health) is called *dreaming*.[65]

---

[64] Michel Eyquem de Montaigne (1533–1592), French essayist, author of the *Essais* (1595). The statement Kant attributes to Montaigne is not quite to be found in the *Essays*. However, in Bk. II, Ch. 13 ("Of Judging of the Death of Others"), Montaigne does cite approvingly Epicharmus' remark that "It is not death, but dying that I fear" (*The Complete Essays of Montaigne*, trans. Donald M. Frame [Stanford: Stanford University Press, 1958], p. 461). See also Bk. I, Ch. 19 ("That our Happiness must not be Judged until after our Death").

[65] *Crossed out in H: dreaming* [that is, with the insensibility of all external sense organs there is an analogue with the laws of experience enduring an involuntary play of imagination, although also he who in waking has submitted to the propensity to mix fantasy among experiences and thereby to merge them into each other is called a dreamer.]

The power of imagination (in other words) is either *inventive* (productive) or merely *recollective* (reproductive). But the productive power of imagination is nevertheless not exactly *creative*, for it is not capable of producing a [168] sense representation that was *never* given to our faculty of sense; one can always furnish evidence of the material of its ideas. To one who has never seen *red* among the seven colors, we can never make this sensation comprehensible, but to the person who is born blind we cannot make any colors comprehensible, not even the secondary colors, for example, green, which is produced from the mixture of two colors. Yellow and blue mixed together give green; but the power of imagination would not produce the slightest idea of this color unless it had *seen* them mixed together.

This is exactly how it is with each one of the five senses, that is, the sensations produced by the five senses in their synthesis cannot be made by means of the power of imagination, but must be drawn originally from the faculty of sense. There have been people for whom the representation of light by their faculty of sight consisted of no greater selection than white or black, and for whom, although they could see well, the visible world seemed like a copperplate engraving. Likewise, there are more people than one would believe who have a good and even extremely sensitive sense of hearing, but who have absolutely no musical ear; whose sense for tone is entirely indifferent not merely to imitating tones (singing) but also to distinguishing them from noise. – The same may be true with the ideas of taste and smell; namely that the *sense* lacks the material of enjoyment for many specific sensations, and one person believes that he understands another in this connection, while the sensations of the one may differ from those of the other not only in degree but specifically and completely. – There are people who lack the sense of smell entirely; they regard the sensation of inhaling pure air through the nose as the sensation of smelling, and consequently they cannot make head or tail of any description which tries to describe the sensation of smell to them. But where the sense of smell is lacking, the sense of taste is also badly missing, and if someone has no sense of taste, it is wasted effort to instruct and teach him about it. But hunger and its satisfaction (satiation) is something quite different from taste.

So, no matter how great an artist, even a sorceress, the power of imagination may be, it is still not creative, but must get the *material* for its images from the senses. But these images, according to the memories [169] formed of them, are not so universally communicable as concepts of understanding. However, sometimes we also name (though only in a figurative

61

sense) the power of imagination's sensitivity for representations through communication as a sense, saying "This human being has no *sense* for it." Though in not grasping communicated representations and uniting them in thought, there exists an inability not of sense, but partly of understanding. He himself does not think about what he says, and therefore others also do not understand him; he speaks *nonsense* (*non sense*) – a mistake that is still to be distinguished from what is *devoid of sense*, where thoughts are paired together in such a way that another person does not know what he should make of them. The fact that the word "sense" (but only in the singular) is used so often for "thought" should signify that it is of a still higher level than that of thinking. The fact that one says of an expression that within it lies a deep or profound sense (hence the word "aphorism"), and that sound human understanding is also called "common sense"[66] and is still placed at the top, even though this expression actually signifies only the lowest level of the cognitive faculty – all of this is based on the fact that the power of imagination, which puts material under the understanding in order to provide content for its concepts (for cognition), seems to provide a reality to its (invented) intuitions because of the analogy between them and real perceptions.

§29

Partaking of intoxicating food and drink is a physical means to excite or soothe the power of imagination.[h] Some of these, as poisons, *weaken* the vital force (certain mushrooms, wild rosemary, wild hogweed, the Chicha of the Peruvians, the Ava of the South Sea Indians, opium); others *strengthen* it or at least elevate its feeling (like fermented beverages,

[170]

---

[66] Sense: *Sinn*, thought: *Gedanken*, aphorism: *Sinnspruch*, common sense: *Gemeinsinn*.

[h] I pass over here what is not a means to a purpose but a natural consequence of a situation in which someone is placed, and where his imagination alone disconcerts him. Examples of this are *dizziness*, caused by looking down from the edge of a steep height (perhaps also by looking down from a narrow bridge without railings) and *seasickness*. – The board on which a human being who feels faint steps would strike no fear in him if it were lying on the ground, but when it is placed over a deep precipice as a footbridge the thought of the mere possibility of taking a false step is so powerful that the person attempting to cross over really is in danger. – Seasickness (which I myself experienced on a voyage from Pillau to Königsberg, if indeed one wants to call this a sea voyage), with its attack of vomiting, came, as I believe I observed, merely by means of my eyes; because the rocking of the ship, as seen from the cabin, made me see now the bay, now the summit of Balga, and the recurrent falling after the rising of the ship provoked, by means of the power of the imagination, an antiperistaltic movement of the intestines by the stomach muscles.

62

wine and beer, or the spirits extracted from them, such as brandy); but all of them are contrary to nature and artificial. He who takes them in such excess that he is for a time incapable of ordering his sense representations according to laws of experience is said to be *drunk* or *intoxicated*; and putting oneself in this condition voluntarily or intentionally is called *getting drunk*. However, all of these methods are supposed to serve the purpose of making the human being forget the burden that seems to lie, originally, in life generally. – This very widespread inclination and its influence on the use of the understanding deserve special consideration in a pragmatic anthropology.

All *silent* intoxication has something shameful in it; that is, intoxication that does not enliven sociability and the reciprocal communication of thoughts – of which opium and brandy are examples. Wine, which merely stimulates, and beer, which is more nourishing and satisfying like a food, serve as social intoxication; but with the difference that drinking-bouts with beer make guests more dreamy and withdrawn, whereas at a wine-party the guests are cheerful, boisterous, talkative, and witty.

Intemperance in social drinking that leads to befuddlement of the senses is certainly rude behavior in a man, not merely in respect to the company with whom he enjoys himself, but also in respect to self-esteem, if he leaves staggering or at least with unsure steps, or merely slurring his words. But there is much to be said for qualifying the judgment of such a mistake, since the borderline of self-control can be so easily overlooked and *overstepped*, for the host desires that the guest leave fully satisfied (*ut conviva satur*) by this act of sociability.

The freedom from care that drunkenness produces, and along with it also no doubt the carelessness, is an illusory feeling of increased vital force: the drunken man no longer feels life's obstacles, with whose over-coming nature is incessantly connected (and in which health also con-sists); and he is happy in his weakness, since nature is actually striving in him to restore his life step by step, through the gradual increase of his powers. – Women, clergymen, and Jews normally do not get drunk, or at [171] least they carefully avoid all appearance of it, because their civil status is weak and they need to be reserved (for which sobriety is required). For their external worth rests simply on others' *belief* in their chastity, piety, and a separatist lawfulness.[67] For, as concerns the last point, all separatists,

---

[67] *separatistische Gesetzlichkeit.*

63

that is, those who submit not only to a public law of the land but also to a special one (of their own sect), are, as oddities and allegedly chosen people, particularly exposed to the attention of the community and the sting of criticism; thus they cannot slacken their attention to themselves, since drunkenness, which removes caution, is a *scandal* for them.[68]

A Stoic admirer of *Cato* said: "his virtue was strengthened by wine (*virtus eius incaluit mero*)";[69] and a modern German said of the ancient Germans: "they formed their counsels (to make a resolution of war) while they were drunk, so that they would not be lacking in vigor, and reflected on them while sober, so that they would not be without understanding."[70]

Drink loosens the tongue (*in vino disertus*).[71] – But it also opens the heart and is an instrumental vehicle of a moral quality, namely frankness. – Holding back one's thoughts is an oppressive state for a sincere heart; and merry drinkers do not readily tolerate a very temperate guest at their revel, because he represents an observer who looks out for the faults of others while he hides his own.[72] Hume also says: "The drinking companion who never forgets is annoying; the follies of one day must be forgotten in order to make room for those of the next."[73] Good-naturedness is presupposed by this permission that man has, for the sake of social pleasure, to go a bit beyond the borderline of sobriety for a short while. The fashionable politics of half a century ago, when the Nordic courts sent envoys who could drink a great deal without getting drunk, but who made others drunk in order to question or persuade them, was deceitful;

---

[68] *Marginal note in H*: The power of imagination is either creative (*productive*) or reproductive (*reproductive*). The latter needs the law of *association* of representations. The characteristic is arbitrary for the aim of *reproduction associi*rende. – In respect to time it is the looking backward, the apprehending, and the foreseeing power of the imagination.

[69] See Horace, *Carmina* 3.21.11–12: "Narratur et prisci Catonis saepe mero caluisse virtus" [trans.: The virtue of even old Cato is said to have been inspired by wine.] However, to judge from similar passages in other versions of the anthropology lectures, Kant probably has not Horace but Seneca in mind. See *Parow* 25: 296, *Pillau* 25: 750, *Menschenkunde* 25: 942, *Mrongovius* 25: 1252. See also *Metaphysics of Morals* 6: 428. Horace wrote about Cato the Elder; Seneca, about Cato the Younger. Cf. Seneca, *De Tranquillitate Animi* 1511: "et Cato vino laxabat animum, curis publicis fatigatum" [trans.: Cato used to relax his mind with wine, when it was worn out with public concerns].

[70] Cf. Tacitus, *Germania* 22. This remark also occurs in many other versions of the anthropology lectures. See *Parow* 25: 295–296, *Pillau* 25: 749, *Menschenkunde* 25: 942, *Mrongovius* 25: 1252.

[71] Trans.: wine makes eloquent.

[72] Külpe draws attention here to a similar remark in Rousseau's *Héloïse* (Bk. I, Letter 23).

[73] David Hume, *An Enquiry Concerning the Principles of Morals*, Sec. 4: "I hate a drinking companion, says the Greek proverb, who never forgets. The follies of the last debauch should be buried in eternal oblivion, in order to give full scope to the follies of the next."

but it has disappeared along with the coarseness of the customs of those times, and a long lecture of warning against this vice may well be superfluous with respect to the civilized classes.[74]

Can one also explore the temperament of the human being who is getting drunk, or his character, while he is drinking? I think not. Alcohol [172] is a new fluid mixed with those flowing in his veins and a further neural stimulus, one that does not *reveal* the *natural* temperature more clearly but rather *introduces* another one. – That is why one person who gets drunk becomes amorous, another boastful, a third cantankerous, a fourth (especially when drinking beer) soft-hearted or pious or altogether silent. But all of them, once they have slept it off and one reminds them of what they said the previous evening, will laugh at this strange humor or ill-humor of their senses.

§30

Originality of the power of imagination (not imitative production), when it harmonizes with concepts, is called *genius*; when it does not harmonize with them, it is called *enthusiasm*. It is noteworthy that we can think of no other suitable form for a *rational* being than that of a human being. Every other form would represent, at most, a symbol of a certain quality of the human being – as the serpent, for example, is an image of evil cunning – but not the rational being himself. Therefore we populate all other planets in our imagination with nothing but human forms, although it is probable that they may be formed very differently, given the diversity of soil that supports and nourishes them, and the different elements of which they are composed. All other forms which we might give them are *caricatures*.[i]

When the lack of a sense (for example, sight) is inborn, then the crippled person cultivates, as far as possible, another sense to use as a *substitute* for it, and exercises the productive power of the imagination to

---

[74] *gesittete Stände*.

[i] Therefore the *Holy Trinity*, an old man, a young man, and a bird (the dove), must not be presented as real forms that are similar to their objects, but merely as symbols. Pictorial expressions of the descent from heaven and the ascension to heaven have exactly the same significance. In order to attach an intuition to our concepts of rational beings, we can proceed in no other way than to anthropomorphize them; however, it is unfortunate or childish if, in doing so, the symbolic representation is raised to a concept of the thing in itself.

65

a high degree. He tries to make the shapes of external bodies conceivable by means of *touch*, and where this sense does not suffice on account of magnitude (for example, with a house), he tries to make the *spaciousness* conceivable by still another sense, possibly *hearing*, that is, through the echo of voices in a room. Finally, however, if a successful operation rescues [173] the organ for sensation, he must first of all *learn* to see and hear, that is, try to bring his perceptions under concepts of this kind of object.

Concepts of objects often prompt a spontaneously produced image (through the productive power of imagination), which we attach to them involuntarily. When we read or have someone tell us about the life and deeds of a great man according to talent, merit, or rank, we are usually led to give him a considerable stature in our imagination; on the other hand, when someone is described as delicate and soft in character we usually form an image of him as smallish and pliable. Not only the peasant but also one fairly acquainted with the ways of the world finds it very strange when the hero, whom he had imagined according to the deeds narrated of him, is presented to him as a tiny little fellow, and, conversely, when the delicate and soft Hume is presented to him as a husky man. – Therefore one must not pitch the expectation of something too high, because the power of imagination is naturally inclined to heighten to extremes; since reality is always more limited than the idea that serves as a pattern for its execution. –

It is not advisable to praise a person too highly before one wishes to introduce him into a social gathering for the first time; on the contrary, it can often be a malicious trick on the part of a rogue to make him seem ridiculous. For the power of imagination raises the representation of what is expected so high that the person in question can only suffer in comparison with our preconceived idea of him. This is exactly what happens when a book, a play, or anything else belonging to gracious manners is announced with exaggerated praise; for when it comes to the presentation, it is bound to fail. Merely having read a play, even a good one, already weakens the impression when one sees it performed. – But if what was praised in advance turns out to be the exact opposite of our strained anticipation of it, then the subject presented, no matter how innocuous, provokes the greatest laughter.

Changing forms set in motion, which in themselves really have no significance that could arouse our attention – things like flickering flames in a fireplace, or the many twists and bubble movements of a brook rippling over stones – entertain the power of imagination with a host of representations of an entirely different sort (than that of sight, in this [174] case): they play in the mind and it becomes absorbed in thought. Even music, for one who does not listen as a connoisseur, can put a poet or philosopher into a mood in which he can snatch and even master thoughts agreeable to his vocation or avocation, which he would not have caught so luckily had he been sitting alone in his room. The cause of this phenomenon seems to lie in the following: when sense, through a manifold that of itself can arouse no attention at all, is distracted by some other object that strikes it more forcibly, thought is not only facilitated but also enlivened, in so far as it requires a more strenuous and enduring power of imagination to provide material for its intellectual ideas. – The English *Spectator*[75] tells of a lawyer who, while pleading a case, was in the habit of taking a thread from his pocket which he incessantly wound and unwound on his finger. When his opponent, the rogue, secretly slipped the thread out of his pocket, the lawyer was completely disconcerted and talked sheer nonsense; and thus it was said that he lost the thread of his discourse. – The sense that is riveted on one sensation pays no attention to other unfamiliar sensations (because of habituation), and therefore it is not distracted by them; but because of this the power of imagination can all the better keep itself on a regular course.

On the productive faculty belonging to sensibility according to its different forms

§31

There are three different kinds of productive faculty belonging to sensibility. These are the *forming* of intuitions in space (*imaginatio plastica*), the *associating* of intuitions in time (*imaginatio associans*), and that of *affinity*, based on the common origin of ideas from each other (*affinitas*).

A On sensibility's productive faculty of constructing forms

Before the artist can present a physical form (palpably, so to speak), he must have produced it in his power of imagination; and this form is then [175]

---

[75] *Spectator* 77.

67

an invention which, if it is involuntary (as perhaps in a dream), is called *fantasy* and does not belong to the artist; but if it is governed by choice, is called *composition, fabrication*. If the artist works from images that are similar to works of nature, his productions are called *natural*; but if he produces forms according to images that cannot be found in experience, then the objects so formed (such as Prince Palagonia's villa in Sicily)[76] are called fantastic, unnatural, distorted forms, and such fancies are like dream images of one who is awake (*velut aegri somnia vanae finguntur species*).[77] – We play with the imagination frequently and gladly, but imagination (as fantasy) plays just as frequently with us, and sometimes very inconveniently.

The play of fantasy with the human being in sleep is called dreaming, and it also takes place in a healthy condition; on the other hand if it happens while the human being is awake, it reveals a diseased condition. – Sleep, as release from every faculty of external perception and especially from voluntary movements, seems to be necessary for all animals and indeed even plants[78] (by analogy of the latter with the former) for the recovery of powers expended while awake. But the same thing also seems to be the case with dreaming: if the vital force were not always kept active in sleep by dreams, it would be extinguished and the deepest sleep would have to bring death along with it. – When we say that we have had a sound sleep, without dreams, this is indeed saying nothing more than that we do not remember anything upon waking up, which, if the products of the imagination change rapidly, can also occur while awake, namely when we are in a state of distraction. If one who fixes his glassy stare on the same point for a while is asked what he is thinking about, the answer obtained is: "I haven't been thinking of anything." If there were not upon awakening many gaps in our memory (from inattention to neglected interconnecting ideas), and if the following night we began to dream again just where we had left off the night before, then I do not know whether we

---

[76] Around 1775, the Prince of Palagonia, Ferdinando Francesco Gravina Agliata, began construction on a villa at Bageria (Sicily) that attracted much attention because of its strange statues. See, e.g., Goethe, *Italienische Reise*, entry of April 9, 1787.

[77] Trans.: chimeras are created like the dreams of a sick person. *Crossed out in H: species* [Therefore we cannot properly (*schicklich*) think of a rational being under any other form except that of a human being].

[78] *Marginal note in H*: Jumping off from the subject matter of the discourse.

would not believe that we were living in two different worlds. – Dreaming is a wise arrangement of nature for exciting the vital force through affects related to involuntary invented events, while bodily movements based on choice, namely muscular movements, are in the meantime suspended. – But one must not take the stories we dream to be revelations from an [176] invisible world.

B On sensibility's productive faculty of association

The law of *association* is this: empirical ideas that have frequently followed one another produce a habit in the mind such that when one idea is produced, the other also comes into being. – It is futile to demand a physiological explanation of this; one may make use of whatever serves as a hypothesis (which is itself, again, an invention), such as Descartes's hypothesis of his so-called material ideas in the brain. At least no explanation of this kind is *pragmatic*; that is, we cannot use it for any technical application, because we have no knowledge of the brain and of the places in it where the traces of the impressions made by ideas might enter into sympathetic harmony with one another, in so far as they touch each other (at least indirectly), so to speak.

This association often extends very far, and the power of imagination often goes so fast from the hundredth to the thousandth that it seems we have completely skipped over certain intermediate links in the chain of ideas, though we have merely not been aware of them. So we must often ask ourselves: "Where was I? Where did I start out in my conversation, and how did I reach this last point?"[j]

---

[j] Therefore he who starts a social conversation must begin with what is near and present to him, and then gradually direct people's attention to what is remote, so long as it can be of interest. Thus a good and common expedient for a person who steps from the street into a social gathering assembled for mutual conversation is the bad weather. For if when stepping into the room he begins with something of the news from Turkey that is just now in the papers, he does violence to others' power of imagination, since they cannot see what has brought him to talk about it. The mind [177] demands a certain order for all communication of thoughts, and much depends on the introductory ideas and the beginning, in conversation as much as in a sermon. [*Marginal note in H: facultas signatrix* belongs to the associative power of imagination.

However, if we perceive real sense representations (not imaginary ones), whose connection is named after a rule of experience, and we perceive our representations by themselves as being connected to each other, then this happens in time and is associative.

On the necessity of two sexes for reproduction.]

C *On sensibility's productive faculty of affinity*

By *affinity* I understand the union of the manifold in virtue of its derivation [177] from one ground. – What interrupts and destroys social conversation is the jumping off from one subject to another entirely different one, for which the ground of the empirical association of representations is merely subjective (that is, with one person the representations are associated differently than they are with another) – this association, I say, is misleading, a kind of nonsense in terms of form. – Only when a subject has been exhausted and a short pause sets in can one introduce another subject of interest. The irregular, roaming power of imagination so confuses the mind, through the succession of ideas that are not tied to anything objective, that he who leaves a gathering of this kind feels as though he has been dreaming. – In silent thinking as well as in the sharing of thoughts, there must always be a theme on which the manifold is strung, so that the understanding can also be effective. However, the play of the power of imagination here still follows the rules of sensibility, which provide the material whose association is achieved without consciousness of the rule, and this association is *in conformity with* the understanding although not derived *from* it.

The word *affinity* (*affinitas*) here recalls a process found in chemistry: intellectual combination is analogous to an interaction of two specifically different physical substances intimately acting upon each other and striving for unity, where this *union* brings about a third entity that has properties which can only be produced by the union of two heterogeneous elements. Despite their dissimilarity, understanding and sensibility by themselves form a close union for bringing about our cognition, as if one had its origin in the other, or both originated from a common origin; but this cannot be, or at least we cannot conceive how dissimilar things could sprout forth from one and the same root.[k]

---

[k] The first two ways of composing representations could be called *mathematical* (of enlargement), but the third would be *dynamic* (of production); whereby an entirely new thing emerges (somewhat like a neutral salt in chemistry). The play of forces in inanimate as well as in animate nature, in the [178] soul as well as in the body, is based on the dissolution and union of the dissimilar. It is true that we arrive at cognition of the play of forces through experience of its effect; but we cannot reach the ultimate cause and the simple components into which its material can be analyzed. – – What is the reason for the fact that all organic beings that we know reproduce their species only through the union of two sexes (which we then call male and female)? We cannot very well assume that the Creator, simply for the sake of curiosity and to establish an arrangement on our planet that pleased him, was so to speak just playing. Rather, it seems that it must be impossible for organic creatures to come into being from the matter of our world through reproduction in any other way than

70

§32 [178]

The power of imagination, however, is not as creative as one would like to pretend. We cannot think of any other form that would be suitable for a rational being than that of a human being. Thus the sculptor or painter always depicts a human being when he makes an angel or a god. Every other figure seems to him to include parts (such as wings, claws, or hooves) which, according to his idea, do not combine together with the structure of a rational being. On the other hand, he can make things as large as he wishes.

Deception due to the *strength* of the human power of imagination often goes so far that a person believes he sees and feels outside himself that which he has only in his mind. Thus the dizziness that seizes the person who looks into an abyss, even though he has a wide enough surface around him so as not to fall, or even stands by a firm handrail. – Some mentally ill people have a strange fear that, seized by an inner impulse, they will spontaneously hurl themselves down. – The sight of others enjoying loathsome things (e.g., when the Tunguse rhythmically suck out and swallow the mucus from their children's noses) induces the spectator to vomit, just as if such a pleasure were forced on him.

The *homesickness* of the Swiss (and, as I have it from the mouth of an experienced general, also the Westphalians and Pomeranians from certain regions) that seizes them when they are transferred to other lands is the result of a longing for the places where they enjoyed the very simple pleasures of life – aroused by the recollection of images of the carefree life and neighborly company in their early years. For later, after they visit these same places, they are greatly disappointed in their expectations and [179] thus also find their homesickness cured. To be sure, they think that this is because everything there has changed a great deal, but in fact it is because they cannot bring back their youth there. It is also noteworthy that this homesickness seizes more the peasants from a province that is

---

through the two sexes established for this purpose. – – In what darkness does human reason lose itself when it tries to fathom the origin here, or even merely undertakes to make a guess at it! [*Marginal note in H*: 1. Formation by means of cold or warm crystallization, in which a solvent (heat or water) escapes, e.g., in calcite

   a) mechanical formation of shape: where the sea [?]
   b) joining together.
     Synthesis of aggregation (mathematical) and of coalition (dynamic).
     Understanding Judgment Reason.]

poor but bound together by strong family ties than those who are busy earning money and take as their motto: *Patria ubi bene*.[79]

If one has heard before that this or that human being is evil, then one believes that one can read malice in his face, and especially when affect and passion appear on the scene, invention mixes here with experience to form a single sensation. According to Helvétius,[80] a lady looked through a telescope and saw the shadows of two lovers in the moon; the clergyman, observing it later, said: "Not at all, Madame; they are the two bell towers of a cathedral."

Furthermore, to all this one can add the effects produced by sympathetic power of imagination. The sight of a human being in a convulsive or epileptic seizure stimulates similar spasmodic movements in the spectator; just as the yawning of another leads one to yawn with him; and the physician Dr. Michaelis[81] states that when a soldier in the army in North America fell into a violent frenzy, two or three bystanders were suddenly thrown into the same state upon seeing him, although this condition was merely temporary. This is why it is not advisable for weak-nerved people (hypochondriacs) to visit lunatic asylums out of curiosity. For the most part, they avoid them of their own accord, because they fear for their sanity. – One also finds that when someone explains something in affect to vivacious people, especially something that may have caused anger to him,[82] their attention is so aroused that they make faces and are involuntarily moved to a play of expression corresponding to this affect. – One may also have noticed that compatibly married people gradually acquire a similarity in facial features, and the cause is interpreted to be that they were married on account of this similarity (*similis simili gaudet*).[83] But this is false; for nature instead strives, in the sexual instinct, for diversity of subjects so that they fall in love with each other and so that all the variety which nature has implanted in their germs[84] will develop. Rather, it is the intimacy and inclination with which they look into each other's eyes so often and at such length when they are close to each other

---

[79] Trans.: Home is where we are doing well.
[80] See Helvétius, *De l'esprit* (1758), 1.2. Kant uses this same example in his 1764 work, *Essay on the Diseases of the Head* 2: 265–266.
[81] Christian Friedrich Michaelis (1754–1804), professor and personal physician in Kassel, Germany. See his "Tollheit aus Mitleidenschaft," in *Medicinisch-praktische Bibliothek* (Göttingen, 1785), vol. 1, Sec. 1, pp. 114–117.
[82] To him] *H*, A2; to them A1. "Something in affect": *etwas im Affekt*.
[83] Trans.: Like takes pleasure in like.   [84] *ihre Keime*.

in solitary conversations that produces sympathetic and similar expres- [180] sions, which, when they become fixed, eventually turn into permanent facial features.

Finally, one can also attribute to this unintentional play of productive power of imagination, which can then be called *fantasy*, the tendency to harmless *lying* that is *always* met with in children and *now* and *then* in adults who, though otherwise good-natured, sometimes have this tendency almost as a hereditary disease. The events and supposed adventures they narrate issue from the power of imagination like a growing avalanche as it rolls down, and they do not have any kind of advantage in view except simply to make their stories interesting. This is like Shakespeare's Sir John Falstaff, who made five people out of two buckram-clad men before he finished his story.[85] –

§33

Because the power of imagination is richer and more fruitful in representations than sense, when a passion appears on the scene the power of imagination is more enlivened through the absence of the object than by its presence. This is evident when something happens that recalls the representation of an object to the mind again, which for a while seemed to be erased through distractions. – Thus a German prince, a rugged warrior but a noble man, took a trip to Italy to drive from his mind his love for a commoner in his residence.[86] But upon his return the first glimpse of her dwelling stirred his imagination so much more strongly than continuous association would have done that he yielded to his resolution without further hesitation, which fortunately was also what was expected. – This sickness, the effect of an inventive power of imagination, is incurable: except through *marriage*. For marriage is truth (*eripitur persona, manet res*. Lucretius).[87]

The inventive power of imagination produces a kind of intercourse with ourselves, which, though it may consist merely of appearances of inner sense, is nevertheless analogous to those of outer sense. The night

---

[85] Shakespeare, *The First Part of King Henry the Fourth*, II, iv. (Actually, Falstaff eventually managed to make *eleven* out of two.) [*Marginal note in H*: Lies of children.]

[86] Prince Leopold of Anhalt-Dessau (1676–1747), i.e., Leopold I. The commoner was Annelise Föse, a pharmacist's daughter. They were married in 1698.

[87] Trans.: When the mask is snatched away, the thing itself remains. Lucretius, *De Rerum Natura* 3.58.

enlivens and raises it above its real content; just as the moon in evening makes a great figure in the heavens, though on a bright day it is seen as an insignificant little cloud. The power of imagination swarms in one who studies by candle-light in the still of the night, or who quarrels with his imaginary opponent, or wanders about in his room building castles in the air. But everything that seems important to him then loses its entire importance the following morning after a night's sleep. With time, how-[181] ever, he feels a weakening of his mental powers from this bad habit. Therefore the taming of the power of imagination, by going to sleep early so that one can get up early, is a very useful rule for a psychological diet. But women and hypochondriacs (who commonly have their ailment for just this reason) enjoy the opposite behavior more. – Why are ghost stories, which are welcomed late at night, found to be distasteful to everyone and entirely inappropriate for conversation as soon as we get up the following morning? Instead we ask if anything new has happened in the household or in the community, or resume our work of the preceding day. The reason is that what is in itself mere *play* is appropriate for the relaxation of powers drained during the day, but what is *business* is appropriate for the human being strengthened and, so to speak, reborn by a night's sleep.

The offenses (*vitia*) of the power of imagination are that its inventions are either merely *unbridled* or entirely *ruleless* (*effrenis aut perversa*). The latter fault is the worst kind. The former inventions could still find their place in a possible world (the world of fable); but ruleless inventions have no place in any world at all, because they are self-contradictory. – Images of the first type, that is, of unbridled imagination, account for the horror with which the Arabs regard human and animal figures hewn in stone that are often encountered in the Libyan desert Ras-Sem; they consider them to be human beings petrified by a curse.[88] – But these same Arabs' opinion that on the day of universal resurrection these statues of animals will snarl at the artist and admonish him for having made them without being able to give them souls is a contradiction. – Unbridled fantasy can always be humbled (like that of the poet who was asked by Cardinal Este on the occasion of a book dedicated to him: "Master Ariosto,[89] where the

---

[88] Külpe surmises that Kant obtained this information from the following article in the *Hamburgisches Magazin* 19 (1757) – "Abhandlung von einer versteinerten Stadt in der Landschaft Tripoli in Afrika" (pp. 631–653).

[89] Ludovico Ariosto (1474–1533), Italian epic and lyric poet. Cardinal Este's remark appears in several different biographies of Ariosto.

devil did you get all this drivel?"). It is luxuriant because of its riches; but ruleless fantasy approaches madness, where fantasy plays completely with the human being and the unfortunate victim has no control at all over the course of his representations.

Moreover, a political artist, just as well as an aesthetic one, can guide and rule the world (*mundus vult decipi*)[90] by deluding it through images in place of reality; for example, the *freedom* of the people (as in the English Parliament), or their rank and *equality* (as in the French Assembly), which consist of mere formalities. However, it is still better to have [182] only the illusion of possessing this good that ennobles humanity than to feel manifestly deprived of it.[91]

On the faculty of visualizing the past and the future by means of the power of imagination

§34

The faculty of deliberately visualizing the past is the *faculty of memory*, and the faculty of visualizing something as taking place in the future is the *faculty of foresight*. Provided that they belong to sensibility, both of them are based on the *association* of representations of the past and future consciousness of the subject with the present; and although they are not themselves perceptions, as a connecting of perceptions *in time*, they serve to connect in a coherent experience what *no longer exists* with what *does not yet exist* through what *presently exists*. They are called the faculties of *memory* and *divination*, of respicience and prospicience (if we may use these expressions), where one is conscious of one's ideas as those which would be encountered in one's past or future state.

A On memory

Memory is distinguished from the merely reproductive power of imagination in that it is able to reproduce the former representations *voluntarily*, so that the mind is not a mere plaything of the imagination. Fantasy, that is, creative power of imagination, must not mix in with it, because

---

[90] Trans.: The world wants to be deceived.
[91] *Marginal note in H*: Do not visit lunatic asylums.

75

then memory would be *unfaithful*. – To *grasp* something quickly in memory, to *recall* it to mind easily, and to *retain* it for a long time are the formal perfections of memory. But these qualities are rarely found together. When we believe that we have something in our memory but cannot bring it to consciousness, we say that we cannot *remember* it (not remember it to *oneself*; for this means much the same as to make oneself senseless).[92] The effort to remember the idea, if one is anxious about it, is mentally exhausting, and the best thing to do is to distract oneself for [183] a while with other thoughts and from time to time look back at the object quickly. Then one usually catches one of the associated representations, which calls it back to mind.

To grasp something *methodically* (*memoriae mandare*) is called *memorizing* (not *studying*, as the common man says of the preacher who merely learns by heart the sermon he intends to give). – Memorizing can be *mechanical*, *ingenious*, or *judicious*. The first is based merely on frequent word-for-word repetition; for example, in learning the multiplication tables, where the pupil must go through the whole series of words following each other in the usual order, in order to reach what is sought after. For instance, when the apprentice is asked how much 3×7 is, he will begin with 3×3 and probably arrive at 21; however, if one asks him how much 7×3 is, he will not be able to remember it so quickly, but must reverse the numbers in order to place them in the usual order. When what is to be learned is a ceremonial formula where no expression can be altered, but which must, as they say, be reeled off, even people with the best of memories are afraid to rely on them (in fact this very fear could make them err). And therefore they regard it as necessary to *read it off*, as the most experienced preachers do, because the least alteration of words in this case would be ridiculous.

Ingenious memorizing is a method of impressing certain ideas on the memory by association with correlative ideas that in themselves (as far as understanding is concerned) have no relationship at all with each other; for example, associating sounds of a language with quite dissimilar images supposed to correspond with them. In this case, in order to grasp something in the memory more easily, we inconvenience it with

---

[92] Remember: *entsinnen*, remember to oneself: *sich entsinnen*, make oneself senseless: *sich sinnlos machen*. Kant is protesting here against the standard German use of the reflexive verb *sich entsinnen*.

still more correlative ideas; consequently it is *absurd*, a ruleless procedure of the power of imagination in pairing together things that cannot belong together under one and the same concept. And at the same time it is a contradiction between means and intention, since it tries to make memory's work easier but in fact makes it more difficult by burdening it unnecessarily with an association of quite disparate representations.[1] The observation that witty people seldom have a trustworthy memory (*inge-* [184] *niosis non admodum fida est memoria*)[93] is explained by this phenomenon.

Judicious memorizing is nothing other than memorizing, in thought, a *table* of the *divisions* of a system (for example, that of Linnaeus)[94] where, if one should forget something, one can find it again through the enumeration of the parts that one has retained; or else through memorizing the *sections* of a whole made visible (for example, the provinces of a country on a map, which lie to the north, to the west, etc.); for here one also needs understanding, and this is reciprocally helpful to the imagination. Most of all, the judicious use of *topics*, that is, a framework for general concepts, called *commonplaces*, facilitates remembering through class division, as when one distributes books in a library on shelves with different labels.

There is no *mnemonic art* (*ars mnemonica*) in the sense of a general doctrine. Among the special tricks belonging to it are maxims in verse (*versus memoriales*), since the rhythm has a regular syllabic stress that is a great advantage to the mechanism of memory. – Concerning the prodigies of memory, such as Pico Mirandola, Scaliger, Angelus Politianus, Magliabecchi,[95] and so on, polyhistorians who carry around in their heads, as material for the sciences, a load of books for one hundred camels: one must not speak disdainfully of them, since they perhaps

---

[1] Thus the illustrated primer, like the picture Bible or even one of the *law digests* presented in pictures, is an optical box that a childish teacher uses to make his pupils even more childish than they were before. As an example of such a manner of teaching, we can use a heading of the *Pandects, de heredibus suis et legitimis* [trans.: we have learned from our heritage, and only the [184] legitimate heritage], to be committed to memory as follows: the first word would be made sensible by a chest of padlocks, the second by a sow, and the third by the two tables of Moses.

[93] Trans.: Wags just do not have a trustworthy memory.

[94] Carl von Linné (1707–1778), Swedish botanist and taxonomist, originator of the modern scientific classification of plants and animals, author of *Systema Naturae* (1735). ("Linnaeus" is a Latinized version of "Linné.")

[95] Giovanni Pico della Mirandola (1463–1494), Italian philosopher and humanist. Julius Caesar Scaliger (1484–1558), Italian philologist and physician who settled in France; father of Joseph Justus Scaliger (1540–1609), French classical scholar. Angelo Poliziano (1454–1494), Italian poet, philologist, and humanist. Antonio Magliabecchi (1633–1714), Italian librarian and book collector.

did not possess the *power of judgment* suitable for choosing among all this knowledge in order to make appropriate use of it. For it is already merit enough to have produced the raw material abundantly, even though later on other heads must come along to process it with *judgment* (*tantum scimus, quantum memoria tenemus*).[96] One of the ancients said: "The art of writing has ruined memory (to some extent made it dispensable)."[97] There is some truth in this proposition, for the common man is more likely to have the various things entrusted to him lined up, so that he can remember them and carry them out in succession, just because memory [185] here is mechanical and no subtle reasoning interferes with it. On the other hand, the scholar, who has many strange ideas running through his head, lets many of his tasks or domestic affairs escape through distraction, because he has not grasped them with sufficient attention. But to be safe with a notebook in the pocket is after all a great convenience, in order to recover precisely and without effort everything that has been stored in the head. And the art of writing always remains a magnificent one, because, even when it is not used for the communication of one's knowledge to others, it still takes the place of the most extensive and reliable memory, and can compensate for its lack.

However, *forgetfulness* (*obliviositas*), where the head, no matter how often it is filled, still remains empty like a barrel full of holes, is all the greater a misfortune. This is sometimes undeserved, as with old people who can easily remember the events of their younger years, but who always lose their thoughts over more recent ones. But it is also often the effect of a habitual distraction, which especially seizes women who are accustomed to reading novels. For since with this type of reading the intention is only to entertain ourselves for the moment, and since we know that it is mere fiction, women readers here thus have complete freedom, while reading, to create things in accordance with the drift of their power of imagination. This is naturally distracting and makes for habitual *absent-mindedness* (lack of attention to the present); as a result the memory is inevitably weakened. – This practice in the art of killing time and making oneself useless to the world, while later complaining about the brevity of life, is one of the most hostile attacks on memory, to say nothing of the mental disposition to fantasy that it produces.

---

[96] Trans.: As much as we have in our memory, so much do we know.   [97] See Plato, *Phaedrus* 275a.

78

B On the faculty of foresight (praevisio)

§35

To possess this faculty interests us more than any other, because it is the condition of all possible practice and of the ends to which the human being relates the use of his powers. Every desire contains a (doubtful or certain) foresight of what is possible through it. Recalling the past (remembering) [186] occurs only with the intention of making foresight of the future possible by means of it: generally speaking, we look about us from the standpoint of the present in order to decide something or to be prepared for something.

Empirical foresight is the *anticipation of similar cases (exspectatio casuum similium)* and requires no rational knowledge of causes and effects, but only the remembering of observed events as they commonly follow one another, and repeated experiences produce an aptitude for it. What the wind and weather will be is of great interest to the mariner and the farmer. But we do not reach much further here than the so–called Farmer's Almanac, whose forecasts are praised when they happen to come true and forgotten when they are not fulfilled; thus they always rest on some trust. – One might almost believe that Providence intentionally made the play of atmospheric conditions such an inscrutable tangle that human beings could not easily make the necessary preparations for every occasion, but rather would need to use their understanding in order to be prepared for all events.

To live for the day (without caution and care) does not bring much honor to human understanding; it is like the Caribbean who sells his hammock in the morning and in the evening is embarrassed about it because he does not know how he will sleep that night. But as long as no offense against morality occurs in this connection, one who is hardened to all eventualities can be regarded as happier than one who always diminishes the joy of life with gloomy outlooks. But of all the outlooks that the human being can have, the most comforting, if his present moral condition warrants it, is the prospect of continuing in this state and progressing even further toward the good. On the other hand, if he courageously makes the resolution from now on to choose a new and better life, he must tell himself: "Nothing will come of it anyway. You have often (because of procrastination) made this promise to yourself, but you have always broken it under the pretext of making an exception just this once." Thus the expectation of similar cases is a bleak state of affairs.

But where what hovers over us depends on fate rather than on the use [187] of our free choice, looking into the future is either presentiment, that is, *premonition* (*praesensio*), or[m] prescience (*praesagitio*). The first suggests as it were a hidden sense for what is not yet present; the second a consciousness of the future produced by reflecting on the law of succession of events (the law of causality).

One can easily see that all premonition is a chimera; for how can one sense what does not yet exist? If there are judgments arising from obscure concepts of such a causal relation, then they are not presentiments; rather we can develop the concepts that lead to them and explain how matters stand with the causal relation and the judgment so conceived. – For the most part, premonitions are of the fearful sort; anxiety, which has its *physical* causes, precedes any definite notion of what the object of fear is. But there are also the joyous and bold premonitions of enthusiasts[98] who scent the imminent revelation of a mystery for which the human being has no such receptivity of sense, and believe that they see the unveiling of the presentiment of what, like the Epoptes,[99] they await in mystical intuition. – The second sight of the Scottish Highlanders also belongs to this class of enchantments. Several of them believed that they saw a man strung up on a mast, the news of whose death they pretended to have received when they actually entered a distant port.

C On the gift of divination (facultas divinatrix)

§36

Predicting, fortune-telling, and prophesying are distinguished as follows: the *first* is foresight according to laws of experience (therefore natural); the *second* is contrary to the familiar laws of experience (contrary to nature); but the *third* is, or is considered to be, inspiration from a cause

---

[m] Recently an attempt has been made to distinguish between *ahnen* and *ahnden*; but the first is not a German word, and there remains only the latter. – *Ahnden* means *to bear in mind. Es ahndet mir* means: I have a vague recollection of it; *etwas ahnden* means to remember someone's action in bad terms (that is, to punish). It is always the same concept, but used in different ways. [*Ahndung* – punishment, vengeance, retribution, was formerly used for *Ahnung* – premonition, presentiment. Both are recognized German words – Ed.]

[98] *Schwärmer*. Again (cf. n. 12), in the German Enlightenment this term had a sense closer to our "fanatics."

[99] Observers who have been initiated into the Eleusinian mysteries. See Plato, *Symposium* 210a ff., *Phaedrus* 250c.

80

that is distinct from nature (supernatural). Because this third capacity [188] seems to result from the influence of a god, it is also properly called the *faculty of divination* (since every shrewd guess about the future is also improperly called divination).

To say of someone that he is able to *foretell* this or that fate can indicate a perfectly natural skill. But if he pretends that he has a supernatural insight into it, we must say that he is a *specious soothsayer*; like the gypsies of Hindu origin, who call fortune-telling from the lines of the hand *reading the planets*; or astrologers and treasure-hunters, and also their associates the alchemists; but the Pythia in Greek antiquity, and in our own time the ragged Siberian Shaman, tower over them all. The sooth-sayings of the auspices and haruspices of the Romans did not purport to discover what is hidden in the course of the world's events so much as to discover the will of the gods, to which in accordance with their religion they had submitted. – But how the poets also came to consider them-selves as inspired (or possessed), and as fortune-tellers (*vates*), and how they could boast of having inspirations in their poetical impulses (*furor poeticus*), can only be explained by the fact that the poet, unlike the prose-orator who composes his commissioned work with leisure, must rather snatch the propitious moment of the mood of his inner sense as it comes over him, in which lively and powerful images and feelings pour into him, while he behaves merely passively, so to speak. For as an old observation goes, genius is mixed with a certain dose of madness. The belief that blindly chosen passages from the works of famous poets (driven by inspiration, so to speak) are oracular utterances (*sortes Virgilianae*)[100] is also based on this supposition. Modern devotees use a jewel-case as a similar means to discover heaven's will. This also applies to the inter-pretation of the Sibylline books,[101] which were supposed to foretell the fate of the Roman state, though the Romans unfortunately lost parts of them on account of injudicious stinginess.[102]

---

[100] I.e., the custom, which seems to have been popular from the second to the sixteenth centuries AD, of predicting the future by opening at random a volume of Virgil and taking as an omen of coming events the first line on which the eyes fell.

[101] Many ancient authors refer to the Sibylline prophecies. Kant seems to be alluding to the story that Tarquinius Priscus' collection of them (to be consulted only at the command of the Senate) was lost in the burning of the Capitol in 83 BC. See, e.g., Dionysius Halicarnassensis 4.62.1–6; Pliny, *Naturalis Historia* 13.88; Lactantius, *Divinae Institutiones* 1.6.10–11; Servius, *Aen.* 6.72.

[102] *Marginal note in H*: Astronomy
   Uselessness of prophecy.

81

All prophesies that foretell an inevitable fate of a people, for which they are themselves still responsible and which therefore is to be brought about by *their own free choice*, contain an absurdity – in addition to the fact that the foreknowledge is *useless* to them, since they cannot escape from [189] it. For in this unconditional fate (*decretum absolutum*) there is thought to be a *mechanism of freedom*, by which the concept contradicts itself.

The extreme limit of absurdity, or of deception, in specious soothsaying may be that a madman has been considered a *seer* (of invisible things); as if a spirit were speaking from him which had taken the place of the soul that had long since departed from its bodily dwelling. And so the poor mental (or merely epileptic) patient was looked upon as an *Energumen* (one possessed), and he was called a *Mantis* by the Greeks if the demon possessing him were considered to be a good spirit. The interpreter of the *Mantis*, however, was called a *prophet*. – Every form of folly must be exhausted in order for us to gain possession of the future, the foreseeing of which interests us a great deal, by leaping over all the steps that might have led us there by means of the understanding working through experience. *O, curas hominum!*[103]

Moreover, there is no science of soothsaying so certain and yet so far-reaching as astronomy, which foretells the revolutions of the heavenly bodies *ad infinitum*. But even this could not prevent a mysticism from promptly joining it which, instead of reckoning the epochs of the world on the basis of events, as reason requires, wanted, on the contrary, to make the events dependent on certain sacred numbers, thus transforming chronology itself, which is such a necessary condition of all history, into a fable.

On involuntary invention in a healthy state, i.e., on dreams

§37

To investigate the natural constitution of *sleep*, of *dreaming*, and of *somnambulism* (to which talking aloud during sleep also belongs) lies outside the field of a *pragmatic* anthropology; for we cannot draw any rules of *conduct* from these phenomena in the state of dreaming, since these rules are valid only for the person who is awake and does not want

---

[103] Trans.: Oh, the troubles of humanity!

to dream, or wants to sleep without thinking. And the judgment of the Greek emperor who condemned a human being to death when he explained to his friends that in his dream he had killed the emperor, under the pretext that "he would not have dreamed it, unless he were thinking about doing it while awake," is both contrary to experience and [190] cruel. "When we are awake we have a world in common, but when we are asleep each has his own world." – Dreaming seems to belong so necessarily to sleeping that sleeping and dying would be one and the same thing if the dream were not added as a natural, although involuntary, agitation of the inner vital organs by means of the power of imagination. Thus I remember well how, as a boy tired because of playing, I went to sleep and, at the moment of falling asleep, quickly awoke because of a dream that I had fallen into water and was being turned around in circles, coming close to drowning, only to soon fall asleep again more peacefully. Presumably this was because the activity of the chest muscles in breathing, which depends completely on choice, had slackened, and with the failure of breathing the movement of the heart was impeded, and thus the power of imagination had to be set into action again by means of the dream. – Here belongs also the beneficial effect of dreaming during a so-called *nightmare* (*incubus*). For without this frightful image of a ghost oppressing us and the straining of every muscle to get into another position, the cessation of blood flow would quickly bring an end to life. This is why nature seems to have arranged for most dreams to contain difficulties and dangerous situations, because such ideas excite the powers of the soul more than when everything goes smoothly. One often dreams that one cannot rise to one's feet, or that one is lost, bogged down in a sermon, or that at a large gathering out of forgetfulness one has put on a nightcap instead of a wig, or that one can hover back and forth through the air at will, or awakens laughing merrily, without knowing why. – How it happens that we are often placed in the long distant past in dreams, speaking with those long dead, or why we are tempted to regard this as a dream and yet feel compelled to regard this image as reality, will always remain unexplained. But one can take it as certain that there could be no sleep without dreaming, and whoever imagines that he has not dreamed has merely forgotten his dream.[104]

---

[104] *Crossed out in H*: According to Sonnerat [Pierre Sonnerat, *Reise nach Ostindien und China* (Zurich, 1783), 1: 60, 69 – Ed.] the Indians on the coast of Malabar have been bound to a large

[191] **On the faculty of using signs (*facultas signatrix*)**

§38

The faculty of cognizing the present as the means for connecting the representation of the foreseen with that of the past is the *faculty of using signs*. – The mental activity of bringing about this connection is *signifying* (*signatio*), which is also called *signaling*, of which the higher degree is called *marking*.

Forms of things (intuitions), so far as they serve only as means of representation through concepts, are *symbols*; and cognition through them is called symbolic or *figurative* (*speciosa*). – *Characters* are not yet symbols; for they can also be mere mediate (indirect) signs which in themselves signify nothing, but only signify something through association with intuitions and then leading through them to concepts. Therefore, *symbolic* cognition must not be opposed to *intuitive* but to *discursive* cognition, in which the character accompanies the concept merely as guardian (*custos*), in order to reproduce the concept when the occasion arises. Symbolic cognition is therefore not opposed to intuitive cognition (through sensuous intuition), but rather to intellectual cognition (through concepts). Symbols are merely means that understanding uses to provide the concept with meaning through the presentation of an object for it. But they are only indirect means, owing to an *analogy* with certain intuitions to which the concept can be applied.

He who can only express himself symbolically still has only a few concepts of understanding, and the lively presentation so often admired in the speeches presented by savages (and sometimes also the alleged wise men among a still uncultivated people) is nothing but poverty in concepts and, therefore, also in the words to express them. For example, when the American savage says: "We want to bury the hatchet," this means: "We want to make peace," and in fact the ancient songs, from Homer to Ossian or from Orpheus to the prophets, owe their bright eloquence merely to the lack of means for expressing their concepts.

extent to a very secret order, whose sign (in the shape of a round tin coin) hangs from a band around the neck directly on the skin. They call it their *tali*, which is accompanied in their initiation ceremony by a mystical word that one person whispers into another's ear only at death. However, the Tibetans have made use of certain sacred things, e.g., flags with certain holy words written on them or also sacred stones, which are planted on or laid over a hill and which they call *mani*. The word *talisman* has probably arisen from the putting together of both words, which appears to correspond in sense and meaning with the *Manitou* of the American savages.

To claim (with Swedenborg)[105] that the real appearances of the world present to the senses are merely a *symbol* of an intelligible world hidden in reserve is *enthusiasm*. But in exhibiting concepts (called ideas) that belong [192] to morality and therefore to pure reason, concepts which constitute the essence of all religion, it is *enlightenment* to distinguish the symbolic from the intellectual (public worship from religion), the temporarily useful and necessary *shell* from the thing itself. Because otherwise an *ideal* (of pure practical reason) is mistaken for an *idol*, and the final end is missed. – It is not disputed that all peoples of the earth have begun with this exchange, and that, when it is a question of what their teachers themselves really thought in their holy writings, one must not interpret them symbolically but rather *literally*; for to twist their words would be dishonest. But when it is a question not merely of the *truthfulness* of the teacher but also, and indeed essentially, of the *truth* of the teaching,[106] then one can and should interpret this teaching as a merely symbolic kind of representation, in which established formalities and customs accompany those practical ideas. Because otherwise the intellectual sense, which constitutes the final end, would be lost.[107]

§39

One can divide signs into *arbitrary* (artificial), *natural*, and *miraculous* signs.

A. To the first group belong: 1) signs of *gesticulation* (mimetic signs, which are also partly natural); 2) *characters* (letters, which are signs for sounds); 3) *tone signs* (notes); 4) purely visual signs that have been agreed upon between individuals (*ciphers*); 5) *signs of social standing* for free

---

[105] Emmanuel Swedenborg (1688–1772), Swedish scientist, religious teacher, and mystic. His religious system is largely incorporated into the Church of the New Jerusalem, founded some years after his death, and his followers are called Swedenborgians. Kant's early work *Dreams of a Spirit-Seer Elucidated by Dreams of Metaphysics* (1766 – 2:315–373) focuses primarily on Swedenborg's religious visions and alleged supernatural powers. While it is predominantly skeptical in tone, occasional moments of admiration are also evident in it. See also Kant's letter to Charlotte von Knobloch of August 10, 1763 (10:43–48).

[106] *Marginal note in H*: On superstition.
Nominal and *real* signs.
Indirect – direct.

[107] *Crossed out in H*: would. [<For the> For the designation of thoughts, not of mere sensation, the human being at first makes use of *mimical* signs, then *sound* signs of language, and finally *allegorical* signs of <visible images of> pictures, which should contain an analogy with <things that are not visible> merely thinkable objects.]

men honored with hereditary rank (coats of arms); 6) *signs of service*, in prescribed clothing (uniforms and liveries); 7) *signs of honor*, for service (ribbons awarded by orders); 8) *signs of disgrace* (brandings and so on). – In writing, signs of pause, question or affect, and astonishment (punctuation marks) also belong to arbitrary signs.

All language is a signification of thought and, on the other hand, the best way of signifying thought is through language, the greatest instrument for understanding ourselves and others. Thinking is *speaking* with oneself (the Indians of Tahiti call thinking "speech in the belly"); consequently it is also *listening* to oneself inwardly (by means of the reproductive power of imagination). To the man born deaf, his speaking is a feeling of the play of his lips, tongue, and jaw; and it is hardly possible to imagine that he does anything more by his speaking than carry on a play [193] with physical feelings, without having and thinking real concepts. – But even those who can speak and hear do not always understand themselves or others, and it is due to the lack of the faculty of signification, or its faulty use (when signs are taken for things, and vice versa), that, especially in matters of reason, human beings who are united in language are as distant as heaven from earth in concepts. This becomes obvious only by chance, when each acts according to his own concepts.

B. Second, as concerns natural signs, the relation of sign to thing signified, depending on the time, is either *demonstrative* or *rememorative* or *prognostic*.

Pulsation signifies to the physician the presence of a feverish condition in the patient, as smoke signifies fire. Reagents reveal to the chemist what hidden substances are present in water, just as the weathervane reveals the wind, etc. But whether *blushing* reveals consciousness of guilt, or rather a delicate sense of honor, or just an imposition of something about which one would have to suffer shame, is uncertain in cases that come before us.[108]

---

[108] *Marginal note in H*: A. Voluntary signs. 1. Of gesture (mimetic) 2. Written signs (letters) 3. Tone signs (notes) 4. Secret guild signs (codes) 5. Signs of social standing (coats of arms) 6. Service signs (uniform or livery) 7. Signs of honor (ribbons of an order) 8. Signs of disgrace (branding with a hot iron) 9. Ear-marking signs (*nota*) 10. Differentiating signs (punctuation) 11. Signs of remembrance (*signum rememorativum*)

B. Natural signs   Signs to regard as things in themselves
C. Signs of wonder   *Zodiac.*

Effects are signs of their causes.
Sign of the zodiac – constellation.

Burial mounds and mausoleums are signs of remembrance of the dead, just as pyramids are also everlasting reminders of the former great power of a king. – Layers of shells in regions far from the sea, the holes of Pholades[109] in the high Alps, or volcanic residue where no fire now bursts forth from the earth, signify to us the ancient condition of the world and establish an *archaeology* of nature. However, they are not as plainly visible as the scarred-over wounds of a warrior. – The ruins of Palmyra, Baalbek, and Persepolis are telling monuments of the state of art in *ancient* states, and sad indications of the change of *all* things.

Generally, *prognostic* signs are the most interesting of all; because in the series of changes the present is only an instant, and the determining ground of the faculty of desire takes to heart the present only for the sake of future consequences (*ob futura consequentia*), and pays careful attention to them. – In regard to future events in the world, the surest prognosis is to be found in astronomy; but it is childish and fantastic when constellations of stars and conjunctions and changes in the positions of the planets are represented (in the *Astrologia iudiciaria*) as allegorical signs written in heaven of impending human fate.

Natural prognostic signs of an impending illness or recovery, or (like the [194] *facies Hippocratica*) of imminent death, are appearances which, based on long and frequent experience, serve the physician as a guide in his course of medical treatment, even after insight into their connection as cause and effect. Such are critical days. But the auguries and haruspices contrived by the Romans for politically shrewd purposes were a superstition sanctified by the state in order to guide the people in dangerous times.

C. As concerns *miraculous signs* (events in which the nature of things reverses itself), apart from those which do not now matter to us (monstrosities among human beings and animals), there are signs and miracles in the sky – comets, balls of light shooting across the sky, northern lights, even solar and lunar eclipses. It is especially when several such signs come together and are accompanied by war, pestilence, and the like, that they are things which seem, to the terrified great masses, to herald the not far distant Judgment Day and the end of the world.

Art of astrology (*astrol. Ind.*), signs of the heavens, comets, eclipses, northern lights. Whether the sacred number (*heil. Zahl*) indicates the way of the world [?]. The dragon chasing the sun and moon *apocalipt.* Signs of divination, mystical signs, holy 7 – x.x. Planets, metals. Weekdays and world epochs. Superstitions of fishermen.

[109] Boring clams, which can bore deeply into mud, wood, and even hard rock.

87

Appendix

In addition, it is worth mentioning here an odd game of the power of imagination with the human being, in which signs are confused with things so that an inner reality is posited for signs, as if things had to conform to them. – Since the course of the moon in its four phases (new moon, first quarter, full moon, and last quarter) cannot be divided into whole numbers any more exactly than into twenty-eight days (and the Zodiac of the Arabians is divided into twenty-eight houses of the moon), of which a quarter makes seven days, the number seven has thereby acquired a mystical importance. Thus, even the creation of the world had to comply with it, especially since (according to the Ptolemaic system) there were supposed to be seven planets, as well as seven tones in the scale, seven primary colors in the rainbow, and seven metals. – From this also the climacteric years[110] emerged (7×7 and, since 9 is also a mystical number for the Indians, 7×9 as well as 9×9), at the end of which human life is supposed to be in great danger. In the Judeo-Christian chronology seventy weeks of years (490 years)[111] also not only constitute the divisions

[195] of the most important changes (between God's call to Abraham and the birth of Christ), but even determine quite exactly their borders, so to speak *a priori*, as if chronology did not have to conform to history, but the reverse, that history had to conform to chronology.

But also in other cases it becomes a habit to make things depend on numbers. When a physician, to whom the patient sends a gratuity through his servant, unwraps the paper and finds therein eleven ducats, he will become suspicious that the servant may have embezzled one; for why not a full dozen? He who buys a complete set of porcelain dishes at an auction will bid less when it is not a full dozen; and if there should be thirteen plates, he will place a value on the thirteenth only in so far as it ensures that if one were to be broken, he would still have the full dozen.

---

[110] *Stufenjahre*. The climacteric year (*annus climacterius*) was based on periods of seven and nine years; the forty-ninth year (7×7), the eighty-first year (9×9), and above all the sixty-third year (7×9) were regarded as the most important. Külpe refers readers to a text by A. Joseph Testa – *Bemerkungen über die periodischen Veränderungen und Erscheinungen im kranken und gesunden Zustande des menschlichen Körpers* (Leipzig, 1790), Ch. 6. See also Kant's letter to A. J. Penzel of August 12, 1777 (12: 362ff.) and *The Conflict of the Faculties*, 7: 62–63n.

[111] See Daniel 9: 24: "Seventy weeks are marked out for your people and your holy city; then rebellion shall be stopped, sin brought to an end, inequity expiated, everlasting right ushered in, vision and prophecy sealed, and the Most Holy Place anointed."

Since one does not invite one's guests by the dozen, what interest can there be in giving a preference to this precise number? In his will a man bequeathed eleven silver spoons to his cousin and added: "He himself will know best why I do not bequeath the twelfth to him" (at his table he noticed that the dissolute young man had secretly stuck a spoon in his pocket, but he didn't want to embarrass him then). With the opening of the will one could easily guess what the meaning of the testator was, but only because of the accepted prejudice that only the dozen would be a full number. – The twelve signs of the zodiac (a number to which the twelve judges in England seem analogous) have also acquired a similar mystical significance. In Italy, Germany, and perhaps elsewhere too, a dinner party of exactly thirteen guests is considered ominous, because it is imagined that one of them, whoever it may be, will die that year; just as at a table of twelve judges, the thirteenth, who finds himself among them, can be no other than the defendant who will be judged. (I once found myself at such a table, where the lady of the house upon sitting down noticed this supposedly evil state of affairs and secretly ordered her son, who was one of the company, to get up and eat in another room, so that the merriment would not be disturbed.) – But even the sheer magnitude of numbers arouses astonishment, when one has enough of the things that they signify, by the fact that the magnitude does not, in counting, complete a round number according to the decadic system (and is consequently arbitrary). Thus the emperor of China is supposed to have a fleet of 9999 [196] ships, and on hearing this number we secretly ask ourselves, why not one more? Although the answer could be: "Because this number of ships is sufficient for his needs"; in reality the intent of the question is not focused on the needs, but rather merely on a kind of number mysticism. – Worse, although not uncommon, is when someone who through miserliness and fraud has brought his fortune to 90,000 thalers in cash now cannot rest until he has a full 100,000, without needing it. And in achieving this goal he perhaps at least deserves the gallows, even if he does not get it.

To what childishness the human being sinks in his ripe old age, when he allows himself to be led by the leash of sensibility! Let us now see how much better or worse he fares when he pursues his course under the illumination of understanding.[112]

---

[112] *Marginal note in H*: The 13th dinner guest.
Many a person stints, deceives, in order to leave 100,000 full.

On the cognitive faculty, in so far as it is based on understanding

Division

§40

Understanding, as the faculty of *thinking* (representing something by means of *concepts*), is also called the *higher* cognitive faculty (as distinguished from sensibility, which is the *lower*), because the faculty of intuition (pure or empirical) contains only the singularity of objects, whereas the faculty of concepts contains the universality of representations, the *rule* to which the manifold of sensuous intuitions must be subordinated in order to bring unity to the cognition of the object. – Therefore understanding certainly is of *higher rank* than sensibility, with which irrational animals can manage provisionally, following implanted instincts, like a people without a sovereign. But a sovereign without a people (like understanding without sensibility) is not able to do anything at all. Therefore between the two there is no dispute about rank, though the one is addressed as higher and the other as lower.

[197] The word *understanding* is, however, also taken in a particular sense, namely when it is subordinated to understanding in a general sense as one member of a division with two other members; and then the higher cognitive faculty (materially, that is, considered not by itself, but rather in relation to the *cognition* of objects) consists of *understanding, the power of judgment*, and *reason*. – Let us now make some observations about human beings, how one differs from another in these mental endowments or in their habitual use or misuse, first in a healthy soul, and then also in mental illness.

Anthropological comparison of the three higher cognitive faculties with one another

§41

A correct understanding is that which is lustrous not only owing to its great number of concepts but also owing to the *appropriateness* of its concepts for cognition of the object; thus it contains the ability and skill to comprehend *truth*. Many a human being has a great many concepts in his head which together amount to a *similarity* with what one wants to learn from him, but which still do not turn out to be true of the object and its determination. He can have concepts of vast scope, and even handle them with *dexterity*. Correct understanding, which is sufficient for concepts of general cognition, is called *sound* understanding (sufficient for everyday needs). It says, with Juvenal's centurion: "*Quod sapio, satis est mihi, non ergo curo – esse quod Arcesilaus aerumnosique Solones.*"[113] It goes without saying that nature's gift of a merely straightforward and correct understanding will limit itself in regard to the range of knowledge expected of it, and that the person endowed with it will proceed *modestly*.[114]

§42

If by the word "understanding" is meant the faculty of cognition of rules (and thus cognition through concepts) in general, so that the understanding composes the entire *higher* faculty of cognition in itself, then the rules are not to be understood as those according to which nature guides the human being in his conduct, as occurs with animals which are driven by natural instinct, but only those that he himself *makes*. What he merely learns, and thus entrusts to his memory, he performs only mechanically (according to laws of reproductive imagination) and without understanding. A servant who has merely to pay a compliment according to a definite formula needs no understanding, that is, he does not need to think for himself. But when in the absence of his master whose household affairs [198] he has to manage, where many rules of behavior will be necessary that cannot be literally prescribed, then he will need understanding.

Correct understanding, *practiced* judgment, and *thorough* reason constitute the entire range of the intellectual cognitive faculty; especially if this faculty is also judged as competence in promoting the practical, that is, competence in promoting ends.

Correct understanding is healthy understanding, provided that it contains an *appropriateness* of concepts for the purpose of its use. By

---

[113] The quotation comes not from Juvenal, but from Persius 3.78f. Trans.: "What I know is enough for me. Therefore I do not worry about being like Arcesilaus and the tormented Solon." Arcesilaus (c. 316–242 BC) was Head of the Academy in the middle of the third century BC. Solon (c. 639–559 BC) was an Athenian statesman and poet.

[114] *Marginal note in H*: 1. What do I want? 2. What does it depend on? 3. What do I gain? (what comes of it?
Correct understanding, practiced power of judgment and thorough reason.

joining together sufficiency (*sufficientia*) and *precision* (*praecisio*) we arrive at *appropriateness*, which constitutes the quality of the concept. Appropriateness contains neither more nor less than the concept demands (*conceptus rem adaequans*).[115] Thus a correct understanding is the first and foremost of all intellectual faculties, because it fulfills its purpose with the *fewest* means.

Craftiness, a head for intrigue, is often regarded as great though misused understanding; but it is only the way of thinking of very limited human beings and is very different from prudence, whose appearance it has. One can deceive the naïve person only once, which in the course of time is very disadvantageous to the personal intention of the crafty person.

The domestic or civil servant under express orders needs only to have understanding. The officer, to whom only the general rule is prescribed for his entrusted tasks, and who is then left alone to decide for himself what to do in cases that come up, needs judgment. The general, who has to judge all possible cases and has to think out the rules for himself, must possess reason. – The talents necessary for these different dispositions are very distinct. "Many a man shines on the second rank who would be invisible on the first." (*Tel brille au second rang, qui s'éclipse au premier.*)[116]

Quibbling is not the same as having understanding, and to draw up maxims for show and yet contradict them by one's actions, like Christina of Sweden,[117] is called being unreasonable. – This is how it was with the Earl of Rochester's answer to King Charles II of England, when the King came upon him in deep reflection and asked: "What are you meditating on so deeply?" – Answer: "I am composing your Majesty's epitaph." – [199] Question: "How does it run?" Answer: "Here lies King Charles II, who said many prudent things in his life, but never did anything prudent."[118]

---

[115] Trans.: the concept has to be adequate to the object.

[116] Kant has quoted from Voltaire's epic poem on Henry IV, *La Henriade* (1718), verse 31.

[117] Christina (1626–1689), Queen of Sweden (1632–1654), daughter and successor of Gustavus II. Descartes was one of a number of scholars and artists invited to her court – he died there on February 11, 1650. See Johann Arckenholz, *Historische Merkwürdiekeiten die Königin Christina von Schweden betreffend* (1751–1760), 4 vols., translated into German by Johann Friedrich Reifstein, esp. the Appendix to vol. 2, pp. 73ff.: "Die Nebenstunden oder Lehrsätze und Denkspruche der Königin C. v. S." See also Kant, *Menschenkunde* 25: 1108.

[118] John Wilmot, 2nd Earl of Rochester (1647–1680), *The Works of the Earl of Rochester* (London: printed for Edmund Curll, 1707): "Here lies our Sovereign Lord the King,/Whose Word no Man rely'd on;/ Who never said a foolish thing,/Nor ever did a wise one" (p. 156).

One who is silent in company and only now and then drops a quite ordinary judgment looks reasonable, just as a certain degree of *coarseness* is passed off as (old German) *honesty*.

***

Natural understanding can be enriched through instruction with many concepts and furnished with rules. But the second intellectual faculty, namely that of discerning whether something is an instance of the rule or not – *the power of judgment* (*iudicium*) – cannot be *instructed*, but only exercised. That is why its growth is called *maturity*, and its understanding that which comes only with years. It is also easy to see that this could not be otherwise; because instruction takes place by means of communication of rules. Therefore, if there were to be doctrines for the power of judgment, then there would have to be general rules according to which one could decide whether something was an instance of the rule or not, which would generate a further inquiry on into infinity. Thus the power of judgment is, as we say, the understanding that comes only with years; it is based on one's long experience, and it is the understanding whose judgment a French Republic searches for in the assembly of the so-called Elders.

This faculty, which is aimed only at that which is feasible, what is fitting, and what is proper (for technical,[119] aesthetic, and practical power of judgment), is not as lustrous as the faculty that extends knowledge. For it merely makes room for sound understanding and forms the association between it and reason.

§43

Now if understanding is the faculty of rules, and the power of judgment the faculty of discovering the particular in so far as it is an instance of these rules, then *reason* is the faculty of deriving the particular from the universal and thus of representing it according to principles and as necessary. – We can therefore also explain reason by means of the faculty of *judging* and (in a practical regard) *acting* according to principles. The human being needs reason for every moral (consequently also religious) judgment, and cannot rest on statutes and established customs. – *Ideas*

---

[119] *H*, ᴀɪ: theoretical.

93

are concepts of reason, to which no object given in experience can be [200] adequate. They are neither intuitions (like those of space and time) nor feelings (such as the doctrine of happiness looks for), both of which belong to sensibility. Ideas are, rather, concepts of a perfection that we can always approach but never completely attain.

Rationalizing[120] (without sound reason) is a use of reason that misses its final end, partly from inability, partly from an inappropriate viewpoint. *To rave with reason* means to proceed according to principles in the form of one's thoughts, but in the matter or end to use means that are directly contrary to it.

Subordinates must not rationalize (wrangle),[121] because the principle that should be employed must often be concealed from them, or at least remain unknown to them. But the commanding officer (general) must have reason, because instructions cannot be given to him[122] for every case that comes up. Yet to require that a so-called layman (*Laicus*) should not use his own reason in matters of religion, particularly since these must be appreciated as moral, but instead should follow the appointed *clergyman* (*Clericus*), thus someone else's reason,[123] is an unjust demand. For in moral matters every man must himself be responsible for what he does and does not do, and the clergyman will not, and indeed cannot, assume the responsibility for it at his own risk.

However, in these cases human beings are inclined to place more security in their own person, so that they renounce completely all use of their own reason and submit passively and obediently to formulas laid down by holy men. But they do this not so much because they feel incapable of insight (for the essence of all religion is surely moral, which soon becomes evident to every human being by himself); rather they do it out of *craftiness*, partly in order to be able to push the blame on to someone else when they have acted wrongly; partly, and above all, to evade gracefully that which is essential (change of heart), and which is much more difficult than cult worship (*Cultus*).

Wisdom, as the idea of a practical use of reason that conforms perfectly with the law, is no doubt too much to demand of human beings. But also, not even the slightest degree of wisdom can be poured into a man by others; rather he must bring it forth from himself. The precept for

---

[120] *Vernünftelei.*   [121] *räsonniren.*   [122] *Marginal note in H*: Provisional judgments.
[123] *fremder Vernunft.*

reaching it contains three leading maxims: 1) Think for oneself, 2) Think into the place of the other (in communication with human beings), 3) Always think consistently with oneself.[124]

The age at which the human being reaches the full use of his reason [201] can be fixed, in respect to his *skill* [the capacity to achieve any purpose one chooses], around the twentieth year; in respect to *prudence* (using other human beings for one's purposes), around the fortieth year; and finally, in respect to *wisdom*, around the sixtieth year. However, in this last period wisdom is more *negative*; it sees the follies of the first two periods. At this point we can say: "It is too bad that we have to die now, just when we have learned for the very first time how we should have lived quite well." But even this judgment is rare in the last period, since the attachment to life becomes stronger the more its value, in terms of action as well as enjoyment, decreases.

§44

Just as the faculty of discovering the particular for the universal (the rule) is the *power of judgment*, so the faculty of thinking up the universal for the particular is *wit* (*ingenium*). The power of judgment is a matter of noting the differences in a manifold that is identical in part; wit is a matter of noting the identity of a manifold that is different in part. – The outstanding talent in both is noticing even the smallest similarity or dissimilarity. The faculty to do this is *acumen* (*acumen*), and observations of this kind are called *subtleties*, which, if they do not advance cognition, are called empty *hairsplitting* or idle *rationalizing* (*vanae argutationes*), and the person who indulges in them is guilty of an admittedly useless, although not exactly untrue, employment of understanding in general.[125] – Therefore acumen is bound not merely to the power of judgment but also befits wit; except that in the first case it is considered valuable more on account of *exactitude* (*cognitio exacta*), while in the second case it is

---

[124] Kant repeats these maxims for enlightened reasoning elsewhere as well. See, e.g., *Critique of the Power of Judgment* 5: 294, *Jäsche Logic* 9: 57.

[125] *Marginal note in H*: On natural and civil immaturity.
How much there is that reason does not clear up in respect to what its own history should be. It is not mere fable but a big lie.
Subtlety and micrological suppositions, preliminary concepts to invention, the capacity of *acumen*. Probability for the power of judgment. Insight for reason. Comprehension of that which one can make himself, *mathematics*. One wonders nevertheless that it takes place like this.

because of the *riches* of the good mind. Thus wit is also said to be *blooming*; and just as nature seems to be carrying on more of a game with its flowers but a business with fruits, so the talent encountered in wit is ranked lower (according to the ends of reason) than talent in the power of judgment. – Common and *sound* understanding makes a claim neither to wit nor to acumen, for it limits itself to true needs; whereas wit and acumen deliver a kind of intellectual luxury.

[202]

On the weaknesses and illnesses of the soul with respect to its cognitive faculty

A General division

§45

The defects of the cognitive faculty are either *mental deficiencies* or *mental illnesses*. Illnesses of the soul with respect to the cognitive faculty can be brought under two main types. One is *melancholia* (hypochondria) and the other is *mental derangement* (mania).[126] With the *former*, the patient is well aware that something is not going right with the course of his thoughts, in so far as his reason has insufficient control over itself to direct, stop, or impel the course of his thoughts. Untimely joys and untimely griefs, hence moods, alternate in him like the weather, which one must take as it comes. – Mental derangement indicates an arbitrary course in the patient's thoughts which has its own (subjective) rule, but which runs contrary to the (objective) rule that is in agreement with laws of experience.

With regard to sense representations, mental derangement is either *amentia* or *dementia*. As a perversity of judgment and reason, it is called *insania* or *vesania*.[127] Whoever habitually neglects to compare his

---

[126] Melancholia: *Grillenkrankheit*; mental derangement: *gestörtes Gemüth*. As Gregor notes in her translation (n. 21, pp. 200–201), Kant's use of psychiatric terms presents multiple difficulties for the translator. His classification scheme does not map well on to modern psychiatric terminology (which itself has changed over time), and many of the terms he uses are obsolete, do not have precise English equivalents, etc. In several cases, I have followed Gregor's practice of using older Latin terms that were still common in the late eighteenth century (terms with which Kant was very familiar, and which he appropriated into his own classification system), rather than offering awkward English translations of the German terms. In thinking about these matters I have also benefited from discussions with Claudia Schmidt.

[127] Amentia: *Unsinnigkeit*; dementia: *Wahnsinn*; insania: *Wahnwitz*; vesania: *Aberwitz*.

imaginings with laws of experience (who dreams while awake) is a *vision-ary* (a melancholic); if he does so with affect, he is called an *enthusiast*. Unexpected fits of the visionary are called attacks of fantasy (*raptus*).

The simpleton, the imprudent person, the stupid person, the cox-comb, the fool, and the buffoon differ from the mentally deranged not merely in degree but in the distinctive quality of their mental discord, and because of their ailments they do not yet belong in the madhouse; that is, a place where human beings, despite the maturity and strength of their age, must still, with regard to the smallest matters of life, be kept orderly through someone else's reason. – Dementia accompanied by affect is *madness*, whose fits, though involuntary, can often be original and which then, like poetic rapture (*furor poeticus*), border on *genius*. But an attack like this of a gentle but unregulated flow of ideas, if it strikes [203] reason, is called *enthusiasm*. Brooding over one and the same idea when there is no possible point to it, e.g., over the loss of a spouse who cannot be called back to life, in order to seek peace in the pain itself, is dumb *madness.* – *Superstition* is more comparable with dementia, *enthusiasm* with insania. The latter type of mental patient is also often called (in milder terms) *over-excited* or even eccentric.

Ravings in fever, or an attack of frenzy related to epilepsy, which may occasionally be caused sympathetically through strong power of imagina-tion at the mere frightening sight of a madman (for which reason it is also not advisable for people with unsteady nerves to extend their curiosity over to the cells of these unfortunates), are temporary and not to be regarded as madness. – However, what is called a *crotchety person* (who is not mentally ill; for by this we usually mean a melancholic perversion of inner sense) is mostly a human *arrogance* that borders on dementia. His unreasonable demand that others should despise themselves in comparison with him is directly counter to his own purpose (like that of a madman), since through this demand he provokes others to undermine his self-conceit in every possible way, to torment him, and to expose him to ridicule because of his offensive foolishness. – The expression of a *whim* (*marotte*) that someone nurtures is milder. It is a principle that should be popular, but which nevertheless never meets with approval among prudent people. For example, he is gifted with presentiment, with certain inspirations similar to those of Socrates' genius, and certain qualities that should be grounded in experience, but which as a matter of fact are based on unclear influences such as sympathy, antipathy, and idiosyncrasy (*qualitates occultae*), which

97

as it were are all chirping inside his head like a house cricket[128] and yet which no one else can hear. – The mildest of all deviations across the borderline of sound understanding is the *hobbyhorse*: a fondness for occupying oneself assiduously, as with a business, with objects of the power of imagination that the understanding merely plays with for amusement – a busy idleness, so to speak. For old people, those retired from business, and those in comfortable circumstances, this frame of mind, which is so to speak like withdrawing again into carefree childhood, is not only conducive to health, as an agitation that keeps the life force constantly moving; it is also charming. At the same time, it is also laughable; but in [204] such a way that the one laughed at can still laugh good-naturedly along with us. – However, with younger people and busy people this hobbyhorse-riding also serves as relaxation, and prigs who denounce these harmless little follies with pedantic seriousness deserve *Sterne's* reprimand: "Let everyone ride his own hobbyhorse up and down the streets of the city, *as long as he does not force you to sit behind him.*"[129]

B On mental deficiencies in the cognitive faculty

§46

He who lacks wit has an *obtuse* head (*obtusum caput*). As for the rest, where it depends on understanding and reason, he can have a very good head; only we must not demand of him that he play the poet. This happened with Clavius,[130] whose schoolmaster wanted to apprentice him to a blacksmith because he could not make verses, but who became a great mathematician when he was given a mathematics book. – A mind that is *slow* in comprehending is for this reason not yet a weak mind; just as he who is *nimble* with concepts is not always profound but is often very shallow.

---

[128] House cricket: *Hausgrille*. Kant's wordplay in this section doesn't come out well in translation. Literally, *Grillenkrankheit* (which I have rendered as "melancholia") would be *cricket-disease*, and *Grillenfänger* (which I have rendered as "melancholic") would be *cricket-catcher*. And one meaning of *Grille* (translated as "whim") is *cricket*, in the sense of "hearing a cricket sound in one's head."

[129] Laurence Sterne (1713–1768), English author, born in Ireland. See his *Tristram Shandy* (1760), vol. 1, Ch. 7.

[130] Christoph Clavius (1537–1612), German astronomer and mathematician. Clavius entered the Jesuit order in 1555 and studied at Coimbra and Rome. In 1582 his proposed reform of the calendar was adopted by Pope Gregory XIII. Clavius is also mentioned in Kant's *Essay on the Diseases of the Head* (1764 – 2: 260). See also *Collins* 25: 133, *Parow* 25: 342, and *Mrongovius* 25: 1314.

Lack of the power of judgment without wit is *stupidity* (*stupiditas*). But the same lack *with* wit is *silliness*. – He who shows judgment in business is *shrewd*. If at the same time he has wit, then he is called *clever*. He who merely affects one of the qualities, the *joker* as well as the *prig*, is a disgusting subject. – Through adversity one is *made wise*; but he who has progressed so far in this school that he can make others clever through their own adversities is *cunning*. – *Ignorance* is not stupidity. As a certain lady replied to the question of an academic, "Do the horses eat at night too?" "How can such a learned man be so stupid!" Otherwise, ignorance is a proof of good understanding, as long as the human being merely knows how to ask good questions (in order to be instructed, either by nature or by another human being).

The *simpleton* is he who cannot grasp *much* through his understanding; but he is not therefore stupid, unless he grasps it incorrectly. "Honest but stupid" (as some improperly describe Pomeranian servants) is a false and highly reprehensible saying. It is false because honesty (observing one's duty from principles) is practical reason.[131] It is highly reprehensible [205] because it presupposes that anyone would deceive if only he felt skillful enough to do so, and that he who does not deceive merely displays his own incapacity. – Hence the sayings: "He didn't invent gunpowder," "He won't betray the country," "He is no wizard," betray misanthropic principles, namely that with the presupposition of a good will in human beings whom we know, we still cannot be sure; rather we can only be sure with the incapacity. – Thus, *Hume*[132] says, the Grand Sultan does not entrust his harem to the virtue of those who are obliged to guard it, but rather to their incapacity (as black eunuchs). – To be very limited (*narrow*) with respect to the *range* of one's concepts does not yet constitute stupidity, rather it depends on the *quality* of one's concepts (principles). – That people allow themselves to be taken in by treasure seekers, alchemists, and lottery agents is not to be attributed to their stupidity but to their evil will: the desire to get rich at others' expense without a proportionate effort of their own. *Craftiness*, cunning, slyness (*versutia*, *astutia*) is skill in cheating others. The question now is: whether the cheater must be *more clever* than the one who is easily cheated, and

---

[131] *Marginal note in H*: Treasure seekers, alchemists, and lottery players – superstitions that all have who count on luck. Fishermen, hunters.
[132] Not Hume but rather Helvétius, in his *De l'esprit* (III.16). See also *Menschenkunde* 25: 1044.

whether it is the latter who is the stupid one? The *true-hearted person* who readily *trusts* (believes, gives credit) is sometimes, but very improperly, called a *fool* because he is an easy catch for rogues, as in the saying "When fools come to market, the merchants rejoice." It is true and prudent that I never again trust someone who has once cheated me, for he is corrupt in his principles. But to trust no *other* human being because *one* has cheated me is misanthropy. The cheater is really the fool. – But what if he once through a great deception knew how to place himself in the position of no longer needing another and his trust? In that case the character under which he *appears* may very well change, but only to the point that, instead of being *laughed at* as a deceived cheater, the lucky person is *spat upon*, and there is really no permanent advantage in that.[n]

[206]

§47

Distraction (*distractio*) is the state of diverting attention (*abstractio*) away from certain ruling ideas by dispersing it among other, dissimilar ones. If

---

[n] The Palestinians living among us since their exile, or at least the great majority of them, have earned the not unfounded reputation of being cheaters, on account of the spirit of usury. Admittedly it seems strange to think of a *nation* of cheaters; but it is just as strange to think of a nation of nothing [206] but merchants, the far greater majority of whom are bound by an ancient superstition recognized by the state they live in, seek no civil honor, but rather wish to make up for their loss through the advantage of outwitting the people under whom they find protection, and even one another. It cannot be otherwise with an entire nation of nothing but merchants, as non-productive members of society (for example, the Jews in Poland). So their constitution, which is sanctioned by ancient statutes and even by us under whom they live (who have certain holy books in common with them), cannot be repealed without inconsistency, even though they have made the saying "Buyer beware" into the highest principle of their morality in dealing with us. – In place of the futile project of moralizing to this people in regard to the matter of cheating and honesty, I prefer rather to give my conjecture of the origin of this peculiar condition (that is, of a people consisting of nothing but merchants). – – In the most ancient times, wealth was brought by trade with India and there over land to the western coast of the Mediterranean Sea and the ports of Phoenicia (to which Palestine belongs). – Indeed, it could have made its way over many other places, for instance, Palmyra, in more ancient times Tyre, Sidon, or also, with some sea crossings, by way of Eziongeber and Elat; as well as from the Arabian coast to Thebes and so across Egypt to the Syrian coast. But Palestine, of which Jerusalem was the capital, was also situated very advantageously for caravan trade. The phenomenon of the one-time wealth of Solomon was probably the result of this, and even the surrounding land up to the time of the Romans was full of merchants. After the destruction of Jerusalem, these merchants, having already acknowledged extensive dealings with other businessmen of their language and faith, could gradually spread into far-distant lands (in Europe), taking language and faith with them and remaining together, finding protection from the states into which they had moved because of the advantage of their business. – So their dispersion throughout the world, with their unity of religion and language, must not be attributed to a *curse* inflicted upon this people, but rather to a *blessing*; especially since their wealth, estimated per capita, probably now exceeds that of any other people of the same number.

the distraction is intentional, it is called *dissipation*; but if it is involuntary it is *absent-mindedness* (*absentia*).

Absent-mindedness is one of the mental deficiencies attached, through the reproductive power of imagination, to a representation on which one has expended great or continuous attention and from which one is not able to get away; that is, one is not able to set the course of the power of imagination free again. If this malady becomes habitual and directed to one and the [207] same object, it can turn into dementia. To be distracted in company is *impolite*, and often laughable as well. Women are not usually subject to this impulse, unless they occupy themselves with learning. A servant who is distracted while waiting on tables usually has something bad in mind: either he is up to something or he fears the consequences of what he has done.

But one can also *distract oneself*, that is, create a diversion for one's involuntary reproductive power of imagination, as, for example, when the clergyman has delivered his memorized sermon and wants to prevent it from echoing in his head afterwards. This is a necessary and in part artificial precautionary procedure for our mental health. Continuous reflection on one and the same object leaves behind it a reverberation, so to speak (as when one and the very same piece of dance music that went on for a long time is still hummed by those returning from a festivity, or when children repeat incessantly one and the same of their kind of *bon mot*, especially when it has a rhythmic sound). Such a reverberation, I claim, molests the mind, and it can only be stopped by distraction and by applying attention to other objects; for example, reading newspapers. – *Recollecting oneself* (*collectio animi*) in order to be ready for every new occupation promotes mental health by restoring the balance between one's powers of soul. The healthiest way of doing this is social conversation filled with varied subjects, similar to a game. But the conversation must not jump from one topic to another, contrary to the natural relationship of ideas, for then the company breaks up in a state of mental distraction, since everything is mixed together and the unity of the conversation is entirely missing. Thus the mind finds itself confused and in need of a new distraction in order to be rid of that one.[133]

One sees from this that there is a (not common) art for busy people belonging to mental diatetics: the art of distracting themselves in order to

---

[133] *Marginal note in H: absentia* – boredom
Reading novels. Distraction to faith, reputation.

collect their powers. – But when one has collected one's thoughts, that is, prepared them to be used for any purpose desired, one nevertheless cannot be called distracted if, in an improper place or while discussing business affairs with others, one gives way to one's thoughts and so pays [208] no attention to these affairs. Rather, one can only be reproached for absent-mindedness, which admittedly is improper in *company*. – Thus to distract oneself without being distracted is an art that is not common. If distraction is habitual, it gives the human being who is subject to this ill the appearance of a dreamer and makes him useless to society, since he blindly follows his power of imagination in its free play, which is not ordered by any reason. – *Reading novels*, in addition to causing many other mental discords, also has the result that it makes distraction habitual. For although through the depiction of characters who actually can be found among human beings (even if with some exaggeration) thoughts are given a *coherence* as in a true story, whose presentation must always be *systematic* in a certain way, the mind is nevertheless at the same time allowed to insert digressions (namely, to insert still other events as inventions) while reading. And the train of thought becomes *fragmentary*, so that one lets representations of one and the same object play in the mind in a scattered way (*sparsim*), not combined (*conjunctim*) in accordance with the unity of understanding. The teacher from the pulpit or in the academic lecture-hall, the prosecutor or defense attorney who has to demonstrate mental composure in free speaking (impromptu), also if need be in conversation, must pay attention to *three* things. First, he must look at what he is saying *now*, in order to present it clearly; second, he must look back to what he *has said*; and then third, he must look ahead to what he just now *intends* to say. If he fails to pay attention to any of these three items, that is to say, fails to arrange them in this order, then he lands himself and his listeners or readers in distraction, and an otherwise good mind cannot reject these rules without being called *confused*.

§48

An understanding that is in itself sound (without mental deficiency) can still be accompanied by deficiencies with regard to its exercise, deficiencies that necessitate either a *postponement* until the growth to proper maturity, or even the *representation* of one's person through that of another in regard to matters of a civil nature. The (natural or legal) incapacity of an otherwise sound human being to use his *own* understanding in civil affairs is called *immaturity*.[134] If this is based on immaturity of age, then it is called *nonage* (being a minor); but if it rests on legal arrangements with regard to civil affairs, it can then be called *legal* or *civil* [209] immaturity.[135]

Children are naturally immature and their parents are their natural guardians. *Woman* regardless of age is declared to be immature in civil matters; her husband is her natural curator. However, if she lives with him and keeps her own property, then another person is the curator. – It is true that when it comes to talking, woman by the nature of her sex has enough of a mouth to represent both herself and her husband, even in court (where it concerns mine and thine), and so could literally be declared to be *over-mature*.[136] But just as it does not belong to women to go to war, so women cannot personally defend their rights and pursue civil affairs for themselves, but only by means of a representative. And this legal immaturity with respect to public transactions makes woman all the more powerful in respect to domestic welfare; because here the *right of the weaker* enters in, which the male sex by its nature already feels called on to respect and defend.

But to *make* oneself immature, degrading as it may be, is nevertheless very comfortable, and naturally it has not escaped leaders who know how to use this docility of the masses (because they hardly unite on their own); and to represent the danger of making use of one's *own* understanding without the guidance of another as very great, even lethal. Heads of state call themselves *fathers of the country*, because they understand better how to make their *subjects* happy than the subjects understand; but the people are condemned to permanent immaturity with regard to their own best interest. And when *Adam Smith*[137] improperly says of these heads of state: "they are themselves, without exception, the greatest spendthrifts of all," he is firmly refuted by the (wise!) sumptuary laws issued in many countries.

---

[134] *Unmündigkeit.*   [135] *Marginal note in H*: fragmentary, not backward and forward.
[136] *übermündig.*
[137] Adam Smith (1723–1790), Scottish economist and professor of moral philosophy at the University of Glasgow. See *An Inquiry into the Nature and Causes of the Wealth of Nations* (London, 1776), II.iii.36. Why does Kant say "(wise!) sumptuary laws," and why does he accuse Smith of speaking "improperly?" Is he being ironic? Did he misunderstand Smith? Is the text corrupt? Smith and Kant generally share a commitment to anti-paternalism.

103

The *clergy* holds the *layperson* strictly and constantly in his immaturity. The people have no voice and no judgment in regard to the path they have to take to the kingdom of heaven. The human being does not need his own eyes in order to reach it; he will soon be led, and even when Holy Scriptures are placed in his hands so that he may see them with his own [210] eyes, he is at once warned by his leaders: "Find in them nothing other than what we assure you is to be found in them." In every field the mechanical handling of human beings under the reign of others is the surest means of maintaining a legal order.

Scholars usually are glad to allow themselves to be kept in immaturity by their wives with regard to domestic arrangements. A scholar, buried in his books, answered the screams of a servant that there was a fire in one of the rooms: "You know, things of that sort are my wife's affair." – Finally, a spendthrift who has already gained maturity can also bring on a relapse into civil immaturity by reasons of state if, after his legal entry into full age, he shows a weakness of understanding with respect to the administration of his estate, which portrays him as a child or an imbecile. However, judgment about this lies outside the field of anthropology.

§49

A man who can be taught nothing, who is incapable of *learning*, is *simple-minded* (*hebes*), like an untempered knife or axe. He who is only skilled at copying is called a *blockhead*; on the other hand, he who can himself be the author of a spiritual or artistic product is a *brain*. Quite different from this is *simplicity* (as opposed to *artificiality*), of which it is said: "Perfect art becomes nature again," and which one only achieves late in life. Simplicity is a faculty of achieving exactly the same end through an economy of means – that is, straightaway. He who possesses this gift (the wise man) is, by virtue of his simplicity, not at all simple-minded.

He who in particular cannot succeed in business is called *stupid*, because he possesses no power of judgment.

A *fool* is one who sacrifices things that have a value to ends that have no value; for example, sacrificing domestic happiness for splendor outside the house. When foolishness is offensive, it is called *buffoonery*. – We can call someone foolish without offending him: he can even admit it to himself. But to become the tool of rogues (according to Pope) and be called a *buffoon* cannot be heard calmly by anyone.° *Arrogance* is buffoonery, for in the first place it is *foolish* to expect others to attach little [211] value to themselves in comparison with me; and so they will always play *tricks* with me, which defeat my purpose. The result, however, is only that I am *laughed at*. But in this unreasonable demand there is also offense, and this produces well-deserved *hate*. The word *buffoon*, used against a woman, does not have the same harsh meaning, because a man does not believe that he can be offended by the conceited presumption of a woman. And so buffoonery appears to be tied merely to the concept of a man's arrogance. – If we call someone who harms himself (temporarily or permanently) a buffoon, and so mix hate in with our contempt of him, although in fact he has not offended us, then we must think of his behavior as an offense to humanity in general and consequently as an offense committed against someone else. Whoever acts directly contrary to his own legitimate interests is also sometimes called a buffoon, although in fact he only harms himself. Arouet, Voltaire's father, said to someone who congratulated him on his well-known sons:[138] "I have two buffoons for sons, one is a buffoon in prose, the other in verse" (one had thrown himself into Jansenism and was persecuted; the other had to pay for his satirical verses in the Bastille). In general, the fool places a greater value on *things* than from a rational point of view he should do; the buffoon, on *himself*.

Calling a human being a *fop* or a *coxcomb* is also based on the concept of imprudence as buffoonery. The fop is a young buffoon; the coxcomb, an old one. Both are misled by rogues or scamps, but where the first incurs pity, the latter incurs bitter scorn. A witty German philosopher and poet[139] clarified the epithets *fat* and *sot* (which come under the generic

---

° If one replies to someone's prank, "You're not being *prudent*," this is a somewhat flat expression for "You're *joking*" or "You're not being shrewd." – A shrewd human being is one who judges [211] correctly and practically, but simply. It is true that experience can make a shrewd human being *prudent*, that is, skilled in the *artificial* use of understanding, but nature alone can make him shrewd.

[138] Külpe refers to the anonymously published *Lebensbeschreibung Voltaires*, translated from the French (Nuremberg, 1787), p. 42.

[139] Abraham Gotthelf Kästner (1719–1800), professor of mathematics at Göttingen University and satirical author. See his *Einige Vorlesungen* (Altenburg, 1768), p. 102. Kant repeats this remark in many other versions of his anthropology lectures – e.g., *Collins* 25: 134, *Menschenkunde* 25: 965, *Mrongovius* 25: 1264.

name *fou*) by an example: "A *fat*," he said, "is a young German moving to Paris; a *sot* is the same man after he has returned from Paris."[140]

***

[212] Complete mental deficiency, which either does not suffice even for animal use of the vital force (as among the *Cretins* of Valais), or which is just sufficient for a mechanical imitation of external actions that are possible through animals (sawing, digging, and so on), is called *idiocy*. It cannot really be called sickness of soul; it is rather absence of soul.

C On mental illnesses

§50

The major division, as already mentioned above,[141] is the division into *melancholia* (hypochondria) and *mental derangement*. The name of the former is taken from the analogy to listening, in the middle of the night, to the chirping noise of a cricket in the house, which disturbs the peace of mind necessary for sleep.[142] Now the illness of the hypochondriac consists in this: that certain internal physical sensations do not so much disclose a real disease present in the body but rather are mere causes of anxiety about it; and that human nature, by virtue of a peculiar characteristic (which animals do not have), can strengthen or sustain a feeling by paying attention to certain *local impressions*. On the other hand, either intentional *abstraction*, or abstraction caused by other distracting occupations, may weaken the feeling, and if the abstraction becomes habitual, make it stay away completely.[P] In this way hypochondria, considered as melancholia, becomes the cause of imagining physical disease: the patient is aware that it is imaginary, but every now and then he cannot refrain from regarding it as something real. Or, conversely, from a real physical ailment (such as unease from flatulent food after having a meal),

---

[140] *Marginal note in H*: Mental illnesses are 1. Weakening 2. Disturbance and a mean between both (*Raptus* or hypochondria) and melancholy.
[141] I.e., at 7: 202, beginning of §45.
[142] See n. 128 above on *Grillenkrankheit* and *Grille*.

[P] I have remarked in another writing that averting attention from certain painful sensations and exerting it on any other object voluntarily grasped in thought can ward off the painful sensations so completely that they are unable to break out into illness. [See Kant's discussion in Part III of *The Conflict of the Faculties*, entitled "On the Power of the Mind to Master its Morbid Feelings by Sheer Resolution" (7: 97–116) – Ed.]

hypochondria will produce imaginings of all sorts of grave external mishaps and worries about one's business, which disappear as soon as digestion has been completed and flatulence has ceased. – – The hypochondriac is a melancholic (visionary) of the most pitiful sort: obstinate, unable to be talked out of his imaginings, and always running headlong to the physician, who has no end of trouble with him, and who can calm him [213] only by treating him like a child (with pills containing bread crumbs instead of medicine). And when this patient, who despite his perpetual sickliness can never be sick, consults medical books, he becomes completely unbearable because he believes that he feels all the ailments in his body that he reads about in books. – – Extraordinary gaiety, in the form of lively wit and joyous laughter, serves as the distinctive feature of this diseased imagination, which the patient sometimes feels himself give way to: thus the ever changing play of his moods. Anxious fear, childish in character, of the thought of *death* nourishes this illness. But whoever does not look away from these thoughts with manly courage will never really be happy in life.

Still on this side of the border of mental derangement is *sudden change of mood* (*raptus*), an unexpected leap from one theme to a totally different one, which no one is prepared for. Sometimes it precedes derangement, which it announces, but often the mind is already so disorganized that these assaults of irregularity become the rule with it. – Suicide is often merely the effect of a *raptus*. For he who cuts his throat in the intensity of affect will soon after patiently allow it to be sewn up again.

Melancholy[143] (*melancholia*) can also be a mere delusion of misery which the *gloomy* self-tormentor (inclined to worry) creates. It is itself not yet mental derangement, but it can very well lead to it.[144] – By the way, it is a mistaken but common expression to speak of a *melancholic* mathematician (for example, Professor Hausen[145]), when one merely means a deep-thinking one.

---

[143] *Tiefsinnigkeit*. As noted earlier (n. 128), I have also translated *Grillenkrankheit* by the Latin "melancholia."

[144] *Marginal note in H*: What do I want? xx –
To think for oneself – In the place of the
The first thing is that it has no governance [?] over oneself in respect to attention to one's feelings, therefore it consists of loud moods.

[145] Christian August Hausen (1693–1745), professor of mathematics at Leipzig. See also *Metaphysics of Morals* 6: 208.

§51

The *delirious raving* (*delirium*) of a person who is awake and in a *feverish* state is a physical illness and requires medical attention. Only the delirious person in whom the physician perceives no such pathological occurrences is called *mad*; for which the word *deranged* is only a euphemistic expression. Thus if someone has intentionally caused an accident, the question arises whether he is liable and to what extent; consequently, the first thing that must be determined is whether or not he was mad at the time. In this case the court cannot refer him to the medical faculty but must refer him to the philosophical faculty (on account of the incompetence of the court). For the question of whether the accused at the time of his act was in possession of his natural faculties of understanding and [214] judgment is a wholly psychological question; and although a physical oddity of the soul's organs might indeed sometimes be the cause of an unnatural transgression of the law of duty (which is present in every human being), physicians and physiologists in general are still not advanced enough to see deeply into the mechanical element in the human being so that they could explain, in terms of it, the attack that led to the atrocity, or foresee it (without dissecting the body). And *forensic medicine* (*medicina forensis*) – when it depends on the question of whether the mental condition of the agent was madness or a decision made with sound understanding – is meddling with alien affairs, which the judge does not understand. He must at least refer it to another faculty, as something not belonging to his competence.[q]

§52

It is difficult to bring a systematic division into what is essential and incurable disorder. It is also of little use to occupy oneself with it, because all methods of cure in this respect must turn out to be fruitless, since the

---

[q] Thus, in the case of a woman who killed a child out of despair because she had been sentenced to the penitentiary, such a judge declared her insane and therefore exempt from the death penalty. – For, he said, he who draws true conclusions from false premises is insane. Now this woman adopted the principle that confinement in the penitentiary is an indelible disgrace, worse than death (which is quite false), and came to the conclusion, by inference from it, that she deserved death. – As a result she was insane and, as such, exempted from the death penalty. – On the basis of this argument it might easily be possible to declare all criminals insane, people whom we should pity and cure, but not punish.

powers of the subject do not cooperate (as is the case with bodily diseases), and yet the goal can only be attained through his own use of understanding. Although anthropology here can only be indirectly pragmatic, namely only command omissions, nevertheless it still requires at least an attempt at a general outline of this most profound degradation of humanity, which still is attributable to nature. One can divide derangement in general into the *tumultuous*, the *methodical*, and the *systematic*.

1) *Amentia*[146] is the inability to bring one's representations into even the coherence necessary for the possibility of experience. In lunatic asylums it is women who, owing to their talkativeness, are most [215] subject to this disease: that is, their lively power of imagination inserts so much into what they are relating that no one grasps what they actually wanted to say. This first type of derangement is *tumultuous*.

2) *Dementia*[147] is that disturbance of the mind in which everything that the insane person relates is to be sure in conformity with the formal laws of thought that make an experience possible; but, owing to the falsely inventive power of imagination, self-made representations are regarded as perceptions. Those who believe that they are surrounded by enemies everywhere, who consider all glances, words, and otherwise indifferent actions of others as aimed against them personally and as traps set for them, belong in this category. – In their unhappy delusion they are often so astute in interpreting that which others do naturally as aimed against them that, if only the data were true, we would have to pay due honor to their understanding. – I have never seen anyone who has been cured of this disease (for to rave with reason is a special predisposition). However, they are not to be reckoned among the hospital buffoons; for, being concerned only with themselves, they direct their supposed craftiness only to their own preservation, without putting others in danger, and therefore do not need to be locked up for reasons of safety. This second type of derangement is *methodical*.

3) *Insania*[148] is a deranged *power of judgment* in which the mind is held in suspense by means of analogies that are confused with concepts of similar things, and thus the power of imagination, in a play resembling understanding, conjures up the connection of disparate things as

---

[146] *Unsinnigkeit.* [147] *Wahnsinn.* [148] *Wahnwitz.*

universal, under which the representations of the universal are contained. Mental patients of this kind are for the most part very cheerful; they write insipid poetry and take pleasure in the richness of what, in their opinion, is such an extensive alliance of concepts all agreeing with each other. – The lunatic of this sort is not curable because, like poetry in general, he is creative and entertaining by means of diversity. – This third kind of derangement is indeed methodical, but only *fragmentary*.

4) *Vesania* is the sickness of a deranged *reason*. – The mental patient flies over the entire guidance of experience and chases after principles that can be completely exempted from its touchstone, imagining that he conceives the inconceivable. – The invention of the squaring of the circle, of perpetual motion, the unveiling of the supersensible forces of nature, and the comprehension of the mystery of the Trinity are in his power. He is the calmest of all hospital patients and, because of his self-enclosed speculation, the furthest removed from raving; for, with complete self-sufficiency, he shuts his eyes to all the difficulties of inquiry. – This fourth kind of derangement could be called *systematic*.[149]

[216]

For in this last kind of mental derangement there is not merely disorder and deviation from the rule of the use of reason, but also *positive unreason*; that is, *another* rule, a totally different standpoint into which the soul is transferred, so to speak, and from which it sees all objects differently. And from the *Sensorio communi*[150] that is required for the unity of *life* (of the animal), it finds itself transferred to a faraway place (hence the word 'derangement')[151] – just as a mountainous landscape sketched from a bird's-eye view prompts a completely different judgment about the region than when it is viewed from level ground. It is true that the soul does not feel or see itself in another place (for it cannot perceive itself according to its position in space without committing a contradiction, since it would then intuit itself as an object of its outer sense, when it itself can only be the object of its inner sense); however, in this way we explain, as best we can, the so-called derangement. – It is

---

[149] *Vesania: Aberwitz. Marginal note in H*: There is a system in lunacy. *Arouet* had two buffoons for sons.
2. Not raving mad.
Disturbed. *mente captus.*
[150] Trans.: common sense.   [151] *Verrückung* – which can also mean "displacement."

astonishing, however, that the powers of the unhinged mind still arrange themselves in a system, and that nature even strives to bring a principle of unity into unreason, so that the faculty of thought does not remain idle. Although it is not working objectively toward true cognition of things, it is still at work subjectively, for the purpose of animal life.

On the other hand, the attempt to observe oneself by physical means, in a condition approaching derangement into which one has voluntarily placed oneself in order to observe better even what is involuntary, shows enough reason for the investigation of the causes of the phenomena. But it is dangerous to conduct experiments with the mind and to make it ill to a certain degree in order to observe it and investigate its nature by the appearances that may be found there. Thus *Helmont*, after taking a specific dose of wolfsbane (a poisonous root),[152] claims to have perceived a sensation as if he were *thinking in his stomach.* Another physician [217] gradually increased his doses of camphor until it seemed to him that everything on the streets was in great tumult. Many have experimented on themselves with opium for so long that they fell into mental deficiency when they gave up further use of this aid to simulating thought. – An artificially induced dementia could easily become a genuine one.

Random remarks

§53

The germ of madness develops together with the germ of reproduction, so that this too is hereditary. It is dangerous to marry into families where even a single such individual has been met with. For no matter how many children of a married couple there are who remain protected from this evil legacy because, for example, they all take after the father or his parents and ancestors, if there has been only one insane child in the mother's family (although she herself is free from this misfortune), one day there nevertheless will appear in this marriage a child who takes after the maternal side (as can also be observed from the resemblance of features) and has a *hereditary* mental derangement.

---

[152] Jan Baptist Helmont (1578–1664), Flemish physician, chemist, and physicist. Külpe notes that Helmont's experiment is mentioned in Sprengel, *Versuch einer pragmatischen Geschichte der Arzneykunde*, 8th ed. (1827), Part IV, p. 302. Wolfsbane or monkshood (*Aconitum napellus*) is a poisonous plant whose dried leaves and roots yield aconite.

People often claim to know how to indicate the accidental causes of this illness, so that it may be represented not as hereditary but rather as acquired, as if the misfortunate one himself were to blame for it. "He became crazy from *love*," they say of one; of another, "He went mad from *pride*"; of yet a third, "He *studied too hard*." – Falling in love with a person from a class of whom to expect marriage is the greatest folly was not the cause but rather the effect of madness; and as far as pride is concerned, the expectation of an insignificant human being that others bow down before him and the decorum that they *hold up* their heads against him *presupposes* a madness without which he would not have fallen into such behavior.

[218] However, as concerns *studying too hard*,[r] there is no need at all to warn young people against it. Here youth more likely needs spurs rather than reins. Even the most intense and sustained exertion on this score, though it can indeed *tire* the mind, so that the human being takes a dislike to science, cannot *upset* the mind unless it was already eccentric and consequently discovered a taste for mystical books and revelations that go beyond sound human understanding. To this also belongs the tendency to devote oneself entirely to the reading of books that have received a certain holy unction, reading them merely for the sake of the letter, without having the moral element in view – for which a certain author has found the expression: "He is scripture-crazy."[153]

I doubt whether there is a difference between general madness (*delirium generale*) and that which is fixed upon a definite object (*delirium circa obiectum*). *Unreason* (which is something positive, not mere lack of reason) is, just like reason, a mere form into which objects can be fitted, and both reason and unreason are therefore dependent on the universal. However, what first comes into the mind at the *outbreak* of a crazy disposition (which usually happens suddenly) henceforth becomes the chief object of the crazy person's ravings (the accidentally encountered *matter* over which he later babbles), because the novelty of the impression fixes it more firmly in his mind than other impressions following later.

---

[r] That businessmen *overextend* themselves and lose their powers in far-flung schemes is a common phenomenon. However, anxious parents have nothing to fear about an excess of diligence in [218] young people (as long as their minds are otherwise sound). Nature itself already prevents such overloads of knowledge by the fact that the student gets disgusted with things over which he has broken his head and brooded in vain.

[153] *schrifttoll.*

112

One also says of someone whose mind has jumped over something: "He has crossed the line," just as if a human being who crosses the equator for the first time were in danger of losing his understanding.[154] But this is only a misunderstanding. It is only to say that the coxcomb who hopes to fish up gold by means of a trip to India, without long effort, draws up his plan here like a buffoon. However, while he is carrying it out the budding folly grows and, upon his return, even if fortune has smiled upon him, it shows itself fully developed.

The person who *talks aloud* to himself or is caught *gesticulating* to himself in his room falls under the suspicion that something is not right with his head. – The suspicion grows even more if he believes that he is blessed with inspirations or visited by higher beings in conversations and [219] dealings. However, it does not apply if he grants that other holy men are perhaps capable of these supersensible intuitions, does not imagine that he has been chosen for them; indeed, does not even once confess to wishing to be chosen for them, and therefore excludes himself.[155]

The only universal characteristic of madness is the loss of *common sense* (*sensus communis*) and its replacement with *logical private sense* (*sensus privatus*); for example, a human being in broad daylight sees a light burning on his table which, however, another person standing nearby does not see, or hears a voice that no one else hears. For it is a subjectively necessary touchstone of the correctness of our judgments generally, and consequently also of the soundness of our understanding, that we also restrain our understanding by the *understanding of others*, instead of *isolating* ourselves with our own understanding and judging *publicly* with our private representations, so to speak. Thus the prohibition of books that advance only theoretical opinions (especially when they have no influence at all on legal commissions and omissions) offends humanity.

---

[154] *Crossed out in H*: understanding [But this is only a <superstitious> saying of the rabble completely unfamiliar with geography, <of which he> who is devoted to seafaring as a business-man knows nothing. Even the fact that some have set out by ship to India because they were possessed by the crazy idea that they would not fail to amass riches there, just because someone once succeeded in doing so, is <the cause of much of this>. But the germ of foolishness, which consists in depending on the good luck of adventure to become wealthy without work, grew in time and matured on the return.]

[155] *Marginal note in H*: Nature and art in products of the faculty of cognition Wit, clever head, sagacity and originality

    1) to make the material (of the same kind) ready
    2) to know how one should search for and invent it
    3) How one without imitation should connect it – *From stock* [*von der Brühe*].

For we are thereby robbed, not of the only, but still of the greatest and most useful means of correcting our own thoughts, which happens on account of the fact that we advance them in public in order to see whether they also agree with the understanding of others; for otherwise something merely subjective (for instance, habit or inclination) would easily be taken for something objective. This is precisely what the illusion consists in that is said to deceive us, or rather by means of which we are misled to deceive ourselves in the application of a rule. – He who pays no attention at all to this touchstone, but gets it into his head to recognize private sense as already valid apart from or even in opposition to common sense, is abandoned to a play of thoughts in which he sees, acts, and judges, not in a common world, but rather in his own world (as in dreaming). – Sometimes, however, it is merely a matter of terminology, through which an otherwise clear-thinking mind wishes to communicate his external perceptions to others that do not agree with the principle of common sense, and he sticks to his own sense. Thus *Harrington*,[156] the gifted author of *Oceana*, fancied that his perspiration (*effluvia*) leaped from his skin in the form of flies. However, this could well have been electrical effects on a body overcharged with this substance, an experience which others

[220] claim to have had; and perhaps he meant only that there was a similarity between his feeling and flies jumping off, not that he saw these flies.

Madness accompanied by *fury* (*rabies*), an affect of anger (toward a real or imaginary object) that makes the subject insensitive to all external impressions, is only a variety of derangement, which often looks more frightening than it is in its consequences. Like a paroxysm during an acute illness, it is not so much rooted in the mind as stimulated by material causes, and can often be removed by the physician with one dose.[157]

---

[156] James Harrington (1611–1677), English political writer. In his *Commonwealth of Oceana* (1656) he described a utopian society in which political authority rested entirely with the landed gentry. Külpe reports that when Harrington fell into a delirium as a result of an overdose of guaiacum he claimed that his animal spirits evaporated in the form of birds, flies, and crickets.

[157] *Crossed out in H*: dose. [On the Talents of the Faculty of Cognition which are at the Command of the Understanding

§39

They are wit, <sagacity>, the gift of inquiry, <and originality> of talent (a witty, reflective, and singular mind <or>, a *genius*). They are natural gifts whose *exercise* serves to promote that which lies in the concepts of the understanding. The fitness for this (*habilitas*) cannot be acquired: nature must have furnished the human being with this. However, one can cultivate it, and one understands by this not merely the faculty but also a propensity (instinct) toward making use of it

On the talents in the cognitive faculty

§54

By *talent* (natural gift) we understand that excellence of the cognitive faculty which depends not on instruction but on the subject's natural predisposition. These talents are *productive wit* (*ingenium strictius s. materialiter dictum*), *sagacity*, and *originality* of thought (genius).

Wit is either *comparative* (*ingenium comparans*) or *argumentative* (*ingenium argutans*). Wit *pairs* (assimilates) heterogeneous representations that often, according to the law of the power of imagination (of association), lie far apart from each other. It is a peculiar faculty of assimilating, which belongs to the understanding (as the faculty of cognizing the universal), in so far as it brings objects under genera. Afterwards, it requires the power of judgment in order to determine the particular under the universal and in order to apply the faculty of thought toward *cognition*. – To be *witty* (in speech or writing) cannot be learned through the mechanism of the school and its constraint, rather it belongs, as a special talent, to the *liberality* of temperament in the mutual communication of thoughts (*veniam damus petimusque vicissim*).[158] It is a quality of understanding in general that is hard to explain – it is as though its *agreeableness* – which contrasts with the *strictness* of judgment (*iudicium discretivum*) in the application of the universal to the particular (the generic concepts to those of the species), *limits* both the faculty of assimilation and also the inclination to use this faculty.[159]

<so that if the understanding as it were involuntarily strives toward it, there is enough material to supply it for thinking>. If the word *Ingenium* is understood in its literal sense, as the innate talent in general, then the first talent would signify *facility* (*promitudo*), the second *sagacity*, the third *originality* of mind in the arrangement of its thought. – The power of imagination provides the material <to the understanding>, and this may be one and the same in different minds; but the talent to work on it for the use of the understanding in this connection can nevertheless differ greatly.

The faculty of <association> reconciling strange conceptual representations by means of the understanding is creative wit (*perspicacia*).]

[158] Trans.: we give pardon and we seek it in turn.

[159] *Crossed out in H*: faculty. [*Sagacity* or the *gift of inquiry* is also a gift of nature: <to know it one> to understand how one should search effectively (with luck) (to question nature or other human beings). It is a talent to *judge provisionally* where the truth might be found and to track it. *Bacon* of Verulam in his *Organon* has given us a brilliant example of this art of judging provisionally (*iudicii praevii*) with regard to himself, through which the method of natural science has been put on its <true> proper track.

Genius, however, is originality in the generation of products of the faculty of cognition; the faculty of thinking and acting in an exemplary manner independently of any other exemplar.]

[221]   ## On the specific difference between comparative and argumentative wit

A On productive wit

§55

It is pleasant, popular, and stimulating to discover similarities among dissimilar things, and so wit provides material to the understanding to make its concepts more general. Judgment, on the other hand, which limits concepts and contributes more to correcting than enlarging them, is indeed praised and recommended; but it is serious, rigorous, and limiting with regard to freedom of thought, and just for this reason it is unpopular. The activity of comparative wit is more like play; but that of judgment is more like business. – Wit is rather like a flower of youth; the power of judgment, more a ripe fruit of old age. – He who unites both to a high degree in a product of the mind is *perspicacious* (*perspicax*).

Wit snatches at *sudden inspiration*; the power of judgment strives for *insight*. Circumspection is a *mayor's virtue*[160] (to protect and administer the town by given laws, under the supreme command of the castle). On the other hand, Buffon,[161] the great author of the system of nature, was considered *bold* (*hardi*) by his countrymen for setting aside the scruples of the power of judgment, even though his daring venture appears rather lacking in modesty (frivolity). – Wit goes more for the *sauce*; the power of judgment, for the *sustenance*. To hunt for *witty sayings* (*bons mots*), such as the Abbot Trublet[162] richly displayed, and in doing so to put wit on the rack, makes shallow minds, or eventually disgusts well-grounded ones. Wit is inventive in *fashions*, that is, assumed rules of behavior, which are pleasing only because of their novelty and which, before they become *custom*, must be exchanged for other forms that are just as transitory.

---

[160] See also *Observations on the Feeling of the Beautiful and the Sublime* 2: 211 and *Mrongovius* 25: 1264, where Kant attributes the remark to Cromwell. Brandt draws attention to the following passage from Hume's *Enquiry Concerning the Principles of Morals*: "To a CROMWELL, perhaps, or a DE RETZ, discretion may appear an alderman-like virtue, as Dr Swift calls it" (Sec. 6).

[161] Georges Louis Leclerc, Comte de Buffon (1707–1788), French naturalist, author of the forty-four-volume *Histoire naturelle* (1749–1804). Kant's theory of race owes a serious debt to Buffon. See, e.g., his endorsement of "Buffon's rule" in *Of the Different Races of Human Beings* 2: 429.

[162] Nicolas Charles Joseph de la Flourie Trublet (1697–1770), in his *Essais sur divers sujets de littérature et de morale*. Kant also mentions Trublet in several other versions of his anthropology lectures. See *Collins* 25: 136, 153; *Parow* 25: 344, 388; *Menschenkunde* 25: 963.

Wit in wordplay is *insipid*; while needless subtlety (micrology) of judgment is *pedantic*. *Humorous wit* means one that comes from a mind disposed to *paradox*, where the (cunning) joker peers from behind the naïve sound of simplicity in order to expose someone (or his opinion) to ridicule by exalting, with apparent eulogy (persiflage), the opposite of [222] what is worthy of approval – for example, "Swift's art of sinking in poetry,"[163] or Butler's *Hudibras*.[164] Such a wit, which uses contrast to make what is contemptible even more contemptible, is very stimulating through the surprise of the unexpected. However, it is an easy wit (like that of Voltaire's), and always only a *game*.[165] On the other hand, the person who presents true and important principles in clothing (like Young[166] in his satires) can be called a very difficult wit, because it is a *serious business* and arouses more admiration than amusement.

A *proverb* (*proverbium*) is not a *witty saying* (*bon mot*), for it is a formula that has become common which expresses a thought that is transmitted by imitation, even though it could well *have been* a witty saying in the mouth of the first speaker. Speaking through proverbs is therefore the language of the rabble, and shows a complete lack of wit in social intercourse with the refined world.

It is true that profundity is not a matter of wit; but in so far as wit, through the graphic element that it adds to thought, can be a vehicle or garb for reason and its management of morally practical ideas, it can be thought of as profound wit (as distinguished from superficial wit). As one of the so-called admirable sayings of *Samuel Johnson* about women goes,

[163] The full title runs: *Peri Bathous s. Anti-Sublime. Das ist: D. Swifts neueste Dichkunst, oder Kunst, in der Poesie zu kriechen*. Translated from English into German, Leipzig, 1733. Dowdell argues that the author was actually Alexander Pope: "On March 8, 1728, appeared *The Last Volume* of the *Miscellanies* of Pope and Swift. The most important piece included in the collection was Pope's prose essay, '*Peri Bathous*, or the Art of Sinking in Poetry,'" (Robert Kilburn Root, *The Poetical Career of Alexander Pope* [Princeton University Press, 1938], p. 128).

[164] Samuel Butler (1612–1680), English poet and satirist. *Hudibras*, published in three parts (1663, 1664, 1678), was a satire directed against the Puritans. See also *Parow* 25: 345, *Pillau* 25: 762, *Menschenkunde* 25: 967, 994, *Mrongovius* 25: 1268–1269.

[165] *Marginal note in H: inanes argutiones*. Crass concepts of sophistical wit, which nevertheless are fine in respect to that which they are being compared to.
All of these talents have their opponents. –
Also here it is necessary to have an inclination for it
On taste in dealing with writings, not with sermons.

[166] Edward Young (1684–1765), English poet and dramatist. See *The Universal Passion* (1725–1727), a collection of seven satires. Kant also refers to Young in several versions of his anthropology lectures – see *Parow* 25: 399, *Friedländer* 25: 517, 575, *Menschenkunde* 25: 967, 1117, *Mrongovius* 25: 1265, 1341, 1391.

which is quoted in *The Life of Waller*: "Doubtless he praised many women whom he would have hesitated to marry, and perhaps he married one he would have been ashamed to praise."[167] Here the play of antitheses constitutes the only admirable thing; reason gains nothing by it. – But when it was a matter of disputed questions for reason, then his friend Boswell could not coax out from Johnson any of those oracular utterances, which he sought so incessantly, that revealed the slightest wit. Rather, everything that Johnson uttered about skeptics in religion, or of the right of government, or even about human freedom in general, fell out with a blunt coarseness because of his natural despotism which the pampering of his flatterers rooted deeply in him. His admirers liked to

[223] call this *roughness*;[s] but it showed his great inability to unite wit with profundity in the same thought. – Also, it appears that men of influence, who refused to listen when Johnson's friends suggested that he would be an exceptionally qualified member of parliament, appreciated his talent very well. For the wit that suffices for the composition of the dictionary of a language[168] is not enough for awakening and enlivening the ideas of reason that are required for insight into important affairs. – – *Modesty* automatically enters into the mind of one who sees himself called to this office, together with a mistrust in one's own talents that leads one not to decide for oneself but rather to take others' judgments into account (unnoticed, if necessary). This was a quality that Johnson never possessed.

B On sagacity, or the gift of inquiry

§56

To *discover* something (that lies hidden either in ourselves or elsewhere) in many cases often requires a special talent of knowing how to search

---

[167] Samuel Johnson (1709–1784), English author, wrote a biography of the poet Edmund Waller (1606–1687). But this anecdote appears in James Boswell's (1740–1795) famous work, *The Life of Samuel Johnson* (1791). Külpe locates the passage in an edition published in 1859, vol. 3, pp. 47f.

[s] Boswell relates that when a certain lord in his presence expressed his regret that Johnson had not had a finer education, *Baretti* said: "No, my lord. You could have done with him whatever you

[223] wanted, he would always have remained a bear." "No doubt, but at least a *dancing bear?*" asked the lord. A third, his friend, thought to soften this by saying: "*He has nothing of the bear but the coat.*" [See Boswell, *Life of Johnson*, ed. Crocker (New York, 1867), 1.252 – Ed.]

[168] Johnson's most famous work was his *Dictionary of the English Language* (1755), the first comprehensive lexicographical work on English ever undertaken.

well: a natural gift for *judging in advance* (*iudicii praevii*) where the truth may indeed be found; for tracking things and using the slightest grounds of relationship to discover or invent that which is sought.[169] The logic of the schools teaches us nothing about this. But Bacon of Verulam[170] gave a brilliant example of the method in his *Organon* of how the hidden constitution of natural things could be uncovered through experiments. However, even this example is insufficient to give instruction according to definite rules as to how one should search successfully, for we must always first presuppose something here (begin with a hypothesis) from which to begin our course of investigation, and this must come about as a result of principles, certain modes of procedure. And it all comes down to how we should scent these out. For to venture forth blindly, trusting good luck until one stumbles over a stone and finds a piece of ore and subsequently a lode as well, is indeed bad advice for inquiry. Still, there are people of talent who, so to speak, with the divining rod in hand track [224] down the treasures of knowledge without having learned to do so; which they then also cannot teach to others but can only demonstrate to them, because it is a natural gift.

C On the originality of the cognitive faculty, or genius

§57

Inventing something is entirely different from *discovering* something. For the thing that one *discovers* is accepted as already existing beforehand, it is only that it was not yet known; for example, America before Columbus. But what one *invents*, for example, *gunpowder*, was not yet known at all before the artist[t] who made it. Both discovery and invention can be meritorious. However, one can *find* something that one doesn't look for

---

[169] *Marginal note in H*: On the necessary modesty in our handling of ideas and through the same. Insight (*perspicacia*) is a faculty of reason which does not depend on wit but whose influence it is better to restrain.
  On Invention, Discovery.
[170] Francis Bacon, Lord of Verulam (1561–1626), English philosopher, essayist, and statesman. His *Novum Organum* (1621) spells out an inductive method that strongly influenced modern science.

  [t] Gunpowder was already in use in the siege of Algeciras, long before the time of the monk *Schwarz*, and its invention seems to belong to the Chinese. But it could still be Schwarz, who obtained this powder, experimented in analyzing it (for example, by leaching out the saltpeter in it, washing away the carbon, and burning the sulphur), and thus *discovered* it, though he did not *invent* it.

at all (like the alchemist who found phosphorus),[171] and there is no merit whatsoever in it. – Now the talent for inventing is called *genius*. But we confer this name only on an *artist*, therefore on one who knows how to *make* something, not on one who is merely acquainted with and *knows* many things. However, it is also not conferred on an artist who merely imitates, but rather on one who is disposed to produce his works *originally*; finally, it is conferred on this artist only when his product is *exemplary*, that is, when it serves as an example (*exemplar*) to be imitated. – So a human being's genius is "the exemplary originality of his talent" (in respect to this or that kind of artistic product). But we also call a mind that has the predisposition to this a genius; then this word is to denote not merely a person's natural gift, but also the person himself. – To be a genius in many departments is to be a *vast* genius (like Leonardo da Vinci).

[225] The proper field for genius is that of the power of imagination, because this is creative and, being less under the constraint of rules than other faculties, it is thus all the more capable of originality. – It is true that mechanism of instruction is indeed disadvantageous to the budding of a genius as far as his originality is concerned, because instruction always requires the student to imitate. But every art still requires certain mechanical basic rules, namely rules concerning the appropriateness of the product to the underlying idea; that is, *truth* in the presentation of the object that one is thinking of. Now this must be learned by means of school rigor,[172] and is indeed always an effect of imitation. However, to free the power of imagination even from this constraint and allow the talent proper to it to proceed without rules and *swoon*,[173] even against nature, might deliver original folly; but it would certainly not be exemplary and thus also would not be counted as genius.[174]

Spirit is the *animating* principle in the human being. In the French language, *spirit* and *wit* bear one and the same name, *Esprit*. In German it is different. One says that a speech, a text, a woman in society, etc. are beautiful but without spirit. The supply of wit makes no difference here; for we can also be put off by it, since its effect leaves nothing permanent. If all these above-mentioned things and persons are to be called *spirited*, then they must arouse an *interest* by means of *ideas*. For this sets the

---

[171] In 1669 an alchemist in Hamburg named Henig Brand obtained phosphorus by distilling concentrated urine; he named it "cold fire."
[172] *mit Schulstrenge.*   [173] *schwärmen.*
[174] *Marginal note in H*: The essence of genius and the power of imagination.

power of imagination in motion, which sees a great playroom for concepts of this kind before it. Therefore how would it be if we were to use the German term *singular spirit* to express the French word *génie*? For our nation permits itself to be persuaded that the French have a word for this in their own language that we do not have in ours but rather must borrow from them. Nevertheless, they *themselves* have borrowed it from the Latin (*genius*), where it means nothing other than a singular spirit.

However, the reason why exemplary originality of talent is designated by this *mystical* name is that the man who has genius cannot explain to himself its outbursts or even make himself understand how he arrived at an art which he could not have learned. For *invisibility* (of the cause of an effect) is an accessory concept of *spirit* (a *genius* which is already assigned to the gifted man at his birth), whose inspiration he only follows, so to speak. The mental powers, however, must move harmoniously with the help of the imagination, because otherwise they would not animate but would disturb one another, and since this must occur owing to the *nature* of the subject, we can also call genius the talent "by which nature gives [226] the rule to art."[175]

§58

Whether the world on the whole is particularly served by great geniuses, because they often take new paths and open new prospects; or whether mechanical minds, with their commonplace understanding that advances slowly on the rod and staff of experience, even if they are not epoch-making (for if none of them excites admiration, it is true that they also cause no disorder), have contributed most to the growth of the arts and sciences, may remain undiscussed here. – But one type of them, called *men of genius* (they are better called apes of genius), have forced their way in under this sign-board which bears the language "minds extraordinarily favored by nature," declaring that difficult study and research are dilettantish and that they have snatched the spirit of all science in one grasp, though they pretend to administer it in small doses that are concentrated and powerful. This type, like that of the quack and the charlatan, is very disadvantageous to progress in scientific and moral

---

[175] For related discussion, see Kant's discussion of genius in the *Critique of the Power of Judgment* 5: 307–320, 344.

121

education[176] when he knows how to conceal his poverty of spirit by dogmatizing from the seat of wisdom in decisive tones over religion, politics, and morals, like one of the initiated or a ruler. What else is there to do against this other than to continue patiently on one's way with diligence, order, and clarity, paying no attention to this trickster?

§59

Genius also seems to have different original seeds within itself and to develop them differently, according to the difference of national type and the soil where it was born. With the Germans it strikes more in the *roots*; with the Italians, in the *foliage*; with the French, in the *blossoms*; and with the English, in the *fruit*.

Still, genius, as the inventive mind, is distinguished from the *universal* mind (which grasps all the various sciences). The latter can be universal about what can be learned; that is, he is a person who possesses historical knowledge of what, with regard to all the sciences, has been done up to now (a *polyhistorian*), like Jul. Cäs. Scaliger. The genius is the man, not so much of wide *range* of mind as of intense greatness, who is epoch-making in everything he undertakes (like Newton or Leibniz). The *architectonic* mind, which methodically examines the connection of all the sciences and how they support one another, is only a subordinate type of genius, [227] but still not a common one. – However, there is also *gigantic* erudition which is still often *cyclopean*, that is to say, missing one eye: namely the eye of true philosophy, by means of which reason suitably uses this mass of historical knowledge, the load of a hundred camels.

Purely natural minds (*élèves de la nature, Autodidacti*) can in many cases also count as geniuses, because, although indeed much of what they know could have been learned from others, they have thought it out for themselves, and in what is not itself a matter of genius, they are nevertheless geniuses – just as, concerning the mechanical arts, there are many in Switzerland who are inventors in these arts. But a prematurely clever prodigy (*ingenium praecox*), like *Heinecke* in Lübeck, or the short-lived *Baratier* in Halle,[177] are deviations from nature's rule, rarities for

---

[176] *wissenschaftliche und sittliche Bildung.*

[177] Christoph Heinrich Heinecke (1721–1725), named the child of Lübeck, caused a great sensation because of the early development of his mind, particularly his extraordinary memory.

a natural history collection. And while their premature ripening arouses admiration, at bottom it is also often cause for repentance on the part of those who promoted it.

***

In the end, since the entire use of the cognitive faculty for its own advancement, even in theoretical cognition, surely requires reason, which gives the rule in accordance with which it alone can be advanced, we can summarize the demand that reason makes on the cognitive faculty in three questions, which are directed to the three cognitive faculties:

> *What do I want?* (asks understanding)[u]
> *What does it matter?* (asks the power of judgment)
> *What comes of it?* (asks reason).

Minds differ greatly in their ability to answer all three of these questions. – The first requires only a clear mind to understand itself; and after some culture this natural gift is fairly common, especially when one draws attention to it. – To answer the second question appropriately is a greater rarity; for all sorts of ways of determining the concept at hand and the apparent solution to the problem present themselves: what is the one solution that is exactly appropriate to this problem (for example, in [228] lawsuits, or at the outset of certain plans of action having the same end)? For this there is a talent for selecting what is exactly appropriate in a given case (*iudicium discretivum*), which is much desired but also very rare. The lawyer who arrives with many principles that are supposed to prove his assertion makes the judge's sentence very difficult, because he himself is only fumbling around. But if the lawyer, after clarifying what he wants to say, knows how to find the point about the matter (for there is only one), then the issue is quickly settled, and the verdict of reason follows by itself.

Understanding is positive and drives out the darkness of ignorance – the power of judgment is more negative, for the prevention of errors from the dim light in which objects appear. – Reason blocks the sources of errors (prejudices), and thereby safeguards understanding through the

---

Jean Philippe Baratier (1721–1740), born in Schwabach. At age five he could already speak three languages; at age eight he could understand the Bible in the original Hebrew and Greek. But he acquired a senile appearance early on, and died before the age of twenty.

[u] "Wanting" is understood here in a purely theoretical sense: What do I want to assert as *true*?

123

universality of principles. – – It is true that book-learning increases knowledge, but it does not extend concepts and insight when reason is not added. However, reason is still different from *rationalizing*,[178] playing with mere experiments in the use of reason without a law of reason. If the question is whether I should believe in ghosts, I can *rationalize* about their possibility in all sorts of ways; but *reason* prohibits the *superstitious* assumption of their possibility, that is, without a principle of explanation of the phenomenon according to laws of experience.

By means of the great difference of minds, in the way they look at exactly the same objects and at each other, and by means of the friction between them and the connection between them as well as their separation, nature produces a remarkable drama of infinite variety on the stage of observers and thinkers. For the class of thinkers the following maxims (which have already been mentioned above, as leading to wisdom) can be made unalterable commands:

1) To think *for oneself*.
2) To think oneself (in communication with human beings) into the place of every *other person*.
3) Always to think *consistently* with *oneself*.

The first principle is negative (*nullius addictus iurare in verba Magistri*),[179] the principle of *freedom from constraint*; the second is positive, the principle of *liberals* who adapt to the principles of others; the

[229] third is the principle of the *consistent* (*consequent*) (logical) way of thinking. Anthropology can furnish examples of each of these principles, but it can furnish even more examples of their opposite.

The most important revolution from within the human being is "his exit from his self-incurred immaturity."[180] Before this revolution he let others think for him and merely imitated others or allowed them to guide him by leading-strings. Now he ventures to advance, though still shakily, with his own feet on the ground of experience.

---

[178] *Vernünfteln*.
[179] Trans.: Nobody is forced to follow the words of the master. See Horace, *Epistles* 1.1.14.
[180] See also Kant's famous definition of enlightenment in the opening sentence of *An Answer to the Question: What is Enlightenment?* 8: 35.

Book II The feeling of pleasure and displeasure [230]

Division

1) *Sensuous pleasure*, 2) *intellectual pleasure*. The *former* is either introduced A) through *sense* (enjoyment), or B) through the *power of imagination* (taste); the second (that is, intellectual pleasure) is either introduced a) through representable *concepts* or b) through *ideas*, – – and thus the opposite, *displeasure*, is also introduced in the same way.

On sensuous pleasure

A On the feeling for the agreeable, or sensuous pleasure in the sensation of an object

§60

Enjoyment is a pleasure through sense, and what amuses sense is called *agreeable*. *Pain* is displeasure through sense, and whatever produces it is *disagreeable*. – They are opposed to each other not as profit and lack of profit (+ and 0), but as profit and loss (+ and −), that is, one is opposed to the other not merely as *opposite* (*contradictorie s. logice oppositum*), but also as *counterpart* (*contrarie s. realiter oppositum*).[1] – – The expressions for what *pleases* or *displeases*, and for what is in between, the *indifferent*, are too *broad*; for they can also refer to intellectual pleasure and displeasure, where they would then not coincide with enjoyment and pain.

---

[1] Translations: contradictory or logically opposed; contrasted or truly opposed.

125

One can also explain these feelings by means of the effect that the [231] sensation produces on our state of mind. What directly (through sense) urges me to *leave* my state (to go out of it) is *disagreeable* to me – it causes me pain; just as what drives me to *maintain* my state (to remain in it) is *agreeable* to me, I enjoy it. But we are led along irresistibly in the stream of time and in the change of sensations connected with it. Now even if leaving one point of time and entering another is one and the same act (of change), there is still a temporal sequence in our thought and in the consciousness of this change, in conformity with the relation of cause and effect. – So the question arises, whether it is the consciousness of *leaving* the present state, or the prospect of *entering* a future state, that awakens in us the sensation of enjoyment? In the first case the enjoyment is nothing other than the ending of a pain and something negative; in the second it would be presentiment of something agreeable, therefore an increase of the state of pleasure, consequently something positive. But we can already guess beforehand that only the first will happen; for time drags us from the present to the future (not the reverse), and the cause of our agreeable feeling can only be that we are first compelled to leave the present, without any certainty into which other state we shall enter, knowing only that it is definitely another one.

Enjoyment is the feeling of promotion of life; pain is that of a hindrance of life. But (animal) life, as physicians also have already noted, is a continuous play of the antagonism of both.

Therefore pain must always precede every enjoyment; pain is always first. For what else but a quick death from *joy* would follow from a continuous promotion of the vital force, which cannot be raised above a certain degree anyway?

Also, no enjoyment can immediately follow another; rather, between one and another pain must appear. Small inhibitions of the vital force mixed in with advancements of it constitute the state of health that we erroneously consider to be a continuously felt well-being; when in fact it consists only of intermittent pleasant feelings that follow one another (with pain always intervening between them). Pain is the incentive[2] of activity, and in this, above all, we feel our life; without pain lifelessness would set in.

[232] *Pains that subside slowly* (like the gradual recovery from an illness or the slow reacquisition of lost capital) *do not result in lively enjoyment*, because

---

[2] *der Stachel.*

126

the transition is imperceptible. – I subscribe with full conviction to these tenets of Count *Veri*.[3]

Elucidation through examples

Why is a game (especially for money) so attractive and, if it is not too selfish, the best distraction and relaxation after a long intellectual exertion, since through idleness one recuperates only slowly? Because a game is a state of incessant movement between fearing and hoping. After a game the evening meal tastes better and also is digested better. – By what means are *plays* (whether tragedies or comedies) so alluring? Because in all of them certain difficulties enter in – anxiety and confusion between hope and joy – and so the play of opposing affects by the conclusion of the piece advances the life of the spectator, since it has stirred up motion within him. – Why does a love story end with the wedding, and why is a supplementary volume added by the hand of a bungler who continues the story into the marriage (as in Fielding's novel)[4] repugnant and in bad taste? Because jealousy, as the pain that comes to lovers between their joys and hopes, is spice to the reader *before* the marriage, but poison *in* marriage; for, to use the language of novels, "the end of love's pain is simultaneously the end of love" (understood as love with affect). – Why is work the best way of enjoying one's life? Because it is an arduous occupation (disagreeable in itself and pleasing only through success), and rest becomes a tangible pleasure, joy, through the mere disappearance of a long hardship; otherwise rest would not be anything enjoyable. – – Tobacco (whether smoked or snuffed) is at first linked with a disagreeable sensation. But just because nature immediately removes this pain (by secreting a mucus from the palate or nose), tobacco (especially when smoked) becomes a kind of company, by entertaining and constantly reawakening sensations and even thoughts; even if in this case they are only fleeting. – Finally, even if no positive pain stimulates us to activity, if necessary a negative one, [233] *boredom*, will often affect us in such a manner that we feel driven to do

---

[3] Intended is Count Pietro Verri (not Veri) (1728–1799), author of *Meditazione sulla felicità* (Milan, 1763), translated into German by the Göttingen philosopher professor Christoph Meiners under the title *Gedanken über die Natur des Vergnügens* (Leipzig, 1777). The sayings paraphrased by Kant are located on pp. 34–37 of the German translation (Brandt).

[4] See Kant's earlier elaboration at 7: 164.

something harmful to ourselves rather than nothing at all. For boredom is perceived as a *void* of sensation by the human being who is used to an alternation of sensations in himself, and who is striving to fill up his instinct for life with something or other.[5]

On boredom and amusement

§61

To feel one's life, to enjoy oneself, is thus nothing more than to feel oneself continuously driven to leave the present state (which must therefore be a pain that recurs just as often as the present). This also explains the oppressive, even frightening arduousness of boredom for everyone

---

[5] *Marginal note in H*: On passing the time as a pure, continuous removal of a pain. – On the boredom which no Carib feels.

How for us each period of time is long and life is short, or the opposite.

How one passes the time (not ordered work)

Crossed out in H: other. [On Boredom

§46

That the incentive of activity, which results in disgust at a sensationless existence (*horror vacui*), accompanies the human being the more his vital power is roused, from the age of childhood until the end of life, and that this always impels him to come out of the present condition, <in fact> is a wise arrangement of nature and its end, and is not to be disputed. But where then does *contentment* (joy in the persistence of his condition) remain, and under these circumstances how highly can he value the worth of his mere life in general? – The phenomenon is strange but nevertheless normal, that for the one who is not burdened every day with compulsory affairs, <the life> the life which has been saved appears too short. – – The cause of this appearance is <exactly the same> one and the same with the fact that German miles, which, however, are not measured ones, are longer the further they are from the capital (e.g., in Pomerania), than when they are nearer to one (e.g., Berlin). Where village upon village, or one farm after another, follows quickly, the traveler believes that he has covered a great stretch of land, <which he naturally also> because he necessarily thinks a long time about it, which contain a great many perceptions following one after another, <which is necessary for it because they> and now after the presumed long time he values the route covered which to him seems <big> long. On the other hand, in a desolate land, because the number of <objects> perceptions following one another in the former case require a long time <for it requires it>, consequently also according to the route of the accomplished trip, the lack of these requires only a short time <afterwards>, so that this is also judged at the end as shorter. Consequently the value of the length of one's life at the end depends on being able <in looking back> to look back on it with contentment, that is, being satisfied with it, and this is based on the number <and man> of occupations which have filled out time (*vitam extendere factis*). The more you have thought, and the more you have done, the longer you yourself have lived according to your <plain> own imagination <estimate of time>.

But what <proves> confirms the above proposition most of all is that all enjoyment consists in the <overcoming of> canceling of a pain, and so is acquired only by continually leaving the present condition, and this is indicated from the ease with which, after looking at one's watch at a party after an entertaining game or a lively conversation, one says "Where has the time gone!"]

who is attentive to his life and to time (cultivated human beings).[a] This pressure or impulse[6] to leave every point of time we are in and pass over into the following one is accelerating and can grow until a man makes the resolution to end his life; for the luxurious person has tried every form of enjoyment, and no enjoyment is new to him any longer. As someone in Paris said of Lord Mordaunt: "The English hang themselves in order to pass the time."[7] – – The void of sensations we perceive in ourselves arouses a horror (*horror vacui*) and, as it were, the presentiment of a slow death which is regarded as more painful than when fate suddenly cuts the thread of life.

This also explains why things that shorten time are taken to be the same thing as enjoyments; because the quicker we make time pass, the more we feel refreshed – as when one member of a party that has conversed for three hours long while taking a pleasure trip in a carriage cheerfully comments upon exiting when a member looks at his watch: [234] "Where has the time gone?" or "How short the time has been for us!" If, on the contrary, we paid attention to time when it was filled with enjoyment and not merely when it brought pain we were endeavoring to leave behind us, how rightly we would regret every loss of time. – Conversations that contain little exchange of ideas[8] are called *boring*, and just because of this also arduous, and an *entertaining* man is still regarded

---

[a] Because of his inborn lifelessness, the Carib is free from this arduousness. He can sit for hours with his fishing rod, without catching anything; thoughtlessness is a lack of incentive to activity, which brings pain with it, from which this one is spared. – Our reading public of refined taste is always sustained by the appetite and even the ravenous hunger for reading ephemeral writings (a way of doing nothing), not for the sake of self-cultivation, but rather for *enjoyment*. So the readers' heads always remain empty and there is no fear of over-saturation. For they give the appearance of work to their busy idleness and delude themselves that it is a worthy expenditure of time, but it is no better than what the *Journal des Luxus und der Moden* offers to the public. [Founded in 1786, the *Journal of Luxury and Fashion* was edited by F. J. Bertuch and J. M. Krause – Ed.]

[6] *Marginal note in H*: On Affects
Taste is the faculty for the play of the power of imagination to choose what is universally valid – therefore the effect of a joy in everyone whose power of the imagination . . . is capable of feelings
   Whether horrible representations also belong to it. Yes – but not the object rather the representation is beautiful
   Why does one rejoice over time that has become short?
   Taste is either the taste that distinguishes or the taste that savors. – The first belongs merely to sense intuition as a faculty of representation, the second belongs to the same as feeling of pleasure and displeasure. Whether and how it tastes good or bad. – *Sapere* – *Gustare*.

[7] Külpe surmises that Kant obtained this remark either from *Lettres de Mr. l'Abbé Le Blanc* (1751), 1: 259 [German edition: *Briefe über die Engländer* (1770), 1: 204f.] or from Alberti, *Briefe über die Engländer* (2nd ed., 1774), 1: 329–338.

[8] *Vorstellungen*.

129

as an agreeable man, even if not exactly an important one. As soon as he merely enters the room, the face of every guest immediately lights up, as with joy at being relieved of a burden.

But how are we to explain the phenomenon that a human being who has tortured himself with boredom for the greatest part of his life, so that every day seemed long to him, nevertheless complains at the end of his life about the *brevity* of life? – The cause of this is to be sought in the analogy with a similar observation: why do German miles (which are not measured or indicated with milestones, like the Russian versts) always become shorter the nearer we are to a capital (e.g., Berlin), and longer the farther we are from one (in Pomerania)? The reason is that the *abundance* of objects seen (villages and farmhouses) produces in our memory the deceptive conclusion that a vast amount of space has been covered and, consequently, that a longer period of time necessary for this purpose has also passed. However, the *emptiness* in the latter case produces little recollection of what has been seen and therefore leads to the conclusion that the route was shorter, and hence the time less, than would be shown by the clock. – – In the same way, the multitude of stages that mark the last part of life with various and different tasks will arouse in an old person the illusion of a longer-traveled lifetime than he would have believed according to the number of years, and filling our time by means of methodical, progressive occupations that lead to an important and intended end (*vitam extendere factis*)[9] is the only sure means of becoming happy with one's life and, at the same time, weary of life. "The more you have thought, and the more you have done, the longer you have lived (even in your own imagination)." – Hence the conclusion of such a life occurs with *contentment*.

But what about *contentment* (*acquiescentia*) during life? – For the human being it is unattainable: neither from the moral point of view [235] (being content with his good conduct) nor from the pragmatic point of view (being content with the well-being that he intends to secure through skill and prudence). As an incentive to activity, nature has put pain in the human being that he cannot escape from, in order always to progress toward what is better, and even in the last moments of life, contentment with the last stage of it can only be called comparative (partly because we compare ourselves with the lot of others, and partly because we compare

---

[9] Trans.: extend life through activity.

ourselves with ourselves); but the contentment is never pure and complete. – To be (absolutely) contented in life would be idle *rest* and the standstill of all incentives, or the dulling of sensations and the activity connected with them. However, such a state is no more compatible with the intellectual life of the human being than the stopping of the heart in an animal's body, where death follows inevitably unless a new stimulus (through pain) is sent.

Remark In this section we should also deal with *affects*[10] as feelings of pleasure and displeasure that transgress the bounds of the human being's inner freedom. But since these are often confused with the *passions* and, indeed, also stand in close relationship to passions, which will be discussed in another section, namely the one on the faculty of desire, I shall undertake a discussion of them when the occasion arises in the third section.[11]

§62

To be habitually disposed to cheerfulness is, to be sure, usually a quality of temperament; but often it can also be an effect of principles, such as Epicurus' *pleasure principle*, so-called by others and for that reason denounced, which actually was intended to designate the *always-cheerful heart* of the sage. – *Even-tempered* is he who is neither delighted nor distressed, and who is quite different from one who is *indifferent* to the coincidences of life and therefore has dull feelings. – Equanimity differs from the *moody* disposition (presumably it was called a *lunatic*[12] disposition at first), which is a subject's disposition to attacks of joy or grief for which the subject himself can give no reason, and which is particularly common with hypochondriacs. It is entirely different from the *witty*[13] *talent* (of a Butler or Sterne); here the wit intentionally places objects in the wrong position (stands them on their head, so to speak), and, with roguish simplicity, gives his audience or readers the pleasure of rearranging them on their own. – *Sensitivity* is not opposed to this equanimity. For it is a *faculty* and a *power* which either permits or [236] prevents the state of pleasure as well as displeasure from entering the

---

[10] *Affekten.* [11] See Book III: **On the Faculty of Desire.**
[12] Moody: *launisch*; lunatic: *lunatisch.* [13] *launicht.*

131

mind, and thus it possesses choice. On the other hand, *sentimentality* is a *weakness* by which we can be affected, even against our will, by sympathy for others' condition who, so to speak, can play at will on the organ of the sentimentalist. Sensitivity is manly; for the man who wants to spare his wife or children difficulties or pain must possess such delicate feeling as is necessary in order to judge their sensation not by *his* own strength but rather by their *weakness*, and *delicacy* of his sensation is necessary for generosity. On the other hand, the ineffectual sharing of one's feelings in order to appear sympathetically in tune with the feelings of others, thus allowing oneself to be affected in a merely passive way, is silly and childish. – So piety can and should be good-humored; we can and should perform difficult but necessary work in good humor, indeed even die in good humor: for all these things lose their value if they are done or endured in bad humor and in a morose frame of mind.

Concerning the grief that someone broods over intentionally, as something that will end only with his life, it is said that he has something *pulling on his mind* (a misfortune). – But one must not allow anything to pull on the mind; what cannot be changed must be driven from the mind: because it would be nonsense to want to make what happened into what has not happened. To better oneself is good and is also a duty; but to want to improve on what is already beyond my power is absurd. On the other hand, *taking something to heart*, which means to make a firm resolution to adopt any good advice or teaching, is the deliberate determination to connect our will with a sufficiently strong feeling for carrying it out. – The penitence of the self-tormentor is completely wasted effort; he should instead quickly apply his disposition to a better way of life. And it has, in addition, the bad consequence that he regards his record of guilt as thereby simply wiped out (through repentance), so that he is spared the effort toward improvement, which under reasonable circumstances should now have been doubled.[14]

§63

One way of enjoying ourselves is also a way of *cultivating* ourselves; that is, increasing the capacity for having more enjoyment of this kind, and

---

[14] *Marginal note in H:* We always place our contentment in comparison with others. Absolute contentment does not occur except at the end of life.

this applies to the sciences and the fine arts. However, *another* way is *overindulgence*, which makes us increasingly less capable of further enjoy- [237] ment. But whichever way we may seek enjoyment, it is a principal maxim, as already stated above, that we indulge only so far that we can climb still further; for being satiated produces that disgusting state that makes life itself a burden for the spoiled human being, and which consumes women in the name of vapors.[15] – – Young man! (I repeat)[16] get fond of work; deny yourself enjoyments, not to *renounce* them, but rather to keep them always in perspective as far as possible! Do not dull your receptivity to enjoyments by savoring them prematurely! The maturity of age, which never lets us regret having done without a single physical enjoyment, will guarantee, even in this sacrifice, a capital of contentment which is independent of either chance or the laws of nature.

§64

However, we also judge enjoyment and pain by a *higher* satisfaction or dissatisfaction within ourselves (namely moral): whether we ought to refuse them or give ourselves over to them.

1) The object can be pleasant, but the enjoyment of it *displeasing*. Therefore we have the expression a *bitter joy*. – He who is in bad circumstances and then inherits the estate of his parents or other appreciative and generous relatives cannot avoid rejoicing over their death; but he also cannot avoid reproaching himself for this joy. The same thing takes place in the mind of an assistant who, with unfeigned sadness, attends the funeral of his esteemed predecessor.
2) The object can be *unpleasant*; but the *pain* concerning it *pleasing*. Therefore we have the expression *sweet sorrow*:[17] for example, the sweet sorrow of a widow who has been left well off but does not want to allow herself to be comforted, which is often interpreted improperly as affectation.

On the other hand, enjoyment can also be pleasing, namely when we find enjoyment in such objects that it does us credit to be occupied with.

---

[15] See also *Observations on the Feeling of the Beautiful and Sublime* 2: 246 n. 2.   [16] See 7: 165.
[17] Pain: *Schmerz*; sweet sorrow: *süßer Schmerz*.

If, for example, someone entertains himself with fine arts instead of mere sensual pleasures, he has the added satisfaction that he (as a refined man) is capable of such pleasures. – Likewise, the pain of a human being can also be displeasing to him. The hatred of an insulted person is pain; but even after satisfaction the well-disposed man can still not refrain from reproaching himself for continuing to retain a grudge against the offender.

[238]

§65

Enjoyment which someone (legally) acquires *himself* is doubly felt; once as *gain* and then also as *merit* (the attribution, inwardly, of being the author himself). – Money acquired by working is enjoyable, at least for a *longer time*, than money won in games of chance; and even if we overlook the general harmfulness of the lottery, there remains, nevertheless, something which a well-disposed human being must be ashamed of if he should win by this means. – A misfortune for which an external cause is to blame *pains* us; but one for which we ourselves are to blame *saddens* and depresses us.

But how do we explain or reconcile that a misfortune which one person has suffered from another leads to two different kinds of explanation? Thus, for example, one sufferer says: "I would accept it, if I were in the least to blame for it"; but the second says: "It is my consolation that I am entirely innocent in the matter." – To suffer innocently is *irritating*, because it is an insult inflicted by another person. – To suffer when one is guilty is *depressing*, because it is a reproach from inside. – It is easy to see that of these two the second is the better human being.

§66

It is not exactly the nicest observation about human beings that their enjoyment increases through comparison with others' pain, while their own pain is diminished through comparison with similar or even greater sufferings of others. However, this effect is purely psychological (according to the principle of contrast: *opposita iuxta se posita magis elucescunt*)[18] and has no bearing on the moral matter of perhaps wishing

---

[18] Trans.: opposites become clearer when they are juxtaposed.

134

suffering on others so that we can feel the comfort of our own condition all the more deeply. One sympathizes with others by means of the power of imagination (for instance, when one sees someone who has lost his balance and is about to fall, one spontaneously and vainly leans toward the opposite side, in order to as it were place him back into balance again), and one is only happy not to be entwined in the same fate.[b] This is why people run with great desire, as to a theater play, to watch a criminal being taken to the gallows and executed. For the emotions and feelings which are expressed in his face and in his bearings [239] have a sympathetic effect on the spectators and, after the anxiety the spectators suffer through the power of the imagination (whose strength is increased even further by means of the ceremony), the emotions and feelings leave the spectators with a mild but nevertheless genuine feeling of relaxation, which makes their subsequent enjoyment of life all the more tangible.

Also, if one compares one's pain with other possible pains of one's own, it thereby becomes more bearable. The misfortune of someone who has broken his leg can be made more bearable if he is shown that he could easily have broken his neck.

The most thorough and easiest means of soothing all pains is the thought, which can well be expected of a reasonable human being, that life as such, with regard to our enjoyment of it, which depends on fortunate circumstances, has no intrinsic value of its own at all, and that life has value only as regards the use to which it is put, and the ends to which it is directed. So it is not luck but only *wisdom* that can secure the value of life for the human being; and its value is therefore in his power. He who is anxiously worried about losing his life will never enjoy life.[19]

---

[b]

Suave, mari magno turbantibus aequora ventis,
E terra magnum alterius spectare laborem;
Non quia vexari quenquam est iucunda voluptas,
Sed quibus ipse malis careas quia cernere suave est.

Lucretius

[Trans.: What joy it is, when out at sea the stormwinds are lashing the waters, to gaze from the shore at the heavy stress some other man is enduring! Not that anyone's afflictions are in themselves a source of delight; but to realize from what troubles you yourself are free is joy indeed. *De Rerum Natura* 2.1–4, trans. Ronald Latham (Harmondsworth: Penguin, 1951) – Ed.]

[19] *Marginal note in H*: Why die for joy. Affect.

135

*B On the feeling for the beautiful, that is, on the partly sensuous,
partly intellectual pleasure in reflective intuition, or taste*

§67

Taste, in the proper sense of the term, is, as has already been stated above,[20] the property of an organ (the tongue, palate, and throat) to be specifically affected by certain dissolved matter in food or drink. In its use it is to be understood either as taste that merely *differentiates* or, at the same time, as taste that also *savors* [for example, whether something is sweet or bitter, or whether what is tasted (sweet or bitter) is *pleasant*]. The former can offer universal agreement as to how certain substances are to be *designated*, but the latter can never offer a universally valid judgment: namely that something (for example, something bitter) which is pleasant to me will also be pleasant to everyone. The reason for this is clear: neither pleasure nor displeasure belongs to the cognitive faculty as [240] regards objects; rather they are determinations of the subject, and so cannot be ascribed to external objects. – The taste that savors therefore contains at the same time the concept of a differentiation between satisfaction and dissatisfaction, which I connect with the representation of the object in perception or imagination.

But the word *taste* is also taken for a sensible faculty of judgment, by which I choose not merely for myself, according to sensation, but also according to a certain rule which is represented as valid for everyone.[21] This rule can be *empirical*, in which case, however, it can make no claim to true universality or, consequently, to necessity either (the judgment of everyone else about taste that savors *must* agree with mine). – So, with regard to meals, the rule of taste that holds for the Germans is to begin with a soup, but the English begin with solid food, because a habit,

---

[20] See §20 above.
[21] *Crossed out in H*: everyone. [Since otherwise pleasure would be appetite in accordance with an object, which one cannot demand of everyone <and>, instead each person must <for oneself through experience> try it out for himself; and this would not be taste, which one represents <describes> *a priori* as <a pleasure> necessary and as a pleasure which one can <must have it> require from everyone. <However> Now this pleasure cannot therefore be sensual pleasure, but it also cannot be intellectual, therefore it must in fact be sensible. However, the faculty of representations is sensible, without nevertheless being representations of sense. Therefore the taste that savors, which serves as a rule for each, is for the power of imagination. From this follows the explanation:
    Taste is the faculty for the play of the power of imagination to choose what is universally valid.

136

gradually extended by imitation, has been made into a rule for arranging a meal.

But there is also a taste that savors, whose rule must be grounded *a priori*, because it proclaims *necessity* and consequently also validity for everyone as to how the representation of an object is to be judged in relation to the feeling of pleasure or displeasure (where reason is accordingly involved in it, although one cannot derive its judgment from principles of reason, and so cannot prove it). And one could call this taste *rationalizing* taste, in distinction to the *empirical* taste that is the taste of the senses (the former is *gustus reflectens*, the latter *reflexus*).[22]

All *presentation* of one's own person or one's art with *taste* presupposes a *social condition* (talking with others) which is not always sociable (sharing in the pleasure of others), but at the beginning is usually *barbaric*, unsociable, and purely competitive. – No one in complete solitude will decorate or clean his house; he will not even do it for his own people (wife and children), but only for strangers, to show himself to advantage. But in *taste* (taste concerning choice), that is, in aesthetic power of judgment, it is not the *sensation* directly (the material of the representation of the object), but rather how the free (productive) power of imagination joins it together through invention, that is, the *form*, which produces satisfaction in the object. For only form is capable of laying claim to a universal rule [241] for the feeling of pleasure. One must not expect such a universal rule from sensations, which can differ greatly, according to the different sense-capacities of subjects. – One can therefore explain taste as follows:[23] "taste is the faculty of the aesthetic power of judgment to choose with universal validity."

Taste is, accordingly, a faculty of making *social* judgments of external objects within the power of imagination. – Here the mind feels its freedom in the play of images (therefore of sensibility); for sociability with

---

[22] *Marginal note in H*: Not the means, but the object of intuition itself immediately!

Naturally this play must then be free and yet in accordance with law, if it is to produce a pleasure in the object.

Taste refers to society and to communication with others, without this it would be a mere choice for the appetite. –

For oneself alone no one would limit one's choice because of the form. –

The sociable, festive meal calls for diversity, but because of freedom of choice also order and unity.

[23] *Crossed out in H*: follows: [Taste is <the power of judgment> the faculty which <connects> unites the free play of the power of imagination with the lawfulness of the understanding. It is therefore the faculty of the aesthetic power of judgment to choose that which is universally valid.]

other human beings presupposes freedom – and this feeling is pleasure. – But the *universal validity* of this feeling for everyone, which distinguishes tasteful choice (of the beautiful) from choice through mere sensation (of what is merely subjectively pleasing), carries with it the concept of a law; for only in accordance with this law can the validity of satisfaction for the person who judges be universal. The faculty of representing the universal, however, is the *understanding*. Therefore the judgment of taste is not only an aesthetic judgment but also a judgment of understanding, but both are thought in combination (consequently the judgment of understanding is not considered as pure). – The judging of an object through taste is a judgment about the harmony or discord of freedom, in the play of the power of imagination and the lawfulness of understanding, and therefore it is a matter only of judging the form aesthetically (the compatibility of the sense representations), not the generation of products, in which the form is perceived. For that would be *genius*, whose passionate vitality often needs to be moderated and limited by the propriety of taste.[24]

Beauty alone belongs to taste; it is true that the *sublime* belongs to aesthetic judgment, but not to taste. However, the *representation* of the sublime can and should nevertheless be beautiful in itself; otherwise it is coarse, barbaric, and contrary to good taste. Even the *presentation* of the evil or ugly (for example, the figure of personified death in Milton) can and must be beautiful whenever an object is to be represented

---

[24] *Marginal note in H*: What one chooses for the pleasure of others can nevertheless be choice without interest.

From whence – *Sapor?*

To choose means to distinguish something in an object through the feeling of pleasure. To choose is not yet to desire, for it is still problematic. Still not interest xx.

Beauty – Sublimity.

In a sermon not spirit and taste 1) the cold and bright theory of the text for the understanding 2) Real life in relation to the text, whether it agrees with this or not. 3) The stimulating application of the same to real life.

Taste results in communication of pleasure in the representation of an object and therefore it is social. No one dresses tastefully or dresses up for oneself.

But whence *Sapor* and *Sapientia*. – The taste that differentiates, which is fine. *Sancho* small iron key xx.

Taste is the faculty of aesthetic judgment, to choose what is universally valid.

Thereby 1) empirical interest is restrained, for this gives no universality. 2) Intellectual interest is restrained, but then also 3) the relation of an object to the feeling of pleasure and displeasure, which also concerns merely the form of the object, is indicated, 4) the freedom of the power of imagination, which is the intuitive representation of its own product, is indicated [?].

aesthetically, and this is true even if the object is a *Thersites*.[25] Otherwise the presentation produces either distaste or disgust, both of which include the endeavor to push away a representation that is offered for enjoyment; whereas *beauty* on the other hand carries with it the concept of an invitation to the most intimate union with the object, that is, to immediate enjoyment. – With the expression "*a beautiful soul*" one says [242] everything that can be said to make one aim at the innermost union with such a soul; for *greatness* and *strength* of soul concern the matter (the instruments for certain ends). *Goodness of soul*, however, concerns the pure form, under which it must be possible to unite all ends, and so wherever it is encountered it is *primordially creative* but also *supernatural*, like the Eros of the world of fable. – Nevertheless, this goodness of soul is the central point around which the judgment of taste gathers all of its judgments of sensuous pleasure that are compatible with the freedom of understanding.

Remark How could it have happened that modern languages in particular have designated the aesthetic faculty of judging with an expression (*gustus, sapor*) that merely refers to a certain sense organ (the inside of the mouth) and to its discrimination as well as choice of enjoyable things? – There is no situation in which sensibility and understanding unite in one enjoyment that can be continued as long and repeated with satisfaction as often as a good meal in good company. – But here the meal is regarded merely as the vehicle for supporting the company. The aesthetic taste of the host shows itself in his skill in choosing with universal validity, something which he cannot bring about through his own sense of taste, because his guests might choose other foods or drinks, each according to his own private sense. Therefore he sets up his meeting with *variety*, so that everyone will find something that suits his sense, which yields a comparative universal validity. In the present discussion we cannot deal with his skill in choosing guests who themselves engage in reciprocal and common conversation (which is indeed also called taste, but which is

---

[25] Milton: see Book II of *Paradise Lost*. Thersites is described in Homer's *Iliad* as being

the ugliest man who came beneath Ion. He was bandy-legged and lame of one foot, with shoulders stooped and drawn together over his chest, and above this his skull went up to a point with the wool grown sparsely upon it. Beyond all others Achilleus hated him, and Odysseus. (*Iliad* 2.216–220, trans. Richmond Lattimore (Chicago: University of Chicago Press, 1951))

actually reason applied to taste, and yet is distinct from it). And so the feeling of an organ through a particular sense has been able to furnish the name for an ideal feeling; the feeling, namely, of a sensible, universally valid choice in general. – It is even more strange that the skill of testing by sense whether something is an object of enjoyment for one and the same subject (not whether the choice of it is universally valid) (*sapor*) has even been exaggerated to designate wisdom (*sapientia*); presumably because an unconditionally necessary end requires neither reflection nor experi-

[243] ment, but comes into the soul immediately by, so to speak, tasting what is wholesome.

§68

The *sublime* is awe-inspiring *greatness* (*magnitudo reverenda*) in extent or degree which invites approach (in order to measure our powers against it); but the fear that in comparison with it we will disappear in our own estimation is at the same time a deterrent (for example, thunder over our heads, or a high rugged mountain).[26] And if we ourselves are in a safe place, the collecting of our powers to grasp the appearance, along with our anxiety that we are unable to measure up to its greatness, arouses *surprise* (a pleasant feeling owing to its continual overcoming of pain).

The *sublime* is the counterweight but not the opposite of the beautiful; because the effort and attempt to raise ourselves to a grasp (*apprehensio*) of the object awakens in us a feeling of our own greatness and power; but the representation in thought of the sublime by *description* or presentation can and must always be beautiful. For otherwise the astonishment becomes a *deterrent*, which is very different from *admiration*, a judgment in which we do not grow weary of being astonished.

The *monstrous* is greatness that is contrapurposive (*magnitudo monstrosa*). Writers, therefore, who wanted to extol the vast extent of the Russian empire have missed badly in calling it monstrous; for herein lies a reproach, as if it were *too great* for a single ruler. – A human being is *adventurous* who has the propensity to become entangled with events whose true account resembles a novel.

---

[26] See also Kant's more extensive discussion of the sublime in the *Critique of the Power of Judgment* 5: 244–280.

The sublime is therefore not an object for taste, but rather an object for the feeling of emotion;[27] however, the artistic presentation of the sublime in description and embellishment (in secondary works, *parerga*) can and should be beautiful, since otherwise it is wild, coarse, and repulsive, and, consequently, contrary to taste.

Taste contains a tendency toward external advancement of morality

[244]

§69

Taste (as a formal sense, so to speak) concerns the *communication* of our feeling of pleasure or displeasure to others, and includes a susceptibility, which this very communication affects pleasurably, to feel a satisfaction (*complacentia*) about it in common with others (sociably). Now satisfaction that can be considered valid not merely for the subject who feels it but also for everybody else, that is, universally valid, must contain necessity (of this satisfaction). So, in order to be considered universally valid, this satisfaction must contain an *a priori* principle. Consequently, it is a satisfaction in the agreement of the subject's pleasure with the feeling of everyone else according to a universal law, which must spring from the subject's giving of universal law and so from reason. That is to say, the choice in accordance with this satisfaction, according to its form, comes under the principle of duty. Therefore ideal taste has a tendency toward the external advancement of morality.[28] – Making the human being *well-mannered*[29] for his social situation to be sure does not mean as much as forming him into a *morally good* person, but nevertheless it prepares him for the latter by the effort he makes in his social situation to please others (to become liked or admired). – In this way one could call taste morality in external appearance; even though this expression, taken literally, contains a contradiction; since being well-mannered after all includes the *appearance* or demeanor of moral goodness, and even a degree of it; namely the inclination to place a value even on the semblance of moral goodness.

---

[27] *das Gefühl der Rührung.*
[28] See also Kant's discussion of the "virtues of social intercourse" in *The Metaphysics of Morals* 6: 473–474, and *Critique of the Power of Judgment* 5: 267.
[29] *gesittet.*

141

§70

To be well-mannered, respectable, well-behaved, polished (with the coarseness planed down) is still only the negative condition of taste. The representation of these qualities in the power of the imagination can be a tasteful, externally *intuitive* way of representing an object, or one's own person, but only for two senses, hearing and sight. Music and the plastic arts (painting, sculpture, architecture, and horticulture) lay claim to taste as a susceptibility of a feeling of pleasure for the mere forms of external intuition, the former in respect to hearing, the latter in respect to sight. On the other hand, the *discursive* way of representing things [245] through speech or writing includes two arts in which taste can manifest itself: *rhetoric* and *poetry*.[30]

Anthropological observations concerning taste[31]

A On taste in fashion

§71

The human being has a natural tendency to compare his behavior to that of a more important person (the child with adults, the lower-ranking person with those of higher rank) in order to imitate the other person's ways. A law of this imitation, which aims at not appearing lower than others, especially in cases where no regard to utility is paid, is called *fashion*. Fashion therefore belongs under the title of *vanity*, because there is no inner worth in its intention; and also of *foolishness*, because in

---

[30] *Marginal note in H*: §51
   On Poetry and Rhetoric, Spirit and Taste.
   The excess of good living with taste is luxury.
   The taste of sense is a matter of only two senses, hearing and sight.
   The taste of reflection is also a matter of manners (*mores*). The latter, which is called beauty, is as it were morality in appearance (virtue, if it appears visibly (*venus orania*), – therefore polished, *poli* – it is the middle step between sensual stimulus and morality. The individuality of the former is left out and delight remains, universality and necessity lead to the good.
   On Taste in Fashion
   Only two senses belong to ideal spirit and taste.
   On splendor and pomp – adventures. Many of them are sugary, like romance novels.
   To be ostentatious is not tasteful but *tasteless*. – To be fashionable is not tasteful, but vain.
[31] *Crossed out in H*: Taste [*Popular* taste (in contrast to *select* taste) is **fashion**. The question: What then is fashion? <means> refers not merely to <what is now> elegant usage which through habit has, as it were, become law, but].

142

fashion there is still a compulsion to let ourselves be led slavishly by the mere example that many in society give us. To be *in fashion* is a matter of taste; he who clings to a past custom that is *out of* fashion is called *old-fashioned*; and he who even places a worth on being out of fashion is an *eccentric*. But it is always better, nevertheless, to be a fool in fashion than a fool out of fashion, if we want to impose such a harsh name on this vanity at all; a title that, indeed, the mania for fashion really deserves if it sacrifices true utility or even duties to this vanity. – All fashions, by their very concept, are mutable ways of living. For when the game of imitation is fixed, it becomes *custom*, and then taste is no longer considered at all. Accordingly, it is novelty that makes fashion popular, and to be inventive in all sorts of external forms, even if they often degenerate into something fantastic and somewhat hideous, belongs to the style of courtiers, especially ladies. Others then anxiously imitate these forms, and those in low social positions burden themselves with them long after the courtiers have put them away. – So fashion is not, strictly speaking, a matter of taste (for it can be quite contrary to taste), but of mere vanity in giving oneself airs, and of rivalry in outdoing one another by it. (The *élégants de la cour*, otherwise called *petits maîtres*, are windbags.)

Splendor can be joined with true, ideal taste, which is therefore something sublime that is at the same time beautiful (such as a splendid starry [246] heaven, or, if it does not sound too vulgar, a St. Peter's church in Rome). Even *pomp*, an ostentatious display for show, can also be joined with taste, but not without firm objection by taste; because pomp is calculated for the masses, which include a great deal of rabble, whose taste, being dull, calls more for sensation than the capacity for judging.

B *On taste in art*

Here I shall take into consideration only the speaking arts: *rhetoric* and *poetry*, because they are aimed at a frame of mind whereby the mind is directly aroused to activity, and thus they have their place in a *pragmatic* anthropology, where one tries to know the human being according to what can be made of him.

The principle of the mind that animates by means of *ideas* is called **spirit**. – *Taste* is a merely regulative faculty of judging form in the combination of the manifold in the power of imagination; *spirit*, however, is the productive faculty of reason which provides a *model* for that *a priori* form of the power of imagination. Spirit and taste: *spirit* to provide ideas, *taste* to limit them to the form that is appropriate to the laws of the productive power of imagination and so to *form* them (*fingendi*) in an original way (not imitatively). A product composed with spirit and taste can be called *poetry* in general and is a work of *beautiful art*; it may be presented directly to the senses by means of the eyes or ears and can also be called *poetic art* (*poetica in sensu lato*); it may include the arts of painting, horticulture, and architecture, as well as the arts of composing music and verse (*poetica in sensu stricto*).[32] But *poetic art* as contrasted with *rhetoric* differs from it only by the way understanding and sensibility are mutually subordinated: poetic art is a *play* of sensibility *ordered* through understanding; rhetoric is a *business* of understanding *animated* through sensibility. However, both the orator and the poet (in the broad [247] sense) are *inventors* and bring forth out of themselves new forms (combinations of the sensible) in their power of imagination.[c]

Because the gift of poetry is an artistic skill and, when it is combined with taste, a talent for beautiful art that aims, in part, at illusion (although one that is sweet and often also indirectly beneficial), it is obvious that no great use (often even detrimental use) of the gift has been made in life. – Accordingly, it is well worth our while to ask some questions and make some observations about the character of the poet, and also about the influence that his occupation has on himself and others and its worthiness.[33]

---

[32] Trans.: poetry in the broad sense; poetry in the strict sense.

[c] *Novelty* in the *presentation* of a concept is a principal demand of beautiful art placed on the inventor, even if the concept itself is not supposed to be new. – But for the understanding (apart from taste) we have the following expressions for increasing our knowledge through new perception. To *discover* something is to perceive something for the first time that was already there, for example, America, the magnetic force directed toward the poles, atmospheric electricity. – To *invent* something (to bring into reality that which was not yet there), for example, the compass, the aerostat. – To *locate* something, to recover that which was lost through searching. – To *devise* and *think out* (for example, with tools for artists, or machines). – To *fabricate*, consciously to represent the untrue as true, as in novels, where it happens only for entertainment. – A fabrication given out as truth, however, is a *lie*.
(*Turpiter atrum desinit in piscem mulier formosa superne.*)
Horace
[Trans.: The woman, well-shaped on top, ends below ugly in a black fish. *Ars poetica* 5.3f. – Ed.]

[33] *Marginal note in H*: The principle in the human being that animates by means of ideas with reason is called – spirit
The painter of *Originalen* the orator the poet – each original author must be a poet and in his product lies his spirit.
Scansion

144

Among the beautiful (speaking) arts, why does poetry win the prize over rhetoric, when both have exactly the same ends? – Because poetry is at the same time music (singable) and tone; a sound that is pleasant in itself, which mere speech is not. Even rhetoric borrows from poetry a sound that approximates tone: *accent*, without which the oration lacks the necessary intervening moments of rest and animation. But poetry wins the prize not merely over rhetoric but also over every other beautiful art: over painting (to which sculpture belongs) and even over music. For music is a *beautiful* (not merely pleasant) *art* only because it serves poetry as a vehicle. Also, among poets there are not so many shallow minds (minds unfit for business) as there are among musicians, because poets also speak to the understanding, but musicians speak only to the senses. – A good poem is the most penetrating means of enlivening the mind. – – But it is true not merely of poets, but of everyone who possesses the gift [248] of beautiful art, that one must be born to it and cannot achieve it by diligence and imitation; also, in order to succeed in his work a lucky mood needs to come over the artist, just like a moment of inspiration (this is why he is also called *vates*). For a work that is made according to precepts and rules turns out to be spiritless (slavish); however, a product of beautiful art requires not merely taste, which can be grounded on imitation, but also originality of thought, which, as self-inspired, is called *spirit*. – The *painter of nature* with paintbrush or pen (in the latter case it is prose or verse) is not the beautiful spirit, because he only imitates; the *painter of ideas* alone is the master of beautiful art.

Why does one usually understand by "poet" a writer who composes in *verse*; that is, in a discourse that is scanned (spoken rhythmically, like music)? Because in announcing a work of beautiful art he enters with a solemnity that must satisfy the finest *taste* (in respect to form); otherwise the work would not be beautiful. – However, since this solemnity is mostly required for the beautiful representation of the sublime, a similarly affected solemnity without verse is called (by Hugh Blair) "*prose run*

---

prose that has become crazy

A witty (also sharp) thought produced in rhyme is therefore not *poesie* – it lacks spirit.

The ancient poems had more spirit than wit.

Uneven length and *naïveté*.

Poets are seldom good businessmen, musicians likewise not, except as lovers, not artists.

Poetry and versemongery

The singability of verse is not a natural language.

mad."[34] – On the other hand, versification is also not poetry, if it is without spirit.

Why is rhyme in the verses of poets of modern times, when the rhyme happily brings the thought to conclusion, an important requirement of taste in our part of the world? On the other hand, why is rhyme a repulsive offense against verse in poems of ancient times, so that now, for example, verse free of rhyme in German is not very pleasing, but a Latin Virgil put into rhyme is even less pleasing? Presumably because with the old classical poets prosody was fixed, but in modern languages prosody is to a large extent lacking, and the ear is compensated for this lack through rhyme, which concludes the verse with a sound similar to the ending of the previous verse. In prosaic, solemn language a rhyme occurring accidentally between other sentences becomes ridiculous.

Where does the *poetic license* to violate the laws of language now and then, to which the orator is not entitled, come from? Presumably from the fact that the orator is not hindered by the law of form too much to express a great thought.

[249] Why is a mediocre poem intolerable, but a mediocre speech still quite bearable? The cause appears to lie in the fact that the solemnity of tone in every poetic product arouses great expectations and, precisely because these expectations are not satisfied, the poem usually sinks even lower than its prose value would perhaps merit. – The conclusion of a poem with a verse which can be preserved as an aphorism produces a pleasant aftertaste and thereby makes amends for much of this staleness; thus it too belongs to the art of the poet.

In old age the *poetic vein* dries up, at a time when the sciences still promise good health and activity in work to a good mind. This is probably so because beauty is a *blossom*, whereas science is the *fruit*; that is, poetry must be a free art which, on account of its variety, requires facility; but in old age this facile sense dwindles away (and rightly so). Furthermore, *habit*, merely advancing along the same track in the sciences, at the same time brings facility along with it; thus poetry, which requires originality and

---

[34] Hugh Blair (1718–1800), *Lectures on Rhetoric* (London, 1783); translated into German by Karl Gottfried Schreiter, *Vorlesungen über Rhetorik und schöne Wissenschaften* (4 vols., Leipzig, 1785–1789). However, the phrase "prose run mad" is not used here. Külpe suggests that Kant's source was the *Epistle to Dr. Arbuthnot*, being the prologue to the satires of Pope, line 188: "It is not poetry, but prose run mad." See also *Reflexion 1485*, 15: 703, *Busolt* 25: 1466, and *Dohna* 25: 1541.

146

novelty in each of its products (and in addition to this agility), does not agree well with old age; except perhaps in matters of *caustic* wit, in epigrams and *xenia*,[35] where poetry is at the same time more serious than playful.

That poets make no such fortune as lawyers and others in the learned professions lies in the predisposition of temperament which is, on the whole, required of the born poet: namely to drive cares away by means of convivial play with thoughts. – However, a peculiarity which concerns *character*, namely, of *having no character*, but being capricious, moody, and (without malice) unreliable, of willfully making enemies for oneself, without even hating anyone, and of mocking one's friend bitingly, without wanting to hurt him, lies in a partly innate predisposition of eccentric *wit* ruling over the practical power of judgment.

On luxury

§72

Luxury (*luxus*) is the excess, in a community, of social high living *with taste* (which is thus contrary to the welfare of the community). Excess *without taste*, however, is public *debauchery* (*luxuries*). – If we take the effects of both on the community's welfare into consideration, then [250] luxury is a *dispensable expenditure* which makes the community *poor*, while debauchery is one that makes it *ill*. Nevertheless, luxury is still compatible with the advancing culture of the people (in art and science); debauchery, however, gorges with pleasure and eventually causes disgust. Both are more ostentatious (glittering on the outside) than self-pleasing; luxury, through elegance (as in balls and spectacles) for the ideal taste; debauchery, through abundance and diversity for the sense of *taste* (for physical taste, as, for example, at the feast of a Lord Mayor). – Whether the government is entitled to limit both of these by sumptuary laws is a question whose answer does not belong here. But since the beautiful as well as the pleasant arts weaken the people to some extent, so that they can be more easily governed, the introduction of a Spartan roughness would work directly against the government's aim.

---

[35] *Xenia* – in Greek, presents to guests or strangers. In German literature, a kind of satirical epigram first introduced by Schiller and Goethe.

The art of good living is the due proportion of living well to sociability (thus, to living with taste). One sees from this that luxury is detrimental to the art of good living, and the expression "he knows how to live," when used of a wealthy or distinguished man, signifies the skillfulness of his choice in social enjoyment, which includes moderation (sobriety) in making pleasure mutually beneficial, and is calculated to last.

Since luxury can properly be reproached not in domestic life but only in public life, one sees from this that the relation of the citizen to the commonwealth, as concerns the freedom to engage in rivalry, to forestall utility, if necessary, for the sake of the embellishment of one's own person or possessions (in festivals, weddings, funerals, and so on down to good tone in common dealings), can hardly be burdened with sumptuary edicts. For luxury still provides the advantage of enlivening the arts, and so reimburses the commonwealth for the expenses that such a display might have entailed for it.

Book III On the faculty of desire

§73

Desire (*appetitio*) is the self-determination of a subject's power through the representation of something in the future as an effect of this representation.[1] Habitual sensible desire is called *inclination*. Desiring without exercising power to produce the object is *wish*. Wish can be directed toward objects that the subject himself feels incapable of producing, and then it is an *empty* (idle) wish. The empty wish to be able to annihilate the time between the desire and the acquisition of the desired object is *longing*. The undetermined desire, in respect of the object (*appetitio vaga*), which only impels the subject to leave his present state without knowing what state he then wants to enter, can be called the *peevish* wish (one that nothing satisfies).

Inclination that can be conquered only with difficulty or not at all by the subject's reason is *passion*. On the other hand, the feeling of a pleasure or displeasure in the subject's present state that does not let him rise to *reflection* (the representation by means of reason as to whether he should give himself up to it or refuse it) is *affect*.

To be subject to affects and passions is probably always an *illness of the mind*, because both affect and passion shut out the sovereignty of reason. Both are also equally vehement in degree; but as concerns their quality they are essentially different from each other, with regard both to the

---

[1] See also Kant's definitions of the faculty of desire in *The Metaphysics of Morals* 6: 211 and the *Critique of the Power of Judgment* 5: 178n.

149

method of prevention and to that of the cure that the physician of souls would have to apply.[2]

On affects in comparison with passion

§74

Affect is[3] surprise through sensation, by means of which the mind's composure (*animus sui compos*) is suspended. Affect is therefore rash, that is, it quickly grows to a degree of feeling that makes reflection impossible (it is thoughtless). – Lack of affect that does not reduce the strength of incentives to action is *phlegm* in the good sense, a property of the valiant man (*animi strenui*), who does not let the strength of affects bring him out of calm reflection. What the affect of anger does not accomplish quickly it does not do at all; and it forgets easily. But the passion of hatred takes its time, in order to root itself deeply and think about its opponent. – If a father or school-master has only had the patience to listen to the apology (not the justification), he cannot punish. – If a person comes into your room in anger in order to say harsh words to you in fierce indignation, politely ask him to sit down; if you succeed in this, his scolding will already be milder, since the comfort of sitting is a relaxation that is not really compatible with the threatening gestures and screaming that can be used when standing. On the other hand, passion (as a state of mind belonging to the faculty of desire) takes its time and reflects, no matter how fierce it may be, in order to reach its end. – Affect works like water that breaks through a dam; passion, like a river that digs itself deeper and deeper into its bed. Affect works on our health like an apoplectic fit; passion, like consumption or emaciation. Affect is like drunkenness that one sleeps off, although a headache follows afterward; but passion is regarded as a sickness that comes from swallowing poison, or a deformity which requires an inner or an

---

[2] See also Kant's discussions in *The Metaphysics of Morals* 6: 407–408 and in *The Conflict of the Faculties*, Part III (7: 95–116).

[3] *Crossed out in H*: is [as it were <the eruption> overflow through the bursting of <the> a dam <of a river>; passion on the other hand is a river, brought about by the steepness of the ground, that digs itself deeper and deeper and makes itself constant.]

outer physician of the soul, one who nevertheless knows how to prescribe remedies that are for the most part not radical, but almost always merely palliative.[4]

Where a great deal of affect is present, there is generally little passion; as with the French, who as a result of their vivacity are fickle in comparison with the Italians and Spaniards (as well as Indians and Chinese), who brood over revenge in their rage or are persistent in their love to the point of dementia. – Affects are honest and open, passions on the other hand are deceitful and hidden. The Chinese reproach the English with being impetuous and hotheaded, "like [253] the Tartars"; but the English reproach the Chinese with being out-and-out (though calm) deceivers, who do not allow this reproach to dissuade them at all in their passion.[5] – – Affect is like *drunkenness* that one sleeps off; passion is to be regarded as a *dementia* that broods over a representation which nestles itself deeper and deeper. – The person who *loves* to be sure can still remain quite clear-sighted; but the person who *falls in love* is inevitably blind to the faults of the beloved object, though the latter person will usually regain his sight eight days after the wedding. – Whoever is usually seized by affect like a fit of madness, no matter how benign these affects may be, nevertheless resembles a deranged person; but since he quickly regrets the episode afterward, it is only a paroxysm that we call *thoughtlessness*. Some people even wish that they could get angry, and Socrates was doubtful as to whether it would not be good to get angry at times; but to have affect so much under one's control that one can cold-bloodedly reflect whether one should get angry or not appears to be somewhat contradictory. – On the other hand, no human being wishes to have passion. For who wants to have himself put in chains when he can be free?

---

[4] *Marginal note in H*: Affect is rash, but does not bear a grudge. If one gives it room, it is even amused at and loves that which has offended it.

> It is not hatred (passion).
> Love can be brought about by means of a momentary impression of a friendly smile, but quickly disappears.

But to be in love is a passion that one is never rid of.

[5] See also *Parow* 25: 416–417 and *Menschenkunde* 25: 1122–1123.

On the affects in particular

A On the government of the mind with regard to the affects

§75

The principle of *apathy* – namely that the wise man must never be in a state of affect, not even in that of compassion with the misfortune of his best friend, is an entirely correct and sublime moral principle of the Stoic school; for affect makes us (more or less) blind. – Nevertheless, the wisdom of nature has planted in us the predisposition to compassion in order to handle the reins *provisionally*, until reason has achieved the necessary strength; that is to say, for the purpose of enlivening us, nature has added the incentive of pathological (sensible) impulse to the moral incentives for the good, as a temporary surrogate of reason. By the way, affect, considered by itself alone, is always imprudent; it makes itself incapable of pursuing its own end, and it is therefore unwise to allow it to come into being intentionally. – Nevertheless, reason, in representing the

[254] morally good by connecting its ideas with intuitions (examples) that have been imputed to them, can produce an enlivening of the will (in spiritual or political speeches to the people, or even in solitary speeches to oneself). Reason is thus enlivening the soul not as effect but rather as cause of an affect in respect to the good, and reason still always handles the reins, causing an *enthusiasm* of good resolution – an enthusiasm which, however, must be attributed to the *faculty of desire* and not to affect, as to a stronger sensible *feeling*.

The *natural gift* of *apathy*, with sufficient strength of soul, is, as I have said,[6] fortunate **phlegm** (in the moral sense). He who is gifted with it is, to be sure, on that account not yet a wise man, but he nevertheless has the support of nature, so that it will be easier for him to become one more easily than others.

Generally speaking, it is not the intensity of a certain feeling that constitutes the affected state, but the lack of reflection in comparing this feeling with the sum of all feelings (of pleasure or displeasure). The rich person, whose servant clumsily breaks a beautiful and rare crystal goblet while carrying it around, would think nothing of this accident if, at the same moment, he were to compare this loss of *one* pleasure with the

---

[6] See the remark on phlegm near the beginning of §74.

multitude of *all* the pleasures that his fortunate position as a rich man offers him. However, if he now gives himself over completely to this one feeling of pain (without quickly making that calculation in thought), then it is no wonder that, as a result, he feels as if his entire happiness were lost.

B *On the various affects themselves*

§76

The feeling that urges the subject to **remain** in the state he is in is *agreeable*; but the one that urges him to **leave** it is *disagreeable*. Combined with consciousness, the former is called *enjoyment* (*voluptas*), the latter *lack of enjoyment* (*taedium*). As affect the first feeling is called *joy*, the other *sadness*. – *Exuberant joy* (which is tempered by no concern about pain) and overwhelming sadness (which is alleviated by no hope), *grief*, are affects that threaten life. Nevertheless, we can see from the register of [255] deaths that more human beings have lost their lives *suddenly* because of exuberant joy than because of grief. For the mind gives itself over completely to *hope* as an affect, owing to the unexpected offering of the prospect of immeasurable good fortune, and so the affect rises to the point of suffocation; on the other hand, continually fearful grief is naturally and always opposed by the mind, so that grief only kills slowly.

Fright is suddenly aroused fear that disconcerts the mind. Similar to fright is the *startling*,[7] something that *puzzles* (though not yet *alarms*) us and arouses the mind to collect itself for reflection; it is the stimulus to *astonishment* (which already contains reflection in itself). This does not happen so easily to the experienced person; but it is proper for art to represent the usual from a point of view that will make it startling. *Anger* is fright that at the same time quickly stirs up powers to resist ill. Fear concerning an object that threatens an undetermined ill is *anxiety*. Anxiety can fasten on to someone without his knowing a particular object for it: an uneasiness arising from merely subjective causes (from a diseased state). *Shame* is anguish that comes from the worried contempt of a person who is *present* and, as such, it is an affect. Moreover, a person can also feel ashamed without the presence of the person before whom he is ashamed; however, then it is not an *affect* but, like grief, a *passion* for

---

[7] *das Auffallende.*

153

tormenting oneself persistently with contempt, but in vain; shame, on the other hand, as an affect, must occur suddenly.

Affects are generally diseased occurrences (symptoms) and can be divided (by an analogy with Brown's system)[8] into *sthenic* affects, which come from strength, and *asthenic* affects, which come from weakness. Sthenic affects are of such a nature as to *excite* the vital force, but in doing so they also often exhaust it as well; asthenic affects are of such a nature as to relax the vital force, but in doing so they often prepare for its recovery as well. – *Laughing* with affect is a *convulsive* cheerfulness. *Weeping* accompanies the *melting* sensation of a powerless wrath against fate or other human beings, like the sensation of an insult suffered from them; and this sensation is *wistfulness*. But both laughing and weeping cheer us up; for they are liberations from a hindrance to the vital force through their effusions (that is, we can laugh till we cry if we laugh till exhaustion). Laughing is *masculine*, weeping on the other hand is *feminine* (with men it is *effeminate*). And when tears glisten in a man's eyes, it is only his *being moved* to tears that can be forgiven, and this only if it comes from magnanimous but powerless sympathy with others' suffering, without letting the tears fall in drops, and still less if he accompanies them with sobs, thereby making a disgusting music.

[256]

On timidity and bravery[9]

§77

Anxiety, anguish, horror, and terror are degrees of fear, that is, degrees of aversion to danger. The composure of the mind to take on fear with reflection is *courage*; the strength of inner sense (*Ataraxia*) through which we do not easily allow ourselves to be put in fear is *intrepidity*. Lack of courage is *cowardice*;[a] lack of intrepidity is *shyness*.[10]

---

[8] John Brown (1735–1788), English physician, author of *Elementa Medicinae* (1780). Brown held that the essence of living organisms consists in excitability, and called an excess of excitability the state of sthenia, and a lack of excitability the state of asthenia.

[9] *Von der Furchtsamkeit und der Tapferkeit.*

[a] The word *poltroon* (derived from *pollex truncates*) was rendered with *murcus* in later Latin and signified a human being who chops off his thumb in order not to be allowed to go to war. [Claudius Salmasius (1588–1653), French humanist and philologist, first created this etymology. However, the derivation is no longer accepted. On *murcus*, see also Ammianus Marcellinus 15.12.3 – Ed.]

[10] *Marginal note in H*: On vigorous and softening affects (tears, which provoke laughter) – On shame and audacity.

Stout-hearted is he who does *not become frightened*; *courage* has he who in reflecting on danger does *not yield*; *brave* is he whose courage is *constant* in danger. *Foolhardy* is the reckless person who ventures into dangers because he does not recognize them. *Bold* is he who ventures into dangers although he is aware of them; *reckless*, he who places himself in the greatest danger at the obvious impossibility of achieving his end (like Charles XII at Bender).[11] The Turks call their brave men (who are perhaps brave through opium) *madmen*. – Cowardice is thus *dishonorable despair*.

Fright is not a *habitual* characteristic to be seized easily with fear, for this is called timidity; it is merely a *state* and accidental disposition, dependent for the most part merely on bodily causes, of feeling not prepared enough against a suddenly arising danger. When the unexpected approach of the enemy is announced to a commander who is in his dressing gown, this can easily stop the blood in the ventricles of the heart for an instant, and a certain general's physician noted that he was faint-hearted and timid when he had acid indigestion. *Stout-heartedness*, however, is merely a quality of temperament. *Courage*, on the other hand, rests on principles and is a virtue. Reason then gives the resolute man strength that nature sometimes denies him. Being frightened in battle [257] even produces salutary evacuations that have proverbially given rise to mockery (not having one's heart in the right place); but it has been noticed that those very sailors who at the call of combat hurry to their place of performance are afterward the most courageous in battle. The same thing has also been noted in the heron when the falcon hovers over him and he prepares himself for battle against it.

Accordingly, *patience* is not courage. Patience is a feminine virtue; for it does not muster the force for resistance, but hopes to make suffering (enduring) imperceptible through habit. He who *cries out* under the surgeon's knife or under the pain of gout or stone is therefore not cowardly or weak in this condition; his cry is like cursing when one is

---

The feeling through which nature strives to maintain itself in exactly the same condition is agreeable; however, that through which it is driven to go beyond it is unpleasant. That which is neither of the two is indifferent

> Anger belongs to the faculty of desire
> Anger is near *Hallucinatio*.
> Affects stimulate the circulation of the blood.

[11] Charles XII (1682–1718), King of Sweden, was defeated by the Russians. See Voltaire, *Histoire de Charles XII*. In Voltaire's entry on "Characters" in his *Dictionary*, he remarks: "Charles XII in his illness on the way to Bender was no longer the same man; he was tractable as a child."

out walking and bumps against a loose cobblestone (with one's big toe, from which the word *hallucinari* is derived)[12] – it is rather an outburst of anger in which nature endeavors to break up the constriction of blood in the heart through cries. – However, the Indians of America display a particular kind of patience: when they are encircled they throw away their weapons and, without begging for mercy, calmly let themselves be massacred. Now in doing this, do they show more courage than the Europeans, who in this situation defend themselves to the last man? To me it seems to be merely a barbaric conceit by means of which to preserve the honor of their tribe, so that their enemy could not force them to lament and groan as evidence of their submission.

However, courage as affect (consequently belonging in one respect to sensibility) can also be aroused by reason and thus be genuine bravery (strength of virtue).[13] If, in doing something worthy of honor, we do not allow ourselves to be intimidated by taunts and derisive ridicule of it, which is all the more dangerous when sharpened by wit, but instead pursue our own course steadfastly, we display a moral courage which many who show themselves as brave figures on the battlefield or in a duel do not possess. That is to say, to venture something that duty commands, even at the risk of being ridiculed by others, requires resoluteness, and even a high degree of courage; because *love of honor* is the constant companion of virtue, and he who is otherwise sufficiently prepared against *violence* seldom feels equal to ridicule if someone scornfully refuses this claim to honor.

[258] The propriety which presents an external semblance of courage, so that one does not compromise one's respect in comparing oneself to others, is called *audacity*; it is the opposite of *timidity*, a kind of shyness and concern not to appear favorably in the eyes of others. – As reasonable confidence in oneself, audacity cannot be reproached.[14] But the kind of

---

[12] Kant, following philologists of the time, derives the word "hallucinate" from the Latin *allex* (the big toe) instead of the Greek *alaomai* (to wander or roam about). This derivation is no longer accepted.

[13] See also Kant's discussion of virtue as fortitude in *The Metaphysics of Morals* 6: 380, as well as his remarks about bravery as moral strength at 6: 405.

[14] *Marginal note in H*: The grotesque, the *gout baroc*, the *a la Grec*, and the *arabesque* are all a false taste.

In all affects the mind is moved by means of *futura consequentia*. Fear is also in all of them. However, not the affects of anger or shame.

Courage, which belongs to virtue (the virtue of bravery), occurs not merely in physical dangers or in those who died for external honors, but also in those who instead risked a little of the ridicule

audacity[b] in propriety that gives someone the semblance of not caring about the judgment of others concerning himself is *impudence*, impertinence, or, in milder terms, immodesty; it thus does not belong to courage in the moral sense of the term.

Whether suicide also presupposes courage, or always despondency only, is not a moral question but merely a psychological one.[15] If it is committed merely in order not to outlive one's honor, therefore out of *anger*, then it appears to be courage; however, if it is due to exhaustion of patience in suffering as a result of *sadness*, which slowly exhausts all patience, then it is an act of *despair*. It seems to be a kind of heroism to the human being to look death straight in the eye and not fear it, when he can no longer love life. But if, although he fears death, he still cannot stop loving life in all circumstances, so that in order to proceed to suicide a mental disorder stemming from anguish must precede, then he dies of cowardice, because he can no longer bear the agonies of life. – To a certain extent the manner of execution of the suicide allows this distinction of mental state to be recognized. If the chosen means are sudden and fatal without possible rescue, as in, for example, a pistol shot or a strong dose of mercury chloride (as a great king carried with him in war, in case he should be taken prisoner),[16] or deep water with one's pockets full of stones, then we cannot contest the courage of the person who has committed suicide. However, if the chosen means are a rope that can still be cut by others, or an ordinary poison that can be removed from his body by the physician, or a slit in the throat that can be sewn up again and healed – attempts in which the subject, when he is saved, is himself normally happy and never attempts it again – then it is cowardly despair [259]

of others, and this is pure moral courage.
  Knight *Bayard Murcus*.

[b] This word should really be written *Dräustigkeit* (from *dräuen* or *drohen*), not *Dreistigkeit*; because the tone or expression of such a human being makes others fear that he could also be crude. In the same way we write *liederlich* for *lüderlich*, although the former signifies a careless, mischievous, but otherwise not useless, good-natured human being, whereas *lüderlich* signifies a depraved human being who disgusts everyone else (from the word *Luder*). [Neither of Kant's etymologies is accepted at present – Ed.]

[15] Kant does discuss suicide as a moral question elsewhere. See, e.g., *The Metaphysics of Morals* 6: 422–424 and *Collins Moralphilosophie* 27: 342, 346, 369–375, 391, 394, 1427–1428.

[16] I.e., Friedrich the Great (1712–1786), King of Prussia (1740–1786). Külpe refers readers to A. F. Büschling, *Charakter Friedrichs des zweyten*, 2nd ed. (1789), p. 431, where the author states that Frederick carried poison with him during the Seven Years War (1756–1763).

from weakness, not vigorous despair, which still requires a strong frame of mind for such an act.

It is not always just depraved, worthless souls who decide to rid themselves of the burden of life in this manner; on the contrary, we need not fear that such people, who have no feeling for true honor, will easily perform an act of this kind. – Although suicide will always remain horrible, and though by committing it the human being makes himself into a monster, still it is noteworthy that in times of public and legally declared injustice during a revolutionary state of affairs (for example, the Public Welfare Committee of the French Republic), honor-loving men (for example, Roland)[17] have sought to forestall execution by law through suicide, which in a constitutional state of affairs they themselves would have declared to be reprehensible. The reason for it is this: in every execution under a *law* there is something disgraceful, because it is *punishment*, and when the punishment is unjust, the man who falls victim to the law cannot acknowledge the punishment as one that is *deserved*. He proves it, however, owing to the fact that, having been doomed to death, he now prefers to choose death as a free human being and he inflicts it on *himself*. That is why tyrants (such as Nero) viewed it as a mark of favor to allow the condemned person to kill himself, because then it happened with more honor.[18] – – However, I do not desire to defend the morality of this.

The courage of the warrior is still quite different from that of the duellist, even if the government takes an indulgent view of *duelling*, though without making it publicly permissible by law, and the army makes it a matter of honor as, so to speak, self-defense against insult, in

---

[17] Jean Marie Roland de la Platière (1734–1793), French revolutionary. Roland rose to power with the Girondists and became minister of the interior in 1792. King Louis XVI dismissed him in July, 1792, but he was restored to office after the overthrow of the monarchy in August, 1792. Accused of royalism in 1793, he resigned and fled Paris. When he learned that his wife (Jeanne Manon Phlipon Roland de la Platière, also a well-known French revolutionary and Girondist) had been executed, he committed suicide on November 15, 1793 by falling upon his sword and piercing his heart.

[18] *Marginal note in H*: Thirst for revenge (faculty of desire) is a weakness

Whether he who pales or blushes from anger is more dangerous?

One can also have a moral love of enjoyment as well as one of benevolence. However, the former can become enthusiastic. (Love of benevolence.) Affect of morality.

On the quantity of enthusiasm in religion, which, the higher it rises, the more it is purified of the sensible ... in what is moral.

which the commander-in-chief does not interfere. – In adopting the terrible principle of winking at the duel, the head of state has not reflected on it properly; for there are also worthless people who risk their lives in order to count for something, and those who put their own life on the line for the preservation of the state are not at all meant here.

Bravery is courage *in conformity with law*; the courage, in doing what duty commands, not to shrink even from the loss of life. Fearlessness alone is of no consequence; rather, it must be joined with moral irreproachability (*mens conscia recti*), as in Sir Bayard (*chevalier sans peur et sans reproche*).[19]

On affects that weaken themselves with respect to their end (*impotentes animi motus*)[20]

[260]

§78

The affects of anger and shame have the peculiarity that they weaken themselves with respect to their end. They are suddenly aroused feelings of an evil[21] in the form of an insult; however, because of their intensity they are at the same time unable to avert the evil.

Who is more to be feared, he who *turns pale* in intense anger, or he who *turns red* in this situation? The first is to be feared immediately; the second is all the more to be feared later (on account of his vindictiveness). In the first case, the disconcerted person is frightened of himself; frightened that he will be carried away by the intensity of his use of violence, which he might later regret. In the second case fright suddenly changes into fear that his consciousness of his inability to defend himself might become *visible*. – Neither affect is detrimental to health if people are able to give vent to anger through the quick composure of the mind; but where this is not possible, then in part they are dangerous to life itself or, when their outbreak is restrained, in part they bequeath a rancor, that is, a mortification at not having responded in the proper way to an insult. Such rancor, however, is avoided if people can only have a chance to express the affects in words. But both affects are of the kind that make

---

[19] Translation of Latin: a mind that knows what is right. Translation of French: the knight without fear or blame. Pierre Terrail, seigneur de Bayard (c. 1474–1524), French military hero, exhibited bravery and genius as a commander in the Italian Wars, and died in the battle of Sesia.
[20] Trans.: The disabled movements of the mind. [21] *ein Übel*.

159

people speechless, and for this reason they present themselves in an unfavorable light.

It is true that *hot temper* can be diminished through inner discipline of the mind; but the weakness of an extremely delicate feeling of honor that manifests itself in shame does not allow itself to be removed so easily. For as Hume says[22] (who himself was affected by this weakness – shyness about speaking in public), if the first attempt at audacity fails, it only makes us more timid; and there is no other remedy but to start our intercourse with people whose judgment concerning propriety matters little to us, and gradually[23] get away from the supposed importance of the judgment of others concerning us, and in this way inwardly to consider ourselves on an equal footing with them. The habit here produces *candor*, which is equally far removed from *shyness* and insulting *audacity*.

[261] We sympathize with another person's *shame* in so far as it is painful to him, but we do not sympathize with his *anger* if he *tells* us with the affect of anger what provoked his anger; for while he is in such a state, the one who listens to his story (of an insult suffered) is himself not safe.[24]

Surprise (confusion at finding oneself in an unexpected situation) at first impedes the natural play of thought and is therefore unpleasant; but later it promotes the influx of thought to the unexpected representation all the more and thus becomes an agreeable excitement of feeling. However, this affect is properly called *astonishment* only if we are thereby quite uncertain whether the perception takes place when we are awake or dreaming. A newcomer in the world is surprised at everything; but he who has become acquainted with the course of things through varied experience makes it a principle to be surprised at nothing (*nihil admirari*). On the other hand, he who thoughtfully and with a scrutinizing eye pursues the order of nature in its great variety falls into *astonishment* at a wisdom he did not expect: an admiration from which he cannot tear himself away (he cannot be surprised enough). However, such an affect is stimulated only by reason, and is a kind of sacred awe at seeing the abyss of the supersensible opening before one's feet.

---

[22] "Of Impudence and Modesty," in *Essays, Moral, Political, and Literary*, ed. Eugene F. Miller (Indianapolis: Liberty Press, 1987), pp. 553f.

[23] *Crossed out in H*: gradually [to progress in dealings with him whose judgment is more significant, and thus further up to that of the most important person's more candid display of himself, which belongs to complete education. toward].

[24] *Marginal note in H*: *ob futura consequentia* [trans.: on account of what the consequences will be].

On the affects by which nature promotes health mechanically

§79

Health is promoted mechanically by nature through several affects. *Laughing* and *crying* in particular belong here. Anger is also a fairly reliable aid to digestion, if one can scold freely (without fear of resistance), and many a housewife has no other emotional exercise[25] than the scolding of her children and servants. Now if the children and servants only submit patiently to it, an agreeable tiredness of the vital force spreads itself uniformly through her body;[26] however, this remedy is also not without its dangers, since she fears resistance by these members of the household.

Good-natured *laughing* (not malicious laughing combined with bitterness) is on the other hand more popular and more fruitful: namely the kind of laughter that someone should have recommended to the Persian king who offered a prize to anyone "who would invent a new pleasure." – [262] The jerky (nearly convulsive) exhaling of air attached to laughter (of which sneezing is only a small but enlivening effect, if its sound is allowed to go unrestrained) strengthens the feeling of vital force through the wholesome exercise of the diaphragm. It may be a hired jester (harlequin) who makes us laugh, or a sly wit belonging to our circle of friends, a wag who seems to have no mischief in mind and does not join in the laughter, but with seeming simplicity suddenly releases a tense anticipation (like a taut string). The resulting laughter is always a shaking of the muscles involved in digestion, which promotes it far better than the physician's wisdom would do. Even a great absurdity of mistaken judgment can produce exactly the same effect, though at the expense of the allegedly cleverer man.[c]

---

[25] *keine andere innigliche Motion.*   [26] *durch die Maschine.*

[c] Many examples of this latter point could be given. But I shall cite only one, which I heard from the lips of the late Countess of K – g, a lady who was a credit to her sex [Countess Charlotte Amalie von Keyserling (1729–1791). Kant was a frequent dinner guest at her estate – Ed.]. Count *Sagramoso*, who had been commissioned to establish the Order of the Knights of Malta in Poland (of Ostrogothic appointment), visited her, and by chance a schoolmaster appeared on the scene who was a native of Königsberg and was visiting his relatives in Prussia, but who had been brought to Hamburg as organizer and curator of the natural history collection that some rich merchants kept as their hobby. In order to talk to him about something, the Count spoke in broken

161

Weeping, an inhaling that occurs with (convulsive) sobs, when it is combined with an outburst of tears, is, as a soothing remedy, likewise a provision of nature for health; and a widow who, as one says, refuses to allow herself to be comforted – that is, who does not want the flow of tears to be stopped – is taking care of her health without knowing it or really wanting to. Anger, which might arise in this situation, would quickly check the flood of tears, but to her detriment; although not only sadness but also anger can bring women and children to tears. –

[263] For *their feeling of powerlessness* against an evil, together with a strong affect (be it anger or sadness), calls upon the assistance of external natural signs which then (according to the right of the weaker) at least disarm a masculine soul. However, this expression of tenderness, as a weakness of the sex, must not move the sympathetic *man* to shedding tears, though it may well bring tears to his eyes; for in the first case he would violate his own sex and thus with his femininity not be able to serve as protector for the weaker sex, and in the second case he would not show the sympathy toward the other sex that his masculinity makes his duty – the duty, namely, of taking the other sex under his protection as befits the character that books of chivalry attribute to the brave man, which consists precisely in this protection.

But why do young people prefer *tragic drama* and also prefer to perform it when they want to give their parents a treat; whereas old people prefer *comedy*, even burlesque? The reason for the former is in part exactly the same as the one that moves children to risk danger: presumably, by an instinct of nature to test their powers. But it is also partly because, given the frivolity of youth, no melancholy is left over from the distressing and terrifying impressions the moment the play has ended, but rather there is only a pleasant tiredness after vigorous

---

German: "*Ick abe in Amberg eine Ant geabt (ich habe in Hamburg eine Tante gehabt); aber die ist mir gestorben*" [I have an aunt in Hamburg; but she is dead – Ed.] The schoolmaster immediately pounced on the word *Ant* and asked: "Why didn't you have her skinned and stuffed?" He took the English word *aunt*, which means *Tante*, for *Ente* [duck – Ed.] and, because it occurred to him that it must have been a very rare specimen, deplored the great loss. One can imagine what laughter this misunderstanding must have caused.

Marginal note in H: I refrain here from examples, but xx.

Deep sigh.

Sagramoso

3. the hieroglyphic, mysterious, intimating (*a la Grecque*)

4. that which is seen in a dream (*arabesque*), both of them at the edges.

internal exercise, which puts them once again in a cheerful mood. On the other hand, with old people these impressions are not so easily blotted out, and they cannot bring back the cheerful mood in themselves so easily. By his antics a nimble-witted harlequin produces a beneficial shaking of their diaphragm and intestines, by which their appetite for the ensuing social supper is whetted, and thrives as a result of the lively conversation.[27]

General remark

Certain internal physical feelings are *related* to the affects, but they are not themselves affects because they are only momentary, transitory, and leave no trace of themselves behind: the *shuddering* that comes over children when they listen at night to their nurses' ghost stories is like this. – *Shivering*, as if one were being doused with cold water (as in a rainstorm), also belongs here. Not the perception of danger, but the mere thought of danger – though one knows that none is present – produces [264] this sensation, which, when it is merely a moment of fright and not an outbreak of it, seems not to be disagreeable.

Dizziness and even *seasickness*[28] seem to belong, according to their cause, to the class of such imaginary dangers.[29] One can advance without tottering on a board that is lying on the ground; but if it lies over an abyss or, for someone with weak nerves, merely over a ditch, then the empty apprehension of danger often becomes really dangerous. The rolling of a ship even in a mild wind is an alternate sinking and being lifted up. With the sinking there occurs the effort of nature to raise itself (because all sinking generally carries the representation of danger with it); consequently the up and down movement of the stomach and intestines is connected mechanically with an impulse to vomit, which is then intensified when the patient looks out of the cabin window, catching alternate glimpses of the sky and the sea, whereby the illusion that the seat is giving way under him is even further heightened.

---

[27] *Marginal note in H*: Striking, the remarkable, what puzzles, what excites the attention as unexpected and in which one cannot immediately find oneself, is an inhibition with an outpouring following thereafter.

[28] See also Kant's footnote at the beginning of §29, where he refers to his own experience with seasickness.

[29] *ideale Gefahren*.

An actor who is himself unmoved, but otherwise possesses understanding and a strong faculty of the power of imagination, can often stir others more by an affected (artificial) affect than by the real one. In the presence of his beloved, a serious lover is embarrassed, awkward, and not very captivating. But a man who merely *pretends* to be in love and has talent can play his role so naturally that he gets the poor deceived girl completely into his trap, just because his heart is unaffected and his head is clear; consequently he is in full possession of the free use of his skill and power to imitate the appearance of a lover very naturally.

Good-natured (openhearted) laughter is *sociable* (in so far as it belongs to the affect of cheerfulness); malicious (sneering) laughter is *hostile*. The distracted person (like Terrasson[30] entering solemnly with his night cap instead of his wig on his head and his hat under his arm, full of the quarrel concerning the superiority of the ancients and the moderns with respect to the sciences), often gives rise to the first type of laughter; he is *laughed at*, but still not *ridiculed*. We smile at the intelligent *eccentric*, but it doesn't cost him anything; he joins in the laughter. – A mechanical (spiritless) laugher is insipid and makes the social gathering tasteless. He who never laughs at all at a social gathering is either sullen or [265] pedantic. Children, especially girls, must be accustomed early to frank and unrestrained smiling, because the cheerfulness of their facial features gradually leaves a mark within and establishes a *disposition* to cheerfulness, friendliness, and sociability, which is an early preparation for this approximation to the virtue of benevolence.

A good-natured and at the same time cultivated way of stimulating a social gathering is to have someone in it as the butt of our wit (to pull his leg) without being caustic (to mock him without being offensive), provided that he is prepared to reply in kind with his own wit, thus bringing a cheerful laughter into the group. But if this happens at the expense of a simpleton whom one tosses to another like a ball, then the laughter is unrefined, to put it mildly, because it is gloating over his misfortune; and if it happens to a parasite who for the sake of revelry abandons himself to the mischievous game or allows himself to be made

---

[30] Abbé Jean Terrasson (1670–1750), French author. Brandt locates the anecdote in Johann Christoph Gottsched, ed., *Des Abbts Terrassons Philosophie, nach ihrem allgemeine Einflusse, auf alle Gegenstände des Geistes und der Sitten* (1756), pp. 45–46. Kant mentions Terrasson in a variety of texts – see, e.g., *Friedländer* 25: 540, *Collins* 25: 27, 136, *Parow* 25: 344, *Mrongovius* 25: 1350, *Critique of Pure Reason* Axix, *Essay on the Diseases of the Head* 2: 269.

a fool of, then it is a proof of bad taste as well as obtuse moral feeling on the part of those who can burst out laughing about this. However, the position of a court jester, whose function is to tease the king's distinguished servants and thus season the meal through laughter for the sake of the beneficial shaking of his diaphragm, is, depending on how one takes it, *above* or *below* all criticism.

On the passions

§80

The subjective *possibility* of the emergence of a certain desire, which *precedes* the representation of its object, is *propensity* (*propensio*); – the inner *necessitation* of the faculty of desire to take possession of this object before one even knows it is *instinct* (like the sexual instinct, or the parental instinct of the animal to protect its young, and so forth). – A sensible desire that serves the subject as a rule (habit) is called *inclination* (*inclinatio*). – Inclination that prevents reason from comparing it with the sum of all inclinations in respect to a certain choice is *passion* (*passio animi*).

Since passions can be paired with the calmest reflection, it is easy to see that they are not thoughtless, like affects, or stormy and transitory; rather, they take root and can even co-exist with rationalizing. – It is also easy to see that they do the greatest damage to freedom, and if affect is *drunkenness*, then passion is an *illness* that abhors all medicine, and it is [266] therefore far worse than all those transitory emotions[31] that at least stir up the resolution to be better; instead, passion is an enchantment that also refuses recuperation.

One uses the term *mania* to designate passion (mania for honor, revenge, dominance, and so on), except for the passion of love, when it is not a case of *being in love*. The reason is that once the latter desire has been satisfied (by enjoyment), the desire, at least with regard to the very person involved, also stops. So one can list being passionately in love [among the passions] (as long as the other party persists in refusal), but one cannot list any physical love as passion, because it does not contain a *constant* principle with respect to its object. Passion always presupposes

---

[31] *vorübergehende Gemüthsbewegungen.*

165

a maxim on the part of the subject, to act according to an end prescribed to him by his inclination. Passion is therefore always connected with his reason, and one can no more attribute passion to mere animals than to pure rational beings. The manias for honor, revenge, and so forth, just because they are never completely satisfied, are therefore counted among the passions as illnesses for which there is only a palliative remedy.

§81

Passions are cancerous sores for pure practical reason, and for the most part they are incurable because the sick person does not want to be cured and flees from the dominion of principles, by which alone a cure could occur. In the sensibly practical too, reason goes from the general to the particular according to the principle: not to please one inclination by placing all the rest in the shade or in a dark corner, but rather to see to it that it can exist together with the totality of *all* inclinations. – The *ambition* of a human being may always be an inclination whose direction is approved by reason; but the ambitious person nevertheless also wants to be loved by others; he needs pleasant social intercourse with others, the maintenance of his financial position, and the like. However, if he is a *passionately* ambitious person, then he is blind to these ends, though his inclinations still summon him to them, and he overlooks completely the risk he is running that he will be hated by others, or avoided in social intercourse, or impoverished through his expenditures. It is folly (making *part* of one's end the *whole*) which directly contradicts the formal principle of reason itself.

[267] That is why passions are not, like affects, merely *unfortunate* states of mind full of many ills, but are without exception *evil* as well. And the most good-natured desire, even when it aims at what (according to matter) belongs to virtue, for example, beneficence, is still (according to form) not merely *pragmatically* ruinous but also *morally* reprehensible, as soon as it turns into passion.

Affect does a momentary damage to freedom and dominion over oneself. Passion abandons them and finds its pleasure and satisfaction in a slavish mind. But because reason still does not ease off with its summons to inner freedom, the unhappy man groans in his chains, which he nevertheless cannot break away from because they have already grown together with his limbs, so to speak.

166

Nevertheless, the passions have also found their eulogists[32] (for where are they not found, once maliciousness has taken its seat among principles?), and it is said that "nothing great has ever been accomplished in the world without intense passions, and that Providence itself has wisely planted passions in human nature just like elastic springs."[33] – Concerning the many *inclinations*, it may readily be admitted that those of a natural and animal need are ones that living nature (even that of the human being) cannot do without. But Providence has not willed that inclinations might, indeed even should, become *passions*. And while we may excuse a poet for presenting them from this point of view (that is, for saying with Pope:[34] "If reason is a magnet, then the passions are the wind"), the philosopher must not accept this principle, not even in order to praise the passions as a provisional arrangement of Providence, which would have intentionally placed them in human nature until the human race had reached the proper degree of culture.

Division of the passions

The[35] passions are divided into passions of *natural* (innate) inclination and passions of inclination that result from human *culture* (acquired).

The passions of the **first** kind are the *inclinations of freedom and sex*, [268] both of which are connected with affect. Those of the **second** kind are the *manias for honor, dominance*, and *possession*, which are not connected with the impetuosity of an affect but with the persistence of a maxim established for certain ends. The former can be called *inflamed* passions (*passiones ardentes*); the latter, like avarice, *cold* passions (*frigidae*). All passions, however, are always only desires directed by human beings to human beings, not to things; and while we can indeed have great inclination toward the utilization of a fertile field or a productive cow,

---

[32] Külpe conjectures that Kant has Helvétius in mind – see *De l'esprit* III.6–8.

[33] *Springfedern.* The source of the remark is not known. See also *Essay on the Diseases of the Head* 2: 267.

[34] Alexander Pope (1688–1744), *Essay on Man*, Epistle 2, line 108: "Reason the card, but Passion is the gale." Kant probably used Brockes's German translation (1740) for this quotation.

[35] *Crossed out in H*: The [are according to the chief classification A.) those of external *freedom*, therefore a passion of negative enjoyment, B. those of *capacity*, therefore passion of positive enjoyment either a.) of the <physically> real concerning the senses or b.) of the ideal in mere possession of the means to this or that enjoyment.]

we can have no *affection* for them (which consists in the inclination toward *community* with others), much less a passion.

A On the inclination to freedom as a passion

§82

For the natural human being this is the most violent[36] inclination of all, in a condition where he cannot avoid making reciprocal claims on others.

Whoever is able to be happy only according to *another* person's choice (no matter how benevolent this other person may be) rightly feels that he is unhappy. For what guarantee has he that his powerful fellow human being's judgment about his well-being will agree with his own? The savage (not yet habituated to submission) knows no greater misfortune than to have this befall him, and rightly so, as long as no public law protects him until the time when discipline has gradually made him patient in submission. Hence his state of continuous warfare, by which he intends to keep others as far away from him as possible and to live scattered in the wilderness. Even the child who has just wrenched itself from the mother's womb seems to enter the world with loud cries, unlike all other animals, simply because it regards the inability to make use of its limbs as *constraint*, and thus it immediately announces its claim to freedom (a representation that no other animal has).[d] – Nomadic peoples, for

---

[36] Natural human being: *Naturmensch*; most violent: *heftigste*.

[d] *Lucretius*, as a poet, interprets this indeed remarkable phenomenon in the animal kingdom differently:

> *Vagituque locum lugubri complet, ut aequumst*
> *Cui tantum in vita restet transire malorum!*
> [Trans.: And fills the air with lamenting cries
> As it befits someone who still has to go through so much evil in his life.
> *De rerum natura* 5.227f. – Ed.]

[269] Now the newborn child certainly cannot have this perspective; but the fact that his feeling of uncomfortableness is not due to bodily pain but to an obscure idea (or a representation analogous to it) of freedom and its hindrance, *injustice*, is disclosed a few months later after the birth by the *tears* which accompany his screaming; they indicate a kind of exasperation when he strives to approach certain objects or in general merely strives to change his position and feels himself hindered in it. – This impulse to have his own way and to take any obstacle to it as an affront is marked particularly by his tone, and manifests a maliciousness that the mother finds necessary to punish, but he usually replies with still louder shrieking. The same thing happens when the child falls through his own fault. The young of other animals play, those of the human being quarrel early with each other, and it is as if a certain concept of justice (which relates to external freedom) develops along with their animality, and is not something to be learned gradually.

example, the Arabs, since they (like pastoral peoples) are not attached [269] to any land, cling so strongly to their way of life, even though it is not entirely free of constraint, and moreover they are so high-spirited, that they look with contempt on *settled* peoples, and the hardship that is inseparable from their way of life has not been able to dissuade them from it over thousands of years. Mere hunting peoples (like the *Olenni-Tungusi*)[37] have really ennobled themselves by this feeling of freedom (which has separated them from other tribes related to them). – Thus it is not only the concept of freedom under moral laws that arouses an affect, which is called enthusiasm,[38] but the mere sensible representation of outer freedom heightens the inclination to persist in it or to extend it into a violent passion, by analogy with the concept of right.

With mere animals, even the most violent inclination (for example, the inclination to sexual union) is not called passion: because they have no reason, which alone establishes the concept of freedom and with which passion comes into collision. Accordingly, the outbreak of passion can be attributed to the human being. – It is said of human beings that they love certain things *passionately* (drinking, gambling, hunting) or hate them passionately (for example, musk or brandy). But one does not exactly call these various inclinations or disinclinations so many passions, because they are[39] only so many different instincts; that is, only so many different states of *mere passivity* in the faculty of desire, and they deserve to be classified, not according to the objects of the faculty of desire as *things* (which are innumerable), but rather according to the principle of the use [270] or abuse that human beings make of their person and of their freedom under each other, when one human being makes another a mere means to his ends. – Passions actually are directed only to human beings and can also only be satisfied by them.

---

[37] A Siberian ethnic group. See also *Lectures on Physical Geography* 9: 401–402.

[38] *Enthusiasm. Crossed out in H*: passion B The inclination toward possession of the capacity in general without using it is also passion. [One can love or hate something passionately, but merely through instinct, where understanding adds nothing, as with physical love of sex (*physische Liebe des Geschlechts*); but then the inclination is directed not to the species of the object but merely to the individual <instead>, and cannot be considered passion according to type and objective, but is merely called subjective inclination. – On the other hand, if the inclination is directed merely to the means and possession of the same toward satisfaction of all inclinations in general, therefore toward mere capacity, it can only be called a passion.]

[39] *Crossed out in H*: are [and only concern the feeling of pleasure and displeasure directly, on the other hand under passion, where the things required].

These passions are the *manias for honor, for dominance*, and *for possession*.

Since passions are inclinations that aim merely at the possession of the means for satisfying all inclinations which are concerned directly with the end, they have, in this respect, the appearance of reason; that is, they aspire to the idea of a faculty connected with freedom, by which alone ends in general can be attained. Possessing the means to *whatever* aims one chooses certainly extends much further than the inclination directed to one single inclination and its satisfaction. – Therefore they can also be called inclinations of delusion, which delusion consists in valuing the mere opinion of others regarding the worth of things as equal to their real worth.[40]

B On the desire for vengeance as a passion

§83

Passions can only be inclinations directed by human beings to human beings, in so far as they are directed to ends that harmonize or conflict with one another, that is, in so far as they are love or hatred. But the concept of right, because it follows directly from the concept of outer freedom, is a much more important and strongly moving impulse to the will than benevolence. So hatred arising from an injustice we have suffered, that is, the *desire for vengeance*, is a passion that follows irresistibly from the nature of the human being, and, malicious as it may be, maxims of reason are nevertheless interwoven with the inclination by virtue of the permissible *desire for justice*, whose analogue it is. This is why the desire for vengeance is one of the most violent and deeply rooted

---

[40] *Marginal note in H:* The capacity to use the power of others for one's purposes
Crossed out in H: worth. Division of the Passions

§30

Passions are inclinations directed by human beings only to human beings, not to things, and even if the inclination to human beings fades away, not in so far as they are considered persons but merely as animal beings of the same species, in the inclination to sex, love to be sure can be passionate, but actually cannot be named a passion, because the latter presupposes maxims (not mere instinct) in proceedings with human beings.

Freedom, law (of justice), and *capacity* (for carrying out) are not mere conditions, but also objects of a faculty of desire of the human being extended to passion, whereby practical reason underlies the inclination, since it proceeds according to maxims.

passions; even when it seems to have disappeared, a secret hatred, called *rancor*, is always left over, like a fire smoldering under the ashes.[41]

The *desire* to be in a state and relation with one's fellow human beings such that each can have the share that justice allots him is certainly no passion, but only a determining ground of free choice through pure [271] practical reason. But the *excitability* of this desire through mere self-love, that is, just for one's own advantage, not for the purpose of legislation for everyone, is the sensible impulse of hatred, hatred not of injustice, but rather against *him who is unjust* to us. Since this inclination (to pursue and destroy) is based on an idea, although admittedly the idea is applied selfishly, it transforms the desire for justice against the offender into the passion for retaliation, which is often violent to the point of madness, leading a man to expose himself to ruin if only his enemy does not escape it, and (in blood vengeance) making this hatred hereditary even between tribes, because, it is said, the blood of someone offended but not yet avenged *cries out* until the innocently spilled blood has once again been washed away with blood – even if this blood should be one of the offending man's innocent descendants.

C On the inclination toward the capacity of having influence
in general over other human beings

§84

This inclination comes closest to technically practical reason, that is, to the maxim of prudence. – For getting other human beings' inclinations into one's power, so that one can direct and determine them according to one's intentions, is almost the same as *possessing* others as mere tools of one's will. No wonder that the striving after such a *capacity* becomes a passion.

---

[41] *Marginal note in H*: Passion is the receptivity of the inner compulsion of a human being through his own inclination in adherence to his ends.

To be sure, passions therefore presuppose a sensible but nevertheless also a counteracting rational faculty of desire (they are therefore not applicable to mere animals), except that inclination in the former takes away pure practical reason, in the latter domination, taking possession of maxims in respect to either one's ends or the use of means toward them. To love or hate passionately. Unnaturalness and vindictiveness.

All passions are directed by human beings only to human beings, in order to use them for one's purposes or also in . . .

This capacity contains as it were a threefold power in itself: *honor*, *authority*, and *money*, through which, if one is in possession of them, one can get to every human being and use him according to his purposes, if not by means of one of these influences, then by means of another. – The inclinations for this, if they become passions, are the *manias for honor, for domination*, and *for possession*. It is true that here the human being becomes the dupe (the deceived) of his own inclinations, and in his use of such means he misses his final end; but here we are not speaking of *wisdom*, which admits of no passions at all, but only of *prudence*, by which one can manage fools.

[272] However, the passions in general, as violent as they may be as sensible incentives, are still sheer *weaknesses* in view of what reason prescribes to the human being.[42] Therefore the clever man's capacity to use the passions for his purposes may be proportionately smaller, the greater the passion is that dominates other human beings.

Mania for honor is the weakness of human beings which enables a person to have influence on them through their *opinion*; *mania for domination*, through their *fear*; and *mania for possession*, through their own *interest*. – Each is a slavish disposition by means of which another person, when he has taken possession of it, has the capacity to use a person's own inclinations for his purposes. – But consciousness of having this capacity and of possessing the means to satisfy one's inclinations stimulates the passion even more than actually using it does.

a The mania for honor

§85

Mania for honor is not *love of honor*, an esteem that the human being is permitted to expect from others because of his inner (moral) worth; rather it is striving after the *reputation of honor*, where semblance[43] suffices. Here arrogance is permitted (an unjustified demand that others think little of themselves in comparison with us, a foolishness that acts contrary to its own end) – this arrogance, I say, needs only to be *flattered*, and one already has control over the fool by means of this passion.

---

[42] *Marginal note in H*: The capacity in itself, the possession of the means increases more the passion than the use of it: it is agreeable for oneself.

[43] *Schein*.

Flatterers,[e] the yes–men who gladly concede high–sounding talk to an important man, nourish this passion that makes him weak, and are the ruin of the great and powerful who abandon themselves to this spell.

Arrogance is an inappropriate desire for honor that acts contrary to its own end, and cannot be regarded as an intentional means of using other human beings (whom it repels) for one's ends; rather the arrogant man is an instrument of rogues, and is called a fool. Once a very intelligent and upright merchant asked me: "Why is the arrogant person always base as well?" (He had known from experience that the man who boasted with his wealth as a superior commercial power later, upon the decline of his fortune, did not hesitate to grovel.) My opinion was this: that, since arrogance is the unjustified demand on another person that he *despise* himself in comparison to others, such a thought cannot enter the head of anyone except one who feels ready to debase himself, and that arrogance itself already supplies a never-deceiving, foreboding sign of the baseness of such human beings.[44] [273]

b The mania for domination

This passion is intrinsically unjust, and its manifestation summons everything against it. It starts, however, from the fear of being dominated by others, and is then soon intent on placing the advantage of force over them, which is nevertheless a precarious and unjust means of using other human beings for one's own purposes: in part it is *imprudent* because it arouses opposition, and in part it is *unjust* because it is contrary to freedom under law, to which everyone can lay claim. – As concerns the *indirect* art of domination, for example, that of the female sex by means of love which she inspires in the male sex, in order to use him for her purposes, it is not included under this title; for it does not employ force, but knows how to dominate and bind its subject through his own inclination. – Not that the female part of our species is free from the

---

[e] The word *Schmeichler* [flatterer – Ed.] was originally supposed to be *Schmiegler* (one who bows and scrapes before people), in order to lead at will a conceited, powerful person through his arrogance; just as the word *Heuchler* [hypocrite – Ed.] (actually it should be written *Häuchler* [breather – Ed.] should have designated a deceiver who feigns his *false humility* before a powerful clergyman by means of *deep sighs* mixed with his speech. [*Marginal note in H*: Arrogance is base bowing and scraping. Valiant passion.]

[44] See also Kant's discussion of arrogance and "pride proper" (*animus elatus*) in *The Metaphysics of Morals* 6: 465–466.

173

inclination to dominate the male part (exactly the opposite is true), but it does not use the same *means* for this purpose as the male part, that is, it does not use the advantage of *strength* (which is here what is meant by the word *dominate*); but rather the advantage of *charm*, which comprehends an inclination of the other part to be dominated.

[274] *c The mania for possession*

Money is the solution, and all doors that are closed to the man of lesser wealth open to him whom Plutus favors. The invention of this means, which does not have (or at least should not have) any use other than that of serving merely as a means for the exchange of human beings' industry, and with it, however, everything that is also physically good among them, has, especially after it was represented by metal, brought forth a mania for possession which finally, even without enjoyment in the mere possession, and even with the renunciation (of the miser) of making any use of it, contains a power that people believe satisfactorily replaces the lack of every other power. This passion is, if not always morally reprehensible, completely banal,[45] is cultivated merely mechanically, and is attached especially to old people (as a substitute for their natural incapacity). On account of the great influence of this universal means of exchange it has also secured the name of a *faculty*[46] purely and simply, and it is a passion such that, once it has set in, no modification is possible. And if the first of the three passions makes one *hated*, the second makes one *feared*, and the third makes one *despised*.[f]

---

[45] *ganz geistlos.*

[46] *Vermögen.* This word can also mean fortune, means, wealth, substance. Kant may be playing on these multiple meanings here.

[f] Contempt is here to be understood in a moral sense; for in a civil sense, if it turns out to be true, as Pope says, that "the devil, in a golden rain of fifty to a hundred falls into the lap of the usurer and takes possession of his soul," the masses on the contrary *admire* the man who shows such great business acumen. [See Pope, *Moral Essays* (3), "Of the Uses of Riches," lines 369–374, in *The Poetical Works* (New York: Worthington, 1884), p. 252 – Ed.]

Crossed out in H: despised [Division On the <formal> natural inclinations (of propensity) that are incurred in comparison with the <material inclinations (of impulse)> (those of habituation and imitation)] Division On formal inclination in the <use> play of vital power in general.

They are 1. inclination to enjoyment in general, 2. to occupation in general, 3. to leisureliness.

a. Because I abstract here from the object of desire (of matter), the aversion of nature to an *emptiness* in the feeling of its existence, that is, *boredom*, is by itself enough of an impulse for every cultivated human being to fill up this emptiness. – The desire for continuous enjoyment, be it physical or even aesthetic (where it is called luxury), is a luxurious living which is at the

174

On the inclination of delusion as a passion

§86

By delusion, as an incentive of desires, I understand the inner practical illusion of taking what is subjective in the motivating cause for objective. – From time to time nature wants the stronger stimulations of passion in order to regenerate the activity of the human being, so that he does not lose the feeling of life completely in mere *enjoyment*. To this end it has very wisely and beneficently simulated objects for the naturally lazy human being, which according to his imagination are real ends (ways of acquiring honor, control, and money). These objects give the person who is reluctant to undertake any *work*[47] enough *to keep him occupied* and *busy* [275] *doing nothing*, so that the interest which he takes in them is an interest of mere delusion. And nature therefore really is playing with the human being and spurring him (the subject) to its ends; while he stands convinced (objectively) that he has set his own end. – These inclinations of delusion, just because fantasy is a self-creator in them, are apt to become *passionate* in the highest degree, especially when they are applied to *competition* among human beings.

The games of the boy in hitting a ball, wrestling, running, playing soldier; later on the games of the man in playing chess and cards (where in the first activity the mere advantage of the understanding is intended, in the second also plain profit); finally, the games of the citizen, who tries his luck in public gatherings with faro or dice – taken together, they are unknowingly the spurs of a wiser nature to daring deeds, to test human beings' powers in competition with others; actually so that their vital

same time an erosion of life, where one becomes hungrier the more one enjoys. (n. This is true also of the aimless mania for reading.)

   b. *Occupation* during *leisure*, which is therefore not called business but *play*, and which aims at victory in conflict with others, contains an incentive to maximal stimulation of inclinations; even if this does not aim at acquisition (without interested intention). However, in *gambling* this is often intensified into the most violent passion; while [the refinement of qualities of intercourse is pretended calmness and even polite behavior in order skillfully to hide the inner raging fury. And the ruined person tries to put on a good face while he is taken advantage of.

     It is not so easy to explain why games of chance exert such a strong fascination among civilized and uncivilized peoples (Chinese and American savages). However, it is even more difficult to explain it as a way to maintain social intercourse, or indeed to explain how it is valued as promoting humanity. – People with unclear concepts: hunters, fishermen, perhaps also sailors, are first and foremost common lottery players and are on the whole superstitious.]

[47] *Geschäft.*

force in general is preserved from weakening and kept active. Two such contestants believe that they are playing with each other; in fact, however, nature plays with both of them – which reason can clearly convince them about, if they consider how badly the means chosen by them suit their end. – But the well-being they feel while stimulated in this way, because it is closely related to ideas of illusion (though ill-construed), is for this very reason the cause of a propensity to the most violent and long-lasting passion.[g]

Inclinations of illusion make weak human beings superstitious and superstitious human beings weak, that is, inclined to expect interesting results from circumstances that cannot be *natural causes* (something to fear or hope for). Hunters, fishermen, gamblers too (especially in lotteries) are superstitious, and the illusion that leads to the *delusion* of taking the subjective for the objective, the voice of inner sense for knowledge of the thing itself, also makes the propensity to superstition comprehensible.

[276]

On the highest physical good

§87

The greatest sensuous enjoyment, which is not accompanied by any admixture of loathing at all, is *resting after work*, when one is in a healthy state. – In this state, the propensity to rest without having first worked is *laziness*. – Nevertheless, a somewhat long refusal to go back again to one's *business*, and the sweet *far niente*[48] for the purpose of collecting one's powers, is not yet laziness; for (even in play) one can be *occupied* agreeably and usefully at the same time, and even changing the type of work according to its specific nature is a varied recreation. On the other hand, it takes considerable determination to return to a piece of hard work that has been left unfinished.

Among the three vices: *laziness*, *cowardice*, and *duplicity*, the first appears to be the most contemptible. But in this judging of laziness,

---

[g] A man in Hamburg, who had gambled away his fortune there, now spent his time watching the players. Someone asked him how he felt when he remembered that he once had such a fortune. The man replied: "If I had it again, I would still not know how to use it in a more agreeable way."

[48] Trans.: doing nothing.

176

one can often do much wrong to a human being. For nature has also wisely placed the aversion to continuous work in many a subject, an instinct that is beneficial both to the subject and to others, because, for example, man cannot stand any prolonged or frequently repeated expenditure of power without exhaustion, but needs certain pauses for recreation. Not without reason *Demetrius*[49] therefore also could have allotted an altar to this demon (laziness); for, if *laziness* did not intervene, *indefatigable* malice would commit far more ill in the world than it does now; if *cowardice* did not take pity on human beings, militant blood-thirst would soon wipe them out; and if there were no *duplicity*, then, because of the innate malice of human nature, entire states would soon be overthrown [for among the many scoundrels united in conspiracy in great number (for example, in a regiment), there will always be one who will betray it].

The strongest impulses of nature are *love of life* and *sexual love*, which represent the invisible reason (of the ruler of the world) that provides generally for the highest physical good[50] of the human race by means of a power higher than human reason, without human reason having to work toward it. Love of life is to maintain the individual; sexual love, the species. For by means of the general mixing of the sexes, the life of our species endowed with reason is *progressively* maintained, despite the fact that this species intentionally works toward its own destruction (by war).[51] Nevertheless, this does not prevent rational creatures, who grow constantly in culture even in the midst of war, from representing [277] unequivocally the prospect of a state of happiness for the human race in future centuries, a state which will never again regress.[52]

---

[49] The reference is uncertain. Külpe suggests that Kant may be referring to Demetrius of Phalerum (345?–283 BC). Brandt, following Adickes, thinks that Demetrius Poliorcetes, King of Macedon (336–283 BC) is intended. See also *Reflexionen* 536 (15: 235) and 1448 (15: 632), and Polybius 18.54.

[50] *das physische Weltbeste.*

[51] *Marginal note in H*: To be sure not a higher level of humanity, as with the Americans, also not to a specifically different one – rather, to a greater humanization *humanisatio.*

Is humanity comprehended in perpetual progress to perfection? Is the human species becoming increasingly better or worse, or does it remain with the same moral content?

From the time the child is in the arms of its nurse until old age, the proportion of cunning, deception, and evil is always the same.

The answer to the question, whether there shall be war or not, is [?] continually determined by the highest persons in power.

The highest level of culture is when the state of war between peoples is in equilibrium, and the means to this is the question of who among them shall inquire whether war shall be or not.

[52] *der nicht mehr rückgängig sein wird.*

On the highest moral-physical good

§88

The two kinds of good, the *physical* and the *moral*, cannot be *mixed* together; for then they would neutralize themselves and not work at all toward the end of true happiness. Rather, inclination to *good living* and *virtue* conflict with each other, and the limitation of the principle of the former through the latter constitute, in their collision, the entire end of the well-behaved[53] human being, a being who is partly sensible but partly moral and intellectual. But since it is difficult to prevent mixing in practice, the end of happiness needs to be broken down by counteracting agents (*reagentia*) in order to know which elements in what proportion can provide, when they are combined, the enjoyment of a *moral happiness*.

The way of thinking characteristic of the union of good living with virtue in *social intercourse* is *humanity*. What matters here is not the degree of good living, since one person requires much, another little, depending on what seems to him to be necessary. Rather, what matters is only the kind of relationship whereby the inclination to good living is limited by the law of virtue.

Sociability is also a virtue, but the *social inclination* often becomes a passion. If, however, social enjoyment is boastfully heightened by extravagance, then this false sociability ceases to be virtue and is a luxurious living[54] that is detrimental to humanity.

***

Music, dance, and games form a speechless social gathering (for the few words necessary for games establish no conversation, which requires a mutual exchange of thoughts). Games, which some pretend should [278] merely serve to fill the void of conversation after the meal, are after all usually the main thing: a means of acquisition whereby affects are vigorously stirred, where a certain convention of self-interest is established so that the players can plunder each other with the greatest politeness, and where a complete egoism is laid down as a principle that no one denies as long as the game lasts. Despite all the culture these manners may bring about, such conversation hardly promises really to

---

[53] *wohlgeartet.*   [54] *ein Wohlleben.*

promote the union of social good living with virtue, and so it hardly promises to promote true humanity.

The good living that still seems to harmonize best with true humanity is *a good meal in good company* (and if possible, also alternating company). Chesterfield[55] says that the company must not number fewer than the *graces* or more than the *muses.*[h]

When I manage a dinner party composed of nothing but men of taste (aesthetically united),[i] in so far as they intend not merely to have a meal in common but to enjoy one another's company (this is why their number cannot amount to many more than the number of graces), this little dinner party must have the purpose not only of physical satisfaction – which each guest can have by himself alone – but also social enjoyment, for which physical enjoyment must seem to be only the vehicle. That number is just enough to keep the conversation from slackening or the guests from dividing into separate small groups with those sitting next to them. The latter situation is not at all a conversation of taste, which must [279] always bring culture with it, where each always talks with all (not merely with his neighbor). On the other hand, so-called festive entertainments (feasts and grand banquets) are altogether tasteless. It goes without saying that in all dinner parties, even one at an inn, whatever is said publicly by an indiscreet table companion to the detriment of someone absent may not be used *outside* this party and may not be gossiped about.

---

[55] Philip Dormer Stanhope, 4th Earl of Chesterfield (1694–1773), English statesman and author. Chesterfield's literary fame rests primarily upon his letters to his illegitimate son, Philip Stanhope (first published in 1774). Kant refers to Chesterfield in other works as well – e.g., *The Metaphysics of Morals* 6: 428, *Busolt* 25: 1482–1483, 1529, *Menschenkunde* 25: 1088, 1152, *Pillau* 25: 776, *Zusätze* 25: 1540, 1543, 1551.

[h] Ten at a table; because the host, who serves the guests, does not count himself along with them. *Crossed out in H: muses* [And <not> neither the candor of the conversation should be anxiously restricted (as at a *Table d'hote*), nor should there be any conversation without choice and context, as at the Lord Mayor's banquet (because every overly large dinner party is vulgar).] *Marginal note in H:* so much for the critique of physical taste.

[i] At a festive table, where the presence of ladies by itself restricts men's freedom within the bounds of good manners, sometimes a sudden silence sets in which is unpleasant because it threatens the company with boredom, and no one trusts himself to introduce something new and appropriate for the resumption of the conversation – he cannot pull it out of thin air, but rather should get it from the news of the day; however, it must be interesting. A single person, particularly the hostess, can often prevent this standstill all by herself and keep the conversation flowing so that, as at a concert, it ends with universal and complete gaiety and, because of this, is all the more beneficial. It is like Plato's symposium, of which the guest said: "Your meals are pleasing not only when one enjoys them, but also as often as one thinks of them." [The reference is not to Plato's dialogue the *Symposium*, but probably to an anecdote from Athenaeus, *Deipnosophistae* 10.14 – Ed.]

179

For even without making a special agreement about it, any such symposium has a certain holiness and a duty of secrecy about it with respect to what could later cause inconvenience, outside the group, to its members; for without this trust, the healthy enjoyment of moral culture within a social gathering and the enjoyment of this social gathering itself would be denied. – Therefore, if something derogatory were said about my best friend in a *so-called* public party (for actually even the largest dinner party is always only a private party, and only the state party[56] as such is public in its idea) – I would, I must say, defend him and, if necessary, take on his cause with severity and bitterness of expression; but I would not let myself be used as the instrument for spreading this evil report and carrying it to the man it concerns. – It is not merely a social *taste* that must guide the conversation; there are also principles that should serve as the limiting condition on the freedom with which human beings openly exchange their thoughts in social intercourse.

There is something analogous here to ancient customs in the trust between human beings who eat together at the same table; for example, those of the Arab, with whom a stranger can feel safe as soon as he has merely been able to coax a refreshment from him (a drink of water) in his tent; or when the deputies coming from Moscow to meet the Russian Tsarina offered her *salt* and *bread*, and by the enjoyment of them she could regard herself as safe from all snares by the right of hospitality. – Eating together at one table is regarded as the formality of such a covenant of safety.

[280]   Eating alone (*solipsismus convictorii*)[57] is unhealthy for a scholar who *philosophizes;*[j] it is not restoration but exhaustion (especially if it becomes

---

[56] *nur die staatsbürgerliche überhaupt.*

[57] Trans.: the solitary person at the table. *Marginal note in H*: For eating alone by oneself refectory.

[j]   For the man who *philosophizes* must constantly carry his thoughts with him, in order to find out through numerous trials what principles he should tie them to; and ideas, because they are not intuitions, float in the air before him, so to speak. The historical or mathematical scholar, on the other hand, can put them down before himself and so, with pen in hand, according to universal rules of reason, arrange them empirically, just like facts; and because his ideas are arranged in certain points, he can continue his work on the following day where he left off. – As concerns the *philosopher*, one cannot regard him as a *worker* on the building of the sciences, that is, not as scholars work; rather one must regard him as an *investigator of wisdom*. He is the mere idea of a person who takes the final end of all knowledge as his object, practically and (for the purposes of the practical) theoretically too, and one cannot use this name "philosopher" in the plural, but only in the singular (the philosopher judges like this or that): for he signifies a mere idea, whereas to say *philosophers* would indicate a plurality of something that is surely absolute unity.

solitary *feasting*): fatiguing work rather than a stimulating play of thoughts. The *savoring* human being who weakens himself in thought during his solitary meal gradually loses his sprightliness, which, on the other hand, he would have gained if a table companion with alternative ideas had offered stimulation through new material which he himself had not been able to track down.

At a full table, where the number of courses is intended only to keep the guests together for a long time (*coenam ducere*),[58] the conversation usually goes through three stages: 1) *narration*, 2) *arguing*,[59] and 3) *jesting*. – A. The first stage concerns the news of the day, first domestic, then foreign, that has flowed in from personal letters and newspapers. – B. When this first appetite has been satisfied, the party becomes even livelier, for in subtle reasoning[60] it is difficult to avoid diversity of judgment over one and the same object that has been brought up, and since no one exactly has the lowest opinion of his own judgment, a dispute arises which stirs up the appetite for food and drink and also makes the appetite wholesome in proportion to the liveliness of this dispute and the participation in it. – C. But because arguing is always a kind of work and exertion of one's powers, it eventually becomes tiresome as a result of engaging in it while eating rather copiously: thus the conversation sinks naturally to the mere play of wit, partly also to please the women present, against whom the [281] small, deliberate, but not shameful attacks on their sex enable them to show their own wit to advantage. And so the meal ends with *laughter*, which, if it is loud and good-natured, has actually been determined by nature to help the stomach in the digestive process through the movement of the diaphragm and intestines, thus promoting physical wellbeing. Meanwhile the participants in the feast believe – one wonders how much! – that they have found culture of the spirit in one of nature's purposes. – Dinner music at a festive banquet of fine gentlemen is the most tasteless absurdity that revelry has ever contrived.

The rules for a tasteful feast that *animates* the company are: a) to choose topics for conversation that interest everyone and always provide someone with the opportunity to add something appropriate, b) not to allow deadly silences to set in, but only momentary pauses in the conversation, c) not to change the topic unnecessarily or jump from one subject to another: for at the end of the feast, as at the end of a drama

---

[58] Trans.: to keep the people at the dinner table.   [59] *Räsonniren.*   [60] *Vernünfteln.*

(and the entire life of a reasonable human being, when completed, is also a drama), the mind inevitably occupies itself with reminiscing on various phases of the conversation; and if it cannot discover a connecting thread, it feels confused and realizes with indignation that it has not progressed in culture, but rather regressed. – A topic that is entertaining must almost be exhausted before proceeding to another one; and when the conversation comes to a standstill, one must know how to slip some related topic into the group, without their noticing it, as an experiment: in this way one individual in the group can take over the management of the conversation, unnoticed and unenvied. d) Not to let *dogmatism*[61] arise or persist, either in oneself or in one's companions in the group; rather, since this conversation should not be business but merely play, one should avert such seriousness by means of a skillful and suitable jest. e) In a serious conflict that nevertheless cannot be avoided, carefully to maintain discipline over oneself and one's affects, so that mutual respect and benevolence always shine forth – here what matters is more the *tone* (which must be neither noisy nor arrogant) of the conversation than the content, so that no guest returns home from the gathering *estranged* from the others.[62]

[282] No matter how insignificant these laws of refined humanity[63] may seem, especially if one compares them to pure moral laws, nevertheless, anything that promotes sociability, even if it consists only in pleasing maxims or manners, is a garment that dresses virtue to advantage, a garment which is also to be recommended in a serious respect. – The *cynic's purism* and the *anchorite's mortification of the flesh*, without social good living,[64] are distorted forms of virtue which do not make virtue inviting; rather, being forsaken by the graces, they can make no claim to humanity.

---

[61] *Rechthaberei.*   [62] *mit dem anderen entzweiet.*
[63] See also Kant's discussions of the meaning of "humanity" in the *Critique of the Power of Judgment* 5: 355 and in *The Metaphysics of Morals* 6: 456–457.
[64] *gesellschaftliches Wohlleben.*

Anthropology[1]

Part II

Anthropological Characteristic.[2] On the way of cognizing the interior of the human being from the exterior[3]

Division

1) The character of the person, 2) the character of the sexes, 3) the character of the peoples, 4) the character of the species.[4]

---

[1] *Marginal note in H*: Anthropology 1st Part Anthropological *Didactic* What is the human being? 2nd Part Anthropological *Characteristic* How is the peculiarity of each human being to be cognized?
The former is as it were the doctrine of elements of anthropology, the latter is the doctrine of method.

[2] *Charakteristik.*

[3] *Von der Art, das Innere des Menschen aus dem Äußeren zu erkennen.*

[4] The terms "person," "sexes," "peoples," and "species" all appear in the singular here as well as in later section titles (7: 285, 303, 311, 321). But the intended meaning of the second and third terms seems to be plural rather than singular.

A The character of the person

From a pragmatic consideration, the universal, *natural* (not civil) doctrine of signs (*semiotica universalis*) uses the word *character* in two senses: because on the one hand it is said that a certain human being has *this* or that (physical) character; on the other hand that he simply has *a* character (a moral character), which can only be one, or nothing at all. The first is the distinguishing mark of the human being as a sensible or natural being; the second is the distinguishing mark of the human being as a rational being endowed with freedom. The man of principles, from whom one knows what to expect, not from his instinct, for example, but from his will, has a character. – Therefore in the Characteristic one can, without tautology, divide what belongs to a human being's faculty of desire (what is practical) into what is *characteristic* in a) his *natural aptitude* or natural predisposition, b) his *temperament* or sensibility, and c) his *character* purely and simply, or way of thinking.[1] – The first two predispositions indicate what can be made of the human being; the last (moral) predisposition indicates what he is prepared to make of himself.

I On natural aptitude

To say that the human being has a good *disposition*[2] means that he is not stubborn but compliant; that he may get angry, but is easily appeased and bears no grudge (is negatively good). – On the other hand, to be [286] able to say of him that "he has a good heart," though this also still

---

[1] Natural aptitude: *Naturell*, natural predisposition: *Naturanlage*, way of thinking: *Denkungsart*.
[2] *ein gut Gemüth*.

185

pertains to sensibility, is intended to say more. It is an impulse toward the practical good, even if it is not exercised according to principles, so that both the person of good disposition and the person of good heart are people whom a shrewd guest can use as he pleases. – Accordingly, natural aptitude has more (subjectively) to do with the *feeling* of pleasure or displeasure, as to how one human being is affected by another (and in this his natural aptitude can have something characteristic), than (objectively) with the *faculty of desire*, where life manifests itself not merely in feeling, internally, but also in activity, externally, though merely in accordance with incentives of sensibility. Now *temperament* exists in this relation, and must still be distinguished from a habitual disposition (incurred through habit), because a habitual disposition is not founded upon any natural predisposition, but on mere occasional causes.

II On temperament

From a *physiological* point of view, when one speaks of temperament one means *physical constitution* (strong or weak build) and *complexion* (fluid elements moving regularly through the body by means of the vital power, which also includes heat or cold in the treatment of these humors).

However, considered *psychologically*, that is, when one means temperament of soul (faculties of feeling and desire), those terms borrowed from the constitution of the blood will be introduced only in accordance with the analogy that the play of feelings and desires has with corporeal causes of movement (the most prominent of which is the blood).

Hence it follows that the temperaments which we attribute merely to the soul may well also have corporeal factors in the human being, as covertly contributing causes: – furthermore, since, *first*, they can be divided generally into temperaments of *feeling* and *activity*, and since, *second*, each of them can be connected with the excitability (*intensio*) or slackening (*remissio*) of the vital power, only **four** simple temperaments can be laid down (as in the four syllogistic figures, by means of the *medius terminus*):[3]
[287] the *sanguine*, the *melancholy*, the *choleric*, and the *phlegmatic*. By this means, the old forms can then be retained, and they only receive a more

---

[3] Trans.: middle term.

comfortable interpretation suited to the spirit of this doctrine of temperaments.

This is why terms referring to the *constitution of the blood* do not serve to indicate the *cause* of the phenomena observed in a sensibly affected human being – whether according to the pathology of humors or of nerves:[4] they serve only to classify these phenomena according to observed effects. For in order properly to give to a human being the title of a particular class, one does not need to know beforehand what chemical blood-mixture it is that authorizes the designation of a certain property of temperament; rather, one needs to know which feelings and inclinations one has observed combined in him.

So the general division of the doctrine of temperaments can be the division into temperaments of *feeling* and temperaments of *activity*; and this division can again be divided into two kinds by means of subdivision, which together give us the four temperaments.[5] – I count the *sanguine*, A, and its opposite, the *melancholy*, B, as temperaments of **feeling**. – The former has the peculiarity that sensations are quickly and strongly affected, but not deeply penetrating (they do not last). On the other hand, in the latter temperament sensations are less striking, but they get themselves rooted deeply. One must locate this distinction of temperaments of feeling *in this*, and not in the tendency to cheerfulness or sadness. For the thoughtlessness of the sanguine temperament disposes it to gaiety; on the other hand, the pensiveness that broods over a sensation deprives gaiety of its easy variability, without thereby exactly producing sadness. – But since every change that one has under one's control generally stimulates and strengthens the mind, he who makes light of whatever happens to him is certainly happier, if not wiser, than he who clings to sensations that benumb his vital power.

---

[4] Adherents of the first group viewed the humors as the starting point of diseases; adherents of the second group, nerves. C. L. Hoffmann (1721–1807) was the chief representative of Humoral-pathology; W. C. Cullen (1712–1790), of Nerves-pathology.

[5] *Marginal note in H*: If one temperament should be mixed with another, they resist each other, they neutralize each other – however, if one at times alternates with another, then it is a mere mood and not a definite temperament. One does not know what one should make of the human being. Cheerfulness and thoughtlessness, melancholy and insanity, high-mindedness and stubbornness, coldness and persistence.

I Temperaments of feeling

A The sanguine temperament of the light-blooded person

The sanguine person indicates his sensibility and is recognizable in the following signs: he is carefree and of good cheer; he attributes a great [288] importance to each thing for the moment, and the next moment may not give it another thought. He makes promises in all honesty, but does not keep his word because he has not reflected deeply enough beforehand whether he will be able to keep it. He is good-natured enough to render help to others, but he is a bad debtor and always asks for extensions. He is a good companion, jocular and high-spirited, he does not like to attribute great importance to anything (*Vive la bagatelle!*),[6] and all human beings are his friends. He is not usually an evil human being, but he is a sinner hard to convert; indeed, he regrets something very much but quickly forgets this regret (which never becomes *grief*). Business tires him, and yet he busies himself indefatigably with things that are mere play; for play involves change, and perseverance is not his thing.

B The melancholy temperament of the heavy-blooded person

He who is *disposed to melancholy* (not the person afflicted with melancholy, for this signifies a condition, not the mere propensity to a condition) attributes a great importance to all things that concern himself, finds cause for concern everywhere and directs his attention first to difficulties, just as the sanguine person, on the other hand, begins with hope of success: therefore the melancholy person also thinks deeply, just as the sanguine person thinks only superficially. He makes promises with difficulty, for keeping his word is dear to him, but the capacity to do so is questionable. Not that all this happens from moral causes (for we are speaking here of *sensible* incentives), but rather that the opposite inconveniences him, and just because of this makes him apprehensive, mistrustful, and suspicious, and thereby also insusceptible to cheerfulness. – Moreover, this state of mind, if it is habitual, is nevertheless contrary to that of the philanthropist, which is more an inherited quality of the sanguine person, at least in its impulse; for

---

[6] Trans.: three cheers for trifles!

he who must *himself* do without joy will find it hard not to begrudge it to others.

II Temperaments of activity [289]

C The choleric temperament of the hot-blooded person

One says of him: he is *hot-tempered*, flares up quickly like straw-fire, readily allows himself to be calmed if the other person gives in, is thereupon angry without hatred, and in fact loves the other person all the more for quickly having given in to him. – His activity is *rash*, but not persistent. – He is busy, but reluctant to undertake business himself just because he is not persistent in it; so he likes to be the mere commander-in-chief who presides over it, but does not want to carry it out himself. Hence his ruling passion is ambition; he likes to take part in public affairs and wants to be loudly praised. Accordingly he loves the *show*[7] and pomp of *formalities*; he gladly takes others under his wing and according to appearances is magnanimous, not from love, however, but from pride, for he loves himself more. – He has a high opinion of *order* and therefore appears to be cleverer than he is. He is avaricious in order not to be stingy; polite, but with ceremony; stiff and affected in social intercourse; likes any flatterer who is the butt of his wit; suffers more wounds because of the opposition of others to his *proud* arrogance than the *miser* ever suffers because of opposition to his *avaricious* arrogance; for a little caustic wit directed at him completely blows away the aura of his importance, whereas the miser is at least compensated for this by his profit. – In short, the choleric temperament is the least happy of all, because it calls up the most opposition to itself.

D The phlegmatic temperament of the cold-blooded person

Phlegm signifies *lack of affect*, not indolence (lifelessness); and therefore one should not immediately call a person who has much phlegm a phlegmatic or say that he is phlegmatic and place him under this title in the class of idlers.

---

[7] *der Schein.*

189

Phlegm, as *weakness*, is the propensity to inactivity, not to let oneself be [290] moved to business even by strong incentives. Insensitivity to such stimuli is voluntary uselessness, and the desires aim only at satiety and sleep.

Phlegm, as *strength*, on the other hand, is the quality of not being moved easily or *rashly* but, if slowly, then *persistently*. – – He who has a good dose of phlegm in his composition warms up slowly, but retains the warmth longer. He does not easily fly into a rage, but reflects first whether he should become angry; when the choleric person, on the other hand, may fall into a rage at not being able to bring the steadfast man out of his cold-bloodedness.

The cold-blooded man has nothing to regret if he has been equipped by nature with a quite ordinary portion of reason, in addition to this phlegm; without being brilliant, he will still proceed from principles and not from instinct. His fortunate temperament takes the place of wisdom, and even in ordinary life one often calls him the philosopher. As a result of this he is superior to others, without offending their vanity. One often calls him *sly* as well; for all the bullets and projectiles fired at him bounce off him as from a sack of wool. He is a conciliatory husband, and knows how to establish dominion over his wife and relatives by seeming to comply with everyone's wishes; for by his unbending but considerate will he knows how to bring their wills round to his – just as bodies with small mass and great velocity penetrate an obstacle on impact, whereas bodies with less velocity and greater mass carry along with themselves the obstacle that stands in their path, without destroying it.

If one temperament should be an associate of another – as it is commonly believed – for example,

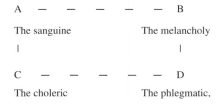

then they either *oppose* each other or *neutralize* each other. The former occurs if one tries to think of the sanguine as united with the melancholy [291] in one and the same subject; likewise the choleric with the phlegmatic: for they (A and B, likewise C and D) stand in contradiction to one another. – The latter, namely neutralization, would occur in the *mixing* (chemical, so to speak) of the sanguine with the choleric, and the melancholy with the phlegmatic (A and C, likewise B and D). For good-natured cheerfulness cannot be conceived of as being fused with forbidding anger in one and the same act, any more than the pain of the self-tormentor can be conceived of as being fused with the contented repose of the self-sufficient mind. – If, however, one of these two states alternates with the other in the same subject, then the result is mere moodiness,[8] not a specific temperament.

Therefore there is no *composite* temperament, for example, a sanguine-choleric temperament (which all windbags want to have, since then they can claim to be the gracious but also stern master). Rather, there are in all only four temperaments, and each of them is simple, and one does not know what should be made of the human being who attributes a mixed one to himself.

Cheerfulness and thoughtlessness, melancholy and insanity, high-mindedness and stubbornness, finally coldness and feeble-mindedness are only distinguished as effects of temperament in relation to their causes.[a]

III On character as the way of thinking

To be able to simply say of a human being: "he has a *character*" is not only to have *said* a great deal about him, but is also to have *praised* him a great deal; for this is a rarity, which inspires profound respect and admiration toward him. [292]

If by this term 'character' one generally understands that which can definitely be expected of a person, whether good or bad, then one usually adds that he has *this* or *that* character, and then the term signifies his

---

[8] *das bloße Launen.*

[a] What influence the variety of temperament has upon public affairs, or vice versa (through the effect which the habitual exercise in public affairs has on temperament), is claimed to have been discovered partly by experience and partly also with the assistance of conjectures about occasional causes. Thus it is said, for example, that

> in religion the choleric is *orthodox*
> the sanguine is *latitudinarian*
> the melancholic is *enthusiast*
> the phlegmatic is *indifferentist.* –

But these are tossed-off judgments which are worth as much for Characteristic as scurrilous wit allows them (*valent, quantum possunt*). [Trans.: they are worth as much as is attributed to them – Ed.]

way of sensing. – But simply to have a character signifies that property of the will by which the subject binds himself to definite practical principles that he has prescribed to himself irrevocably by his own reason. Although these principles may sometimes indeed be false and incorrect, nevertheless the formal element of the will in general, to act according to firm principles (not to fly off hither and yon, like a swarm of gnats), has something precious and admirable in it; for it is also something rare.

Here it does not depend on what nature makes of the human being, but on what the human being *makes of himself*; for the former belongs to temperament (where the subject is for the most part passive), and only the latter enables one to recognize that he has a character.

All other good and useful properties of the human being have a *price* that allows them to be exchanged with other things that have just as much use; talent has a **market price**, since the sovereign or lord of the manor can use a talented human being in all sorts of ways; – temperament has a **fancy price**,[9] one can have an enjoyable time with such a person, he is a pleasant companion; – but character has an inner **worth**,[b] and is beyond all price.

[293] ## On the qualities that follow merely from the human being's having or not having character

1) The *imitator* (in moral matters) is without character; for character consists precisely in originality in the way of thinking. He who has

---

[9] *ein Affektionspreis.*

[b] A seafarer listened to the dispute in a society led by scholars over the rank of their respective faculties. He decided it in his own way, namely: how much would a human being he had captured bring in for him at the sale in the marketplace in Algiers? No human being there can use a theologian or jurist, but the physician knows a trade and can be worth cash. – King James I of England was asked by the wet nurse who had breast-fed him to make her son a *gentleman* (a man of refinement). James answered: "That I cannot do. I can make him an earl, but he must make himself a gentleman." – Diogenes (the Cynic), as the story goes [see Diogenes Laertius, *Lives of Eminent Philosophers* 6.74 – Ed.], was captured on a sea voyage near the island of Crete and offered for sale at a public slave market. "What can you do? What do you know?" asked the broker who had put
[293] him on the stand. "I know how *to rule*," answered the philosopher, "and you find me a buyer who needs a *master*." The merchant, moved by this strange demand, concluded the sale by this strange transaction: he turned his son over to Diogenes for education, to make of him what he wanted; meanwhile he himself conducted business in Asia for several years, and then upon his return he received his previously uncouth son transformed into a skillful, well-mannered, virtuous human being. – Thus, approximately, can one estimate the gradation of human worth.

character derives his conduct from a source that he has opened by himself.[10] However, the rational human being must not be an *eccentric*; indeed, he never will be, since he relies on principles that are valid for everyone. The imitator is the *mimicker* of the man who has a character. Good-naturedness from temperament[11] is a painting of watercolors and not a trait of character; but a trait of character drawn in caricature is an outrageous mockery pushed on the man of true character: because he does not take part in evil once it has become public custom (fashion), and, consequently, he is presented as an eccentric.

2) Maliciousness from temperamental predisposition is nevertheless less bad than good-naturedness from temperamental predisposition without character; for by character one can get the upper hand over maliciousness from temperamental predisposition. – Even a human being of evil character (like Sulla), though he arouses disgust through the violence of his firm maxims, is nevertheless also an object of admiration: as we admire *strength of soul* generally, in comparison with *goodness of soul*. Both must be found united in the same subject in order to bring out what is more an ideal than something that exists in reality; namely the right to the title of *greatness of soul*.

3) The rigid, inflexible disposition[12] which accompanies a formed resolution (as, for example, in Charles XII) is indeed a natural predisposition very favorable to character, but it is not yet a determinate character as such. For character requires maxims that proceed from reason and morally practical principles. Therefore one cannot rightly say that the malice of this human being is a quality of his character; for then it would be diabolic. The human being, however, never *sanctions* the evil in himself, and so there is actually no malice from principles; [294] but only from the forsaking of them. –

***

Accordingly, it is best to present negatively the principles that relate to character. They are:

a. Not intentionally to say what is false; consequently, also to speak with caution so that one does not bring upon oneself the disgrace of retraction.

---

[10] *aus einer von ihm selbst geöffneten Quelle.*   [11] *Die Gutartigkeit aus Temperament.*
[12] *Der steife, unbeigsame Sinn.*

b. Not to dissemble; appearing well disposed in public, but being hostile behind people's backs.

c. Not to break one's (legitimate) promise;[13] which also includes honoring even the *memory* of a friendship now broken off, and not abusing later on the former confidence and candor of the other person.

d. Not to enter into an association of taste with evil-minded human beings, and, bearing in mind the *noscitur ex socio* etc.,[14] to limit the association only to business.

e. Not to pay attention to gossip derived from the shallow and malicious judgment of others; for paying attention to it already indicates weakness. Also, to moderate our fear of offending against fashion, which is a fleeting, changeable thing; and, if it has already acquired some importance in its influence, then at least not to extend its command into morality.[15]

The human being who is conscious of having character in his way of thinking does not have it by nature; he must always have *acquired* it. One may also assume that the grounding of character is like a kind of rebirth, a certain solemnity of making a vow to oneself; which makes the resolution and the moment when this transformation took place unforgettable to him, like the beginning of a new epoch. – Education, examples, and teaching generally cannot bring about this firmness and persistence in principles *gradually*, but only, as it were, by an explosion which happens one time as a result of weariness at the unstable condition of instinct. Perhaps there are only a few who have attempted this revolution before the age of thirty, and fewer still who have firmly established it before they are forty. – Wanting to become a better human being in a fragmentary way is a futile endeavor, since one impression dies out while one works on

[295] another; the grounding of character, however, is absolute unity of the inner principle of conduct as such. – It is also said that *poets* have no character, for example, they would rather insult their best friends than give up a witty inspiration; or that character is not to be sought at all

---

[13] *Sein (erlaubtes) Versprechen.*

[14] The *Dohna* version of the anthropology lectures contains the full proverb: *Noscitur ex socio, qui non cognoscitur ex se* (p. 314). Trans.: He who cannot be characterized by his own merits can be characterized by the company he keeps. See also *Parow* 25: 393, *Mrongovius* 25: 1390, *Reflexion* 7187, 19: 267.

[15] *ihr Gebot wenigstens nicht auf die Sittlichkeit auszudenken.* A1 and A2: "then ... morality." *H reads*: "then it is still better, as one says, to be a fool in fashion than a fool out of fashion."

among courtiers, who must put up with all fashions; and that with clergymen, who court the Lord of Heaven as well as the lords of the earth in one and the same pitch, firmness of character is in a troublesome condition; and, accordingly, it probably is and will remain only a pious wish that they have inner (moral) character. But perhaps the *philosophers* are to blame for this, because they have never yet isolated this concept and placed it in a sufficiently bright light, and have sought to present virtue only in fragments but have never tried to present it *whole*, in its beautiful form, and to make it interesting for all human beings.

In a word: the only proof within a human being's consciousness that he has character is that he has made truthfulness his supreme maxim, in the heart of his confessions to himself as well as in his behavior toward everyone else; and since to have this is the minimum that one can demand of a reasonable human being, but at the same time also the maximum of inner worth (of human dignity), then to be a man of principles (to have a determinate character) must be possible for the most common human reason and yet, according to its dignity, be superior to the greatest talent.[16]

On physiognomy

Physiognomy is the art of judging a human being's way of sensing or way of thinking according to his visible form; consequently, it judges the interior by the exterior. – Here one does not judge him in his unhealthy, but in his healthy condition; not when his mind is agitated, but when it is at rest. – It goes without saying that if he who is being judged for this purpose perceives that someone is observing him and spying out his interior, his mind is not at rest but in a state of constraint and inner agitation, indeed even indignation, at seeing himself exposed to another's censure.

If a watch has a fine case, one cannot judge with certainty from this (says a famous watchmaker) that the interior is also good; but if the case is poorly made, one can with considerable certainty conclude that the interior is also no good; for the craftsman will hardly discredit a piece of work on which he has worked diligently and well by neglecting its exterior, which costs him the least labor. But it would be absurd to [296]

---

[16] *Marginal note in H*: Cut stones
Camee and intaglio

195

conclude here, by the analogy of a human craftsman with the inscrutable Creator of nature, that the same holds for Him: that, for example, He would have added a good soul to a beautiful body in order to recommend the human being, whom he created, to other human beings and promote him, or, on the other hand, frighten one person away from another (by means of the *hic niger est, hunc tu Romane caveto*).[17] For *taste*, which contains a merely subjective ground of satisfaction or dissatisfaction of one human being with another (according to their beauty or ugliness), cannot serve as a guide to *wisdom*, which has its existence objectively with certain natural qualities as its end (which we absolutely cannot understand), in order to assume that these two heterogeneous things[18] are united in the human being for one and the same end.

On the guidance of nature to physiognomy

If we are to put our trust in someone, no matter how highly he comes recommended to us, it is a natural impulse to look him in the face first, particularly in the eyes, in order to find out what we can expect from him. What is revolting or attractive in his gestures determines our choice or makes us suspicious even before we have inquired about his morals, and so it is incontestable that there is a physiognomic Characteristic, which, however, can never become a science, because the peculiarity of a human *form*, which indicates certain inclinations or faculties of the subject being looked at, cannot be understood by description according to concepts but only by illustration and presentation in intuition or by an imitation of it; whereby the human form in general is set out to judgment according to its *varieties*, each one of which is supposed to point to a special inner quality of the human being.

The caricatures of human heads by *Baptista Porta*,[19] which present animal heads compared analogically with certain characteristic human faces, and from which conclusions were supposed to be drawn about a [297] similarity of natural predispositions in both, have long been forgotten.

---

[17] Trans.: This one is black-hearted; therefore, Roman, beware of him. See Horace, *Satires* 1.4.85.

[18] "These two heterogeneous things" refers to body and soul. But as Gregor notes, the sentence as a whole is difficult to follow.

[19] Giambattista Porta (1540–1615), author of *De Humana Physiognomia* (1580), in which human faces are explained by means of animal faces. See also *Reflexion* 918, 15: 403–405.

Lavater[20] spread this taste widely by silhouettes, which became popular and inexpensive wares for a while, but recently they have been completely abandoned. – Now almost nothing remains of this, except perhaps the ambiguous remark (of von Archenholz)[21] that the face of a human being which one imitates by means of a grimace to oneself alone also stirs up certain thoughts and sensations, which agree with the imitated person's character. Thus there is no longer any demand for physiognomy as the art of searching out the interior of the human being by means of certain external, involuntary signs; and nothing remains of it but the art of cultivating taste, and to be more precise not taste in things but in morals, manners, and customs, in order to promote human relations and knowledge of human beings generally by means of a critique which would come to the aid of this knowledge.

Division of physiognomy

On Characteristic: 1. in the *structure of the face*, 2. in the *features of the face*, 3. in the *habitual gesture of the face* (mien).

A On the structure of the face

It is noteworthy that the Greek artists – in statues, cameos, and intaglios – also had an ideal in mind of the structure of the face (for gods and heroes), which was meant to express eternal youth and at the same time a repose free from all affects, without putting in anything *charming*. – The *Greek* perpendicular *profile* makes the eyes deeper set than they should be according to our taste (which leans toward what is charming), and even a Venus de Medici lacks charm. – The reason for this may be that since the ideal should be a firm, unalterable norm, a nose springing out of the face from the forehead at an angle (where the angle may be greater or smaller) would yield no *firm* rule of form, as is nevertheless required of that which belongs to the norm. The modern Greeks, despite their otherwise

---

20 Johann Caspar Lavater (1741–1801), Swiss theologian and mystic. He wrote several books on metaphysics, but is remembered chiefly for his work on physiognomy. See also Lavater's letter to Kant of April 8, 1774 and Kant's two replies (10: 165–166, 175–180).

21 Johann Wilhelm von Archenholz (1743–1812), editor of the journal *Literatur und Völkerkunde* from 1782 to 1791. In vol. 4 (1784): 857–860 of this journal there appears an article entitled "Ein Scherflein zur Physiognomik" (signed with the initials "M. Y."), which Külpe surmises is the source of Kant's remark. (See esp. p. 859.)

[298] beautifully formed bodies, still do not have that severe perpendicularity of profile in their faces, which seems to prove that these ideal facial structures in works of art were *prototypes*. – According to these mythological models, the eyes happen to lie deeper and have been placed somewhat in the shade of the base of the nose; on the other hand nowadays one considers human faces more beautiful that have a nose with a slight deviation from the direction of the forehead (an indentation at the base of the nose).

When we pursue our observations of human beings as they actually are, it becomes apparent that an exactly measured *conformity to the rule* generally indicates a very ordinary human being who is without spirit. The *mean* seems to be the basic measurement and the basis of beauty; but it is far from being beauty itself, because for this something characteristic is required. – However, one can also come across this characteristic in a face without beauty, where the expression speaks very well for the face, though in some other respect (perhaps moral or aesthetic). That is, one may find fault with a face here, there a forehead, nose, chin, or color of hair, and so on, and yet admit that it is still more pleasing for the individuality of the person than if it were in perfect conformity to the rule, since this generally also carries lack of character with it.

But one should never reproach a face with *ugliness* if in its features it does not betray the expression of a mind corrupted by vice or by a natural but unfortunate propensity to vice; for example, a certain feature of sneering as soon as one begins to speak, or of looking another person in the face with impudence that is untempered by gentleness, and thereby showing that one thinks nothing of his judgment. – There are men whose faces are (as the French say) *rebarbaratif*,[22] faces with which, as the saying goes, one can drive children to bed; or who have a face lacerated and made grotesque by smallpox; or who have, as the Dutch say, a *wanschapenes*[23] face (a face imagined as it were in delusion or in a dream). But at the same time people with such faces still show such good-naturedness and cheerfulness that they can make fun of their own faces, which therefore by no means can be called ugly, although they would not be offended if a lady said of them (as was said of *Pelisson*[24] at the **Académie**

---

[22] Trans.: forbidding, repulsive. (The correct French word is *rébarbatif*.)
[23] Trans.: misshapen, shapeless.
[24] Paul Pellisson-Fontanier (1624–1693), French philosopher and member of the Academy in Paris. The remark was made by Madame de Sévigné.

française): "Pelisson abuses the privilege men have of being ugly." It is even more wicked and stupid when a human being from whom one may expect manners behaves like rabble by reproaching a handicapped person [299] with his physical defects, which often serve only to enhance his spiritual merits. If this happens to someone who has met with an accident in his early youth (for example, if he is called "you blind dog," or "you lame dog"), it makes that person really malicious and gradually embitters him toward people who, because they are well formed, think that they are better.

Generally, people who have never left their country make an object of ridicule of the unfamiliar faces of strangers. Thus little children in Japan run after the Dutch businessmen there, calling out "Oh, what big eyes, what big eyes!," and the Chinese find the red hair of many Europeans who visit their country horrid, but their blue eyes ridiculous.

As concerns the bare skull and its structure which constitutes the basis of its shape, for example, that of the Negroes, the Kalmyks, the South Sea Indians, and so on, as they have been described by Camper and especially Blumenbach,[25] observations about it belong more to physical geography than to pragmatic anthropology. A mean between the two can be the remark that even among us the forehead of the male sex is generally *flat*, while that of the female is more *rounded*.

Whether a hump on the nose indicates a satirist – whether the peculiarity of the shape of the Chinese face, of which it is said that the lower jaw projects slightly beyond the upper, is an indication of their stubbornness – or whether the forehead of the Americans, overgrown with hair on both sides, is a sign of innate feeble-mindedness, and so forth, these are conjectures that permit only an uncertain interpretation.[26]

---

[25] The Kalmyks, a semi-nomadic branch of the Oirat Mongols, migrated from Chinese Turkistan to the steppe west of the mouth of the Volga river in the mid seventeenth century. Petrus Camper (1722–1789), Dutch anatomist and naturalist, author of *On the Natural Difference of Facial Features* (Berlin, 1792). See also *Anth* 7: 322; *Critique of the Power of Judgment* 5: 304, 428; *The Conflict of the Faculties* 7: 89; *Zusätze* 25: 1552. Johann Friedrich Blumenbach (1752–1840), German anatomist and naturalist, professor of medicine at Göttingen, author of *Manual of Natural History* (Göttingen, 1779). See also *Critique of the Power of Judgment* 5: 424, *The Conflict of the Faculties* 7: 89. In his letter to Blumenbach of August 5, 1790, Kant writes: "I have found much instruction in your writings" (11: 185).

[26] *Marginal note in H: Hume* in thought and *Rousseau*
    On skulls according to Camper and Blumenbach. Spherical head, not flat forehead.
    Heydegger

B On what is characteristic in the features of the face

It does a man no harm, even in the judgment of the female sex, if his face has been disfigured and made unpleasing because of the coloring of his skin or pockmarks; for if good-naturedness shines forth from his eyes, and if at the same time from his glance the expression of a man valiant in the consciousness of his power and at peace shines forth, then he can always be liked and lovable, and this holds good universally. – One jokes [300] with such people and their amiability (*per antiphrasin*); and a woman can be proud to have such a husband in her possession. Such a face is not a *caricature*; for a caricature is an intentionally exaggerated sketch (a *distortion*) of the face in affect,[27] devised for derision and belonging to mimicry. It must rather be included among a variety that lies in nature, and must not be called a distorted face (which would be repulsive); for even if it is not lovely it can inspire love, and although it is without beauty it is still not ugly.[c]

C On what is characteristic in facial expressions[28]

Expressions are facial features put into play, and this results more or less from strong affect, the propensity to which is a characteristic trait of the human being.

It is difficult not to betray the imprint of an affect by any expression; it betrays itself by the painstaking restraint in gesture or in the tone itself, and he who is too weak to govern his affects will expose his interior through the play of expressions (against the wish of his reason), which he would like to hide and conceal from the eyes of others. But if one finds

---

[27] *des Gesichts im Affekt.*

[c] *Heidegger*, a German musician in London, was a grotesquely formed but bright and intelligent man, with whom refined people liked to associate for the sake of conversation. – Once it occurred to him at a drinking party to claim to a lord that he had the ugliest face in London. The lord reflected and wagered that he could present a face still uglier, and then sent out for a drunken woman, at whose appearance the whole party burst into laughter and called out: "Heidegger, you have lost the bet." "Not so fast," he replied, "let the woman wear my wig and I shall put on her headdress; then we shall see." As this happened, everyone fell into laughter, to the point of suffocation, for the woman looked like a very well-bred man, and the man like a witch. This proves that in order to call anyone beautiful, or at least tolerably pretty, one must not judge absolutely but always only relatively, and that someone must not call a man ugly just because he is perhaps not pretty. – Only repulsive physical defects of the face can justify this verdict.

[28] *Von dem Charakteristischen der Mienen.*

out about them, those who are masters in this art are not exactly regarded as the best human beings with whom one can deal in confidence, especially if they are practiced in affecting expressions that contradict what they do.

The art of interpreting expressions that unintentionally reveal one's [301] interior, while nevertheless thereby lying about it, can provide the occasion for many fine remarks, of which I wish to consider only one. – If someone who is otherwise not cross-eyed looks at the tip of his nose while relating something and consequently crosses his eyes, then what he is relating is always a lie. – However, one must not include here the defective eye condition of a cross-eyed person, who can be entirely free from this vice.

Moreover, there are gestures established by nature, by which human beings of all races[29] and climates understand each other, even without prior agreement. To these gestures belong *nodding the head* (in affirmation), *shaking the head* (in disavowal), *raising the head* (in defiance), *shaking the head* (in astonishment), *turning up one's nose* (in derision), *laughing derisively* (sneering), making a *long face* (upon refusal of a request), *frowning* (in annoyance), *quickly opening and closing the mouth* (bah!), *beckoning toward and waving away from oneself with the hands*, *beating the hands together over the head* (in surprise), *making a fist* (in threatening), *bowing, putting the finger on the mouth (compescere labella)*,[30] in order to command silence, *hissing*, and so forth.

Random remarks

Frequently repeated expressions that accompany emotion,[31] even involuntarily, gradually become permanent facial features, which, however, disappear in death. Consequently, as Lavater remarks, the terrifying face that betrays the scoundrel in life ennobles itself (negatively) in death, so to speak: for then, when all the muscles relax, there remains as it were the expression of repose, which is innocent. – Thus it can also happen that a man who has gone through his youth uncorrupted may still in later years, despite his good health, acquire another face because of debauchery. But from this nothing should be inferred about his natural predisposition.

---

[29] *von allen Gattungen.*   [30] Trans.: to close the lips (with one's finger).   [31] *Gemüthsbewegung.*

One also speaks of a *common* face in contrast with one that is refined. The latter signifies nothing more than an assumed importance, combined with a courtly manner of ingratiation, which thrives only in big cities, where human beings rub against one another and grind away their roughness. Therefore, when civil servants, born and brought up in the country, are promoted with their families to notable municipal positions, [302] or even when they only qualify for such service in accordance with their rank, they show something common, not merely in their manners, but also in their facial expression. For, having dealt almost exclusively with their subordinates, they felt free and easy in their sphere of activity, so that their facial muscles did not acquire the flexibility required for cultivating the play of expression appropriate to dealings with people in all relationships – toward superiors, inferiors, and equals – and to the affects connected with them. To have this play of expression without compromising oneself is required for a good reception in society. On the other hand, when human beings of equal rank accustomed to urbane manners become conscious of their superiority over others in this respect, this consciousness, if it becomes habitual by long practice, molds their faces with permanent features.

Devotees of a dominant[32] religion or cult, when they have long been disciplined and, so to speak, hardened in the mechanical practices of devotion, introduce national features into a whole people, within the boundaries of that religion or cult, traits that even characterize them physiognomically. Thus Herr Fr. Nicolai[33] speaks of the embarrassing *sanctimonious* (*fatale gebenedeiete*) faces in Bavaria; whereas *John Bull* of old England carries even on his face the freedom to be impolite wherever he may go in foreign lands or toward foreigners in his own country. So there is also a national physiognomy, though it should not necessarily be thought of as innate. – There are characteristic marks in societies that the law has brought together for punishment. Regarding the prisoners in Amsterdam's *Rasphuis*, Paris's *Bicêtre*, and London's *Newgate*, a skillful and well-traveled German physician remarks that they were mostly bony fellows and conscious of their superiority, but that there were none about

---

[32] *machthabende.*
[33] Christoph Friedrich Nicolai (1733–1811), writer, publisher, and merchant in Berlin; one of the *Popularphilosophen* and founding editor of the journal *Allgemeine deutsche Bibliothek*. See his *Beschreibung einer Reise durch Deutschland und die Schweiz im Jahre 1781*, vol. 6, pp. 544, 752f. See also *Zusätze* 25: 1549, 1556.

whom it would be permissible to say, with the actor Quin:[34] "If this fellow is not a scoundrel, then the Creator does not write a legible hand." For in order to pass sentence so strongly, more power of discrimination would be needed than any mortal may claim to possess between the play that nature carries on with the forms it develops in order to produce mere diversity of temperaments, and what this does or does not do for morality.

[34] The German physician is Johann Friedrich Grimm (1737–1821). See his *Bemerkungen eines Reisenden durch Deutschland, Frankreich, England, und Holland in Briefen* (Altenburg, 1775), p. 334. See also *Friedländer* 25: 668, *Pillau* 25: 828, *Menschenkunde* 25: 1180–1181, *Mrongovius* 25: 1307, 1384, 1402. The actor is James Quin (1693–1766), who worked in England. See also *Friedländer* 25: 672.

[303]

B The character of the sexes

In all machines that are supposed to accomplish with little power just as much as those with great power, **art** must be put in. Consequently, one can already assume that the provision of nature put more art into the organization of the female part than of the male; for it furnished the man with greater power than the woman in order to bring both into the most intimate *physical* union, which, in so far as they are nevertheless also *rational* beings, it orders to the end most important to it, the preservation of the species. And moreover, in this quality of theirs (as rational animals), it provided them with social inclinations in order to make their sexual companionship persist in a domestic union.

Two persons convening at random is insufficient for the unity and indissolubility of a union; one partner must *yield* to the other, and, in turn, one must be superior to the other in some way, in order to be able to rule over or govern him. For in the *equality* of claims of two people who cannot do without each other, self-love produces nothing but squabbling. In the *progress* of *culture*, each partner must be superior in a different way: the man must be superior to the woman through his physical power and courage, while the woman must be superior to the man through her natural talent for mastering his desire for her; on the other hand in still uncivilized conditions superiority is simply on the side of the man. – For this reason, in anthropology the characteristic features of the female sex, more than those of the male sex, are a topic of study for the philosopher. In the crude state of nature one can no more recognize these characteristic features than those of crab apples and wild pears, which reveal their diversity only through grafting or

204

inoculation; for culture does not introduce these feminine qualities, it only allows them to develop and become recognizable under favorable conditions.

Feminine ways are called weaknesses. One jokes about them; fools ridicule them, but reasonable people see very well that they are just the levers women use for governing men and using them for their own purposes. Man is easy to study, woman does not betray her secret, [304] although she is poor at keeping another person's secret (because of her loquacity). He loves *domestic peace* and gladly submits to her regime, simply in order not to find himself hindered in his own concerns; she does not shy away from *domestic warfare*, which she conducts with her tongue, and for which nature endowed her with loquacity and eloquence full of affect,[1] which disarms the man. He relies on the right of the stronger to give orders at home because he is supposed to protect it against external enemies; she relies on the right of the weaker to be protected by the male partner against men, and disarms him by tears of exasperation while reproaching him with his lack of generosity.[2]

In the crude state of nature it is certainly different. There the woman is a domestic animal. The man leads the way with weapons in his hand, and the woman follows him loaded down with his household belongings. But even where a barbaric civil constitution makes polygamy legal, the most favored woman in his kennel (called a harem) knows how to achieve dominion over the man, and he has no end of trouble creating a tolerable peace amid the quarrel of many women to be the one (who is to rule over him).

In civil society the woman does not give herself up to the man's desire without marriage, and indeed *monogamous* marriage. Where civilization has not yet ascended to feminine freedom in *gallantry* (where a woman openly has lovers other than her husband), the man punishes his wife if

---

[1] *affektvolle Beredtheit.*
[2] *Marginal note in H*: Why a woman (*Venus*) also marries the ugliest man (*Vulcan*) and is not laughed at about it
Among unrefined groups of people the woman is a beast of burden.
Hearne of Hudson Bay. [Samuel Hearne (1745–1792), British fur trader. Hired by the Hudson's Bay Company, Hearne made three expeditions to northern Canada. See his *Journey from Prince of Wales Fort on Hudson's Bay to the Northern Ocean* (1795) – Ed.]
– On the last favor of the *Cicisbeo*.
The beatings of the Russians out of love and jealousy.

she threatens him with a rival.[a] But when gallantry has become the fashion and jealousy ridiculous (as never fails to happen in a time of [305] luxury), the feminine character reveals itself: by extending favors toward men, woman lays claim to freedom and, at the same time, to the conquest of the entire male sex. – This inclination, though it indeed stands in ill repute under the name of coquetry, is nevertheless not without a real basis of justification. For a young wife is always in danger of becoming a widow, and this causes her to extend her charms over all men whose fortunate circumstances make them marriageable; so that, should this situation occur, she would not be lacking in suitors.

Pope[3] believes that one can characterize the female sex (the cultivated part of it, of course) by two points: the inclination to *dominate* and the inclination to *enjoyment*. – However, by the latter one must understand not domestic but public enjoyment, where woman can show herself to advantage and distinguish herself; and then the latter inclination also dissolves into the former, namely: not to yield to her rivals in pleasing others, but to triumph over them all, if possible, by her taste and charm. – – However, even the first-mentioned inclination, like inclination generally, is not suitable for characterizing a class of human beings in general in their conduct toward others. For inclination toward what is advantageous to us is common to all human beings, and so too is the inclination to dominate, so far as this is possible for us; therefore it does not *characterize* a class. – However, the fact that this sex is constantly feuding with itself, whereas it remains on very good terms with the other sex, might rather be considered

---

[a] The old saying of the Russians that women suspect their husbands of keeping other women if they do not get a beating now and then by them is usually regarded as fiction. [Külpe refers readers here to "Von Weibern, die erst dann, wenn sie geschlagen werden, ihre Männer lieben," *Berlinische Monatsschrift* 13 (1789), pp. 551ff., as well as to Carl Friedrich Flögel, *Geschichte des Groteskekomischen* (1788), p. 181. Brandt has found a much earlier text where a similar saying occurs – Sigmund von Herberstein, *Moscoviter wunderbare Historien* (1567), p. LVIII – Ed.] However, in Cook's Travels one finds that when an English sailor on Tahiti saw an Indian punishing his wife by beating her, the sailor, wanting to be gallant, attacked the husband with threats. The woman turned on the spot against the Englishman and asked how it concerned him: the husband must do this! [See James Cook, *Captain Cooks dritte und letzte Reise, oder Geschichte einer Entdeckungsreise nach dem stillen Ocean* (1789), esp. the reports on Tahiti (3: 45–46) and on Friendship Island (4: 394) – – Ed.] – Accordingly, one will also find that when the married woman openly practices gallantry and her husband pays no attention to it, but compensates himself for it by drinking and card parties, or wooing other women, then not merely contempt but also *hatred* overcomes the female partner: because the woman recognizes by this that he now places no worth at all in her, and that he abandons his wife indifferently to others to gnaw on the same bone.

[3] Alexander Pope, *Moral Essays*, Epistle 2, lines 209–210. See also *Menschenkunde* 25: 1190.

as its character, were this not merely the natural *result* of rivalry to win the advantage of one over others in the favor and devotion of men. In that case, inclination to *dominate* is woman's real aim, while *enjoyment in public*, by which the scope of her charm is widened, is only the means for providing the effect for that inclination.[4]

One can only come to the characterization of this sex if one uses as one's principle not what we *make* our end, but what *nature's end* was in establishing womankind; and since this end itself, by means of the foolishness of human beings, must still be wisdom according to nature's purpose, these conjectural ends can also serve to indicate the principle for characterizing woman – a principle which does not depend on our choice but on a higher purpose for the human race. These ends are: 1) the preservation of the species, 2) the cultivation of society and its refinement by womankind.   [306]

I.   When nature entrusted to woman's womb its dearest pledge, namely the species, in the fetus by which the race[5] is to propagate and perpetuate itself, nature was frightened so to speak about the preservation of the species and so implanted this *fear* – namely fear of *physical* injury and *timidity* before similar dangers – in woman's nature; through which weakness this sex rightfully demands male protection for itself.

II. Since nature also wanted to instill the finer feelings that belong to culture – namely those of sociablity and propriety – it made this sex man's ruler through her modesty and eloquence in speech and expression. It made her clever while still young in claiming gentle and courteous treatment by the male, so that he would find himself imperceptibly fettered by a child through his own magnanimity, and led by her, if not to morality itself, to that which is its cloak, moral decency,[6] which is the preparation for morality and its recommendation.

Random remarks

Woman wants to dominate, man to be dominated (especially before marriage). – This was the reason for the gallantry of ancient knighthood. – She

---

[4] *Marginal note in H*: Woman seeks to please all men because, if her man dies, she has hope for another, whom she has pleased.
[5] Species: *Species*; race: *Gattung*.   [6] *zu dem, was ihr Kleid ist, dem gesitteten Anstande.*

acquires confidence early in her ability to please. The young man is always afraid of displeasing and, consequently, is embarrassed (self-conscious) in the company of ladies. – She maintains, merely from the claim of her sex, this pride of the woman to restrain all man's importunities through the respect that she inspires, and the right to demand respect for herself without even deserving it. – The woman *refuses*, the man *woos*; her surrender is a favor. – Nature wants that the woman be sought after, therefore she herself does not need to be so particular in her choice (in matters of taste) as the man, whom nature has also built more coarsely, and who already pleases the woman if only his physique shows that he has the strength and ability to protect her. For if she were disgusted with regard to the beauty of his physique and refined in her choice, then she would have to do the wooing in order to be able to fall in love, while he would have to appear to refuse; which would entirely degrade the value of her sex, even in the eyes of the

[307] man. – She must appear to be cold in love, whereas the man must appear to be full of affect. Not to respond to an amorous advance seems to be shameful to the man, but to lend an ear easily seems shameful to the woman. – The desire of the latter to allow her charms to play on all refined men is coquetry, the affectation of appearing to be in love with all women is gallantry; both can be a mere affectation that has become the fashion, without any serious consequence: as with *cicisbeism*,[7] an affected freedom of the married woman, or, in the same way, the *courtesan system* that formerly existed in Italy. (In the *Historia Concilii Tridentini* it is reported, among other things: *erant ibi etiam 300 honestae meretrices, quas cortegianas vocant.*)[8] It is said of this courtesan system that its well-mannered *public* associations contained more refined culture than did mixed companies in private houses. – In marriage the man woos only his *own* wife, but the woman has an inclination for *all* men; out of jealousy, she *dresses up* only for the eyes of her own sex, in order to outdo other women in charm or

---

7 *Marginal note in H*: Of all female virtues none is required except that she firmly stand her ground against the attempt on her female honor (not to give herself away without honor). [Concerning the cicisbeo or cavaliere servente, Külpe refers readers to Samuel Sharp, *Letters from Italy 1765–66* (London, 1767), pp. 18ff., 73ff., 257; and *Neues Hamburgisches Magazin* 2 (1767), pp. 249ff.: "Einige Briefe über Italien und über die Sitten und Gewohnheiten diese Landes von Samuel Sharp," pp. 255 f., 263ff. See also *Encyclopedia Britannica*, 11th ed., s.v. "cicisbeo": "The cicisbeo was the professional gallant of a married woman, who attended her at all public entertainments, it being considered unfashionable for the husband to be the escort" – Ed.]

8 Trans.: there were also 300 kept mistresses, who are called courtesans. The author of the text (which was originally published in Italian) is Paolo Sarpi (1552–1623). Külpe reports that he could not locate Kant's citation after searching through the eight-volume Latin translation.

fashionableness. The man, on the other hand, dresses up only for the feminine sex; if one can call this dressing up, when it goes only so far as not to disgrace his wife by his clothes. – The man judges feminine mistakes leniently, but the woman judges them very strictly (in public); and young women, if they were allowed to choose whether a male or female tribunal should pass judgment on their offenses, would certainly choose the former for their judge. – When refined luxury has reached a high level, the woman appears demure only by compulsion and makes no secret of wishing that she might rather be a man, so that she could give her inclinations larger and freer latitude; no man, however, would want to be a woman.

The woman does not ask about the man's continence before marriage; but for him this same question on the part of the woman is of infinite importance. – In marriage, women scoff at intolerance (the jealousy of men in general), but it is only a joke of theirs; on this subject the *unmarried* woman judges with great severity. – As concerns scholarly women: they use their *books* somewhat like their *watch*, that is, they carry one so that it will be seen that they have one; though it is usually not running or not set by the sun.[9]

Feminine virtue or lack of virtue is very different from masculine virtue or lack of virtue, not only in kind but also as regards incentive. – She should be *patient*; he must be *tolerant*. She is *sensitive*; he is *sentimental*.[10] – Man's economic activity consists in *acquiring*, woman's [308] in *saving*. – The man is jealous *when he loves*; the woman is jealous even when she does not love, because every lover won by other women is one lost from her circle of admirers. – The man has his *own* taste,[11] the woman makes herself the object of *everyone's* taste. – "What the world says is *true*, and what it does, *good*" is a feminine principle that is hard to unite with a *character* in the narrow sense of the term. However, there have still been heroic women who, in connection with their own household, have upheld with glory a character suitable to their vocation. – Milton[12] was encouraged by his wife to accept the position of Latin Secretary, which was offered to him after Cromwell's death,

---

[9] See also Maria Charlotta Jacobi's letter to Kant of June 12, 1762 (10: 39); *Observations on the Feeling of the Beautiful and the Sublime* 2: 229–230; *Reflexion* 1299, 15: 572.

[10] Patient: *geduldig*; tolerant: *duldend*; sensitive: *empfindlich*; sentimental: *empfindsam*. (In these two sentences Kant is playing on the sound and meaning of related German adjectives.)

[11] *hat Geschmack für sich*.

[12] John Milton (1608–1674), English poet. Külpe, referring to a book by Alfred Stern (*Milton und seine Zeit* [1879], Part II, Book IV, pp. 12, 196), claims that the following anecdote is false.

though it was against his principles now to declare a government lawful which he had previously described as unlawful. "Ah, my dear," he replied; "you and others of your sex want to travel in coaches, but I – must be an honorable man." – Socrates' wife, perhaps also Job's, were similarly driven into the corner by their valiant husbands; but masculine virtue upheld itself in these men's characters, without, however, diminishing the merit of feminine virtue in theirs, given the relation in which they were placed.

Pragmatic consequences

The feminine sex must train and discipline itself in practical matters; the masculine sex understands nothing of this.

The *young* husband rules over his *older* spouse. This is based on jealousy, according to which the party that is subordinate to the other in sexual power[13] guards itself against encroachment on its rights by the other party and thus feels compelled to submit to being obliging and attentive in its treatment of the other party. – This is why every experienced wife will advise against marriage with a young man, even with one of just the *same* age; for with the passing of years the female party certainly ages earlier than the male, and even if one disregards this inequality, one cannot safely count on the harmony that is based on equality. A young, intelligent woman will have better luck in marriage with a healthy but, [309] nevertheless, noticeably older man. However, a man who perhaps has already lewdly squandered his *sexual power* before marriage will be the fool in his own house, for he can have this domestic domination only in so far as he does not fail to fulfill any reasonable demands.

Hume notes[14] that women (even old maids) are more annoyed by satires on *marriage* than by *gibes* against their *sex*. – For these gibes can never be serious, whereas the former could well become serious if the difficulties of the married state are correctly illuminated, which the unmarried person is spared. However, skepticism on this topic is

---

[13] *Geschlechtsvermögen.*

[14] In the opening statement of his essay "Of Love and Marriage," Hume writes: "I know not whence it proceeds, that women are so apt to take amiss every thing which is said in disparagement of the married state; and always consider a satyr upon matrimony a satyr upon themselves" (in *Essays, Moral, Political, and Literary*, ed. Eugene F. Miller [Indianapolis: Liberty Press, 1987], p. 557). See also *Reflexion* 1283, 15: 565, *Parow* 25: 458, *Menschenkunde* 25: 1193, *Mrongovius* 25: 1393.

bound to have bad consequences for the whole feminine sex, because this sex would be degraded to a mere means for satisfying the desire of the other sex, which, however, can easily result in boredom and unfaithfulness. – Woman becomes free by marriage; man loses his freedom by it.

It is never a woman's concern to spy out the moral properties in a man, especially a young man, *before* the wedding. She believes that she can improve him; an intelligent woman, she says, surely can set right a badly behaved man, in which judgment she generally finds herself deceived in the most lamentable manner. This also applies to the naïve woman who believes that the debaucheries of her husband before marriage can be overlooked, because, if only he has not exhausted himself, this instinct will now be sufficiently provided for by his wife. – These good children do not consider that dissoluteness in this area consists precisely in change of pleasure, and that the monotony[15] of marriage will soon lead him back to his former way of life.[b]

Who, then, should have supreme command in the household? – for there certainly can be only one who coordinates all transactions[16] in accordance with one end, which is his. – I would say, in the language of gallantry (though not without truth): the woman should *dominate* and the man should *govern*; for inclination dominates, and understanding governs. – The husband's behavior must show that to him the welfare of his [310] wife is closest to his heart. But since the man must know best how he stands and how far he can go, he will be like a minister to his monarch who is mindful only of enjoyment. For example, if he undertakes a festival or the building of a palace, the minister will first declare his due compliancy with the order, even if at present there is no money in the treasury, and even if certain more urgent necessities must first be attended to, and so on – so that the most high and mighty master can do all that he wills, but under the condition that his minister suggests to him what this will is.[17]

Since the woman is to be sought after (this is required for the refusal necessary to her sex), even in marriage she will be generally seeking to

[15] *das Einerlei.*

[b] The consequence of this is, as in Voltaire's *Voyage de Scarmentado*: "Finally," he says, "I returned to my fatherland, Candia, took a wife there, soon became a cuckold, and found that this is the most comfortable life of all." [See the conclusion to Voltaire's *Histoire des voyages de Scarmentado* – Ed.]

[16] *alle Geschäfte.*

[17] The most high and mighty master: *der höchstgebietende Herr*; suggests to him what this will is: *diesen Willen ihm sein Minister an die Hand giebt.*

please; so that, if she by chance should become a widow while young, she will find suitors for herself. – With the matrimonial alliance, the man lays aside all such claims. Therefore jealousy caused by this coquetry of women is unjust.

Conjugal love, however, is by its nature *intolerant*. Women occasionally ridicule this intolerance, but, as has already been mentioned above, they do so in jest; for if a husband were patient and indulgent when a stranger encroached upon his rights, this would result in his wife's contempt and also hatred toward such a husband.

The fact that fathers generally *spoil* their daughters and mothers their sons; and that among the latter the wildest son, if only he is daring, is usually spoiled by the mother, appears to have its cause in the prospect of each parent's needs *in case the other should die*; for if the wife dies before the husband, he can still have a mainstay in his oldest daughter, and if the wife loses her husband, then the grown-up, well-behaved son has the duty incumbent on him, and also the natural inclination within him, to honor her, to support her, and to make her life as a widow pleasant.

***

I have dwelt longer on this section of Characteristic than may seem proportionate to the other divisions of anthropology; but nature has also put into her economy here such a rich treasure of arrangements for her end, which is nothing less than the maintenance of the species, that [311] when the occasion arises for closer researches there will still be more than enough material, in its problems, to admire the wisdom of gradually developing natural predispositions and to use it for practical purposes.

C The character of the peoples

By the word *people* (*populus*) is meant a *multitude* of human beings united in a region, in so far as they constitute a *whole*. This multitude, or even the part of it that recognizes itself as united into a civil whole through common ancestry, is called a *nation* (*gens*). The part that exempts itself from these laws (the unruly crowd within this people) is called a *rabble* (*vulgus*),[a] whose illegal association is *the mob* (*agere per turbas*),[1] – conduct that excludes them from the quality of a citizen.

Hume thinks that if each individual in a nation is intent on assuming his own particular character (as with the English), the nation itself has no character.[2] It seems to me that he is mistaken; for affectation of a character is precisely the general character of the people to which he himself belongs, and it is contempt for all foreigners, particularly because the English believe that they alone can boast of a respectable constitution that combines civil freedom internally with power against outsiders.[3] – A character like this is *arrogant rudeness*, in contrast to the *politeness* that easily becomes familiar; it is obstinate behavior toward every other

---

[a] The abusive name *la canaille du peuple* probably has its origin in *canalicola*, an idler going to and fro along the canal in ancient Rome and teasing the crowd of working people (*cavillator et ridicularius, vid. Plautus, Curcul.*). [The terms *cavillator* and *ridicularius* do not appear in Plautus' *Curculio*, but rather in his *Miles Gloriosus* 3.1.47. See also his *Truculentus* 3.2.15–16, and Gellius, *Noctes Atticae* 4.20.3. Kant's etymology is also false. *Canaille* actually means "dog-people," and is derived from the Latin *canis* (dog) – Ed.]

[1] Trans.: acting like rabble. Quality: *Qualität*.

[2] Hume, in his essay "Of National Characters," writes: "the ENGLISH, of any people in the universe, have the least of a national character; unless this very singularity may pass for such" (in *Essays, Moral, Political, and Literary*, ed. Eugene F. Miller [Indianapolis: Liberty Press, 1987], p. 207). See also *Friedländer* 25: 630, *Pillau* 25: 832, *Mrongovius* 25: 1398, *Reflexion* 1113, 15: 496.

[3] *Macht gegen Außen.*

person from supposed self-sufficiency, where one believes that one has no need of anybody else and so can be excused from kindness toward other people.

Thus the two *most civilized* peoples on earth,[b] England and France, have contrasting characters, and perhaps chiefly because of this are in a [312] constant feud with each other. Also because of their innate character, of which the acquired and artificial character is only the result, England and France are perhaps the only peoples to which one can assign a definite and – as long as they do not become mixed by the violence of war[4] – unchangeable character. – That French has become the universal language *of conversation*, especially in the feminine world, and English the most widely used language *of commerce*,[c] especially among business people, probably lies in the difference in their continental and insular situation. However, as concerns their natural aptitude, what they actually have at present, and its formation by means of language, this must be derived from the innate character of the original people of their ancestry; but the documents for this are lacking. – In an anthropology from a pragmatic point of view, however, the only thing that matters to us is to present the character of both, as they are now, in some examples, and, as far as possible, systematically; which makes it possible to judge what each can expect from the other and how each could use the other to his own advantage.

Hereditary maxims, or those which have become, as it were, second nature through long usage, as well as those maxims grafted upon them, which express the sensibility of a people, are only so many risky attempts to classify[5] the *varieties* in the natural tendency of entire peoples, and

---

[b] It is understood that in this classification the German people is disregarded; for otherwise the praise of the author, who is German, would be self-praise.

[4] *Crossed out in H*: war [which, because of the difference in their natural predispositions, is difficult to avoid].

[c] The commercial spirit also shows certain modifications of its pride in the difference of tone used in bragging. The Englishman says: "The man is *worth* a million"; the Dutchman: "He *commands* a million"; the Frenchman: "He *has* a million."

[5] *Crossed out in H*: classify [The Frenchman characterizes himself to his advantage through his excellent talent <skill> and the propensity to consistently agreeable and philanthropic relations. The *Etranger* is, under this title, already under his protection. His liveliness makes him inclined to surprise, which can often be healthy, but more often <nevertheless> also neck-breaking, and he participates in all national pleasures or interests].

more empirically for geographers than according to principles of reason for philosophers.[d]

To claim that the kind of character a people will have depends entirely [313] on its form of government is an ungrounded assertion that explains nothing; for from where does the government itself get its particular character? – Climate and soil also cannot furnish the key here; for migrations of entire peoples have proven that they do not change their character as a result of their new place of residence; instead they merely adapt it to the circumstances, while language, type of occupation, and even type of dress always reveal traces of their ancestry, and consequently also their character. – – I shall sketch their portrait somewhat more from the side of their faults and deviations from the rule than from the more beautiful side (but, nevertheless, not in caricature); for, in addition to the fact that flattery *corrupts* while criticism *improves*, the critic offends less against the self-love of human beings when he merely confronts them all, without exception, with their faults than when, by praising some more and others less, he only stirs up the envy of those judged against one another.

1. *The French nation* is characterized among all others by its taste for conversation, with regard to which it is the model for all the rest. It is *courteous*, especially toward foreigners who visit France, even if it is now out of fashion to be *courtly*. The Frenchman is courteous, not because of interest, but rather because of taste's immediate need to talk with others. Since this taste particularly concerns association with women of high society, the language of ladies has become the common language of high society, and it is indisputable that an inclination of this kind must also have an influence on willingness in rendering services, helpful benevolence, and, gradually, on universal philanthropy according to principles. And so it must make such a people as a whole *lovable*.

---

[d] If the *Turks*, who call Christian Europe *Frankestan*, traveled in order to get to know human beings and their national character (which no people other than the European does, and which proves the limitedness in spirit of all others), they would perhaps divide the European people in the following way, according to the defects shown in its character: 1) The *land of fashion* (France). – 2) *The land of moods* (England). – 3) The *land of ancestry* (Spain). – 4) The *land of splendor* (Italy). – 5) *The land of titles* (Germany, together with Sweden and Denmark, as German peoples). – 6) The *land of lords* (Poland), where every citizen wants to be a lord but none of these lords, except him who is not a citizen, wants to be a subject. – – Russia and European Turkey, both largely of Asiatic ancestry, would lie outside Frankestan: the first is of *Slavic*, the other of *Arabic* origin, both are descended from two ancestral peoples who once extended their domination over a larger part of Europe than any other people, and they have fallen into the condition of a constitution of law without [313] freedom, where no one therefore is a citizen.

The other side of the coin is a *vivacity* that is not sufficiently kept in check by considered principles,[6] and to clear-sighted reason it is thoughtlessness not to allow certain forms to endure for long, when they have proved satisfactory, just because they are old or have been praised excessively; and it is an infectious *spirit of freedom*, which probably also [314] pulls reason itself into its play, and, in the relations of the people to the state, causes an enthusiasm that shakes everything and goes beyond all bounds. – The peculiarities of this people, sketched plainly[7] but nevertheless according to life, easily permit without further description the delineation of a whole merely through disconnected fragments jotted down, as materials for Characteristic.

The words *esprit* (instead of *bon sens*), *frivolité*, *galanterie*, *petit maître*, *coquette*, *étouderie*, *point d'honneur*, *bon ton*, *bureau d'esprit*, *bon mot*, *lettre de cachet*, and so forth, cannot easily be translated into other languages, because they denote more the peculiarity of the sensibility of the nation that uses them than the object that the thinking person[8] has in mind.

2. The *English people*. The ancient tribe of *Britons*[e] (a Celtic people) seem to have been human beings of a capable kind, but the immigrations of tribes of German and French peoples (for the brief presence of the Romans could leave no noticeable trace) have obliterated the originality of this people, as their mixed language proves. And since the insular situation of their land, which protects them fairly well against attacks from without and rather invites them to become aggressors, made them a powerful people of maritime commerce, they have a character that they have acquired for themselves when they actually have none by nature. Accordingly the character of the Englishman cannot signify anything other than the principle learned from early teaching and example, that he must make a character for himself, that is, affect to have one. For an inflexible disposition to stick to a voluntarily adopted principle and not to deviate from a certain rule (no matter which) gives a man the

---

[6] As Brandt notes, here Kant is describing the character of the French in light of the French Revolution, which began in 1789. See also Kant's more supportive remarks about the Revolution (and public reaction to it) in *The Conflict of the Faculties* 7: 85–86.

[7] *in schwarzer Kunst.*   [8] *der Denkende.*

[e] As Professor Büsch correctly writes it (after the word *britanni*, not *brittani*). [Johann Georg Büsch (1728–1800), professor of mathematics at the Hamburg Handelsakademie, author of many popular works in applied and commercial science. Külpe notes that he was not able to locate Büsch's dictum concerning the spelling of "Britons." – Ed.]

significance that one knows for certain what one has to expect from him, and he from others.

That this character is more directly opposed to that of the French people than to any other is evident from the fact that it renounces all amiability toward others, and indeed even among the English people, whereas amiability is the most prominent social quality of the French. The Englishman claims only respect, and by the way, each wants only to live as he pleases. – For his compatriots the Englishman establishes great, benevolent institutions, unheard of among all other peoples. – However, [315] the foreigner who has been driven to England's soil by fate and has fallen on hard times can die on the dunghill because he is not an Englishman, that is, not a human being.

But even in his own country the Englishman isolates himself when he pays for his own dinner. He prefers to eat alone in a separate room than at the *table d'hôte*, for the same money: for at the *table d'hôte*, some politeness is required. And abroad, for example, in France, where Englishmen travel only to proclaim all the roads and inns as abominable (like D. Sharp),[9] they gather in inns only for the sake of companionship among themselves. – But it is curious that while the French generally love the English nation and praise it respectfully, nevertheless the Englishman (who has never left his own country) generally hates and scorns the French. This is probably not due to rivalry among neighbors (for in this respect England considers itself indisputably superior to France), but to the commercial spirit in general, which makes the English merchants very unsociable in their assumption of high standing.[f] Since both peoples are close to each other with respect to their coasts and are separated only by a channel (which could very well be called a sea), their rivalry nevertheless causes in each of them a different kind of political character modified by their feud: *concern* on the one side and *hatred* on the other. These are the two forms of their incompatibility, of

---

[9] Kant spells the name "Scharp" – Külpe corrects it to "Sharp," referring readers to Dr. Samuel Sharp. See *Neues Hamburgisches Magazin* 2 (1767), pp. 259, 261. Sharp is called a "splenetic" doctor in *Das deutsche Museum* 1 (1786), p. 387.

[f] The commercial spirit itself is generally unsociable, like the aristocratic spirit. One *house* (as the merchant calls his establishment) is separated from another by its business, as one *castle* is separated from another by a drawbridge, and friendly relations without ceremony are hence proscribed, except with people under the *protection* of the house, who then, however, would not be regarded as members of it.

217

which one aims at *self-preservation*, the other at *domination*; however, in the contrary case[10] the aim is destruction of the other.

We can now formulate more briefly the characterization of the others, whose national peculiarity is derivable not so much from their different types of culture – as is for the most part so in the preceding two cases – as from the predispositions of their nature, which results from the mixture of their originally different tribes.

[316]   3. The *Spaniard*, who arose from the mixture of European with Arabian (Moorish) blood, displays in his public and private behavior a certain *solemnity*; and even toward superiors, to whom he is lawfully obedient, the peasant displays a consciousness of his own *dignity*. – The Spanish grandeur and the grandiloquence found even in their colloquial conversation point to a noble national pride. For this reason the familiar playfulness of the French is entirely repugnant to the Spaniard. He is moderate and wholeheartedly devoted to the laws, especially those of his ancient religion. – This gravity also does not hinder him from enjoying himself on days of amusement (for example, bringing in the harvest with song and dance), and when the *fandango* is fiddled on a summer evening, there is no lack of working people now at their leisure who dance to his music in the streets. – – This is his good side.

The worse side is: he does not learn from foreigners; does not travel in order to get to know other peoples;[g] remains centuries behind in the sciences; resists any reform; is proud of not having to work; is of a romantic temperament of spirit, as the bullfight shows; is cruel, as the former *Auto da Fé* proves; and shows in his taste an origin that is partly non-European.

4. The *Italian* unites French vivacity (gaiety) with Spanish seriousness (tenacity), and his aesthetic character is a taste that is linked with affect; just as the view from his Alps down into the charming valleys presents matter for courage on the one hand and quiet enjoyment on the other.

---

[10] *im entgegesetzten Falle.* Kant's meaning here is not clear. *Marginal note in H:* Russians and Poles are not capable of any autonomy. The former, because they want to be without absolute masters; the latter, because they all want to be masters.
French wit is superficial
Gondoliers and *Lazzaroni.*

[g] The limitation of spirit of all peoples who are not prompted by disinterested curiosity to get to know the outside world with their own eyes, still less to be transplanted there (as citizens of the world), is something characteristic of them, whereby the French, English, and Germans favorably differ from other peoples.

Temperament here is neither mixed nor unsteady (for then it would yield no character), rather it is a tuning of sensibility toward the feeling of the sublime, in so far as it is also compatible with the feeling of the beautiful. – His countenance manifests the strong play of his sensations, and his face is full of expression. The pleading of an Italian advocate before the bar is so full of affect that it is like a declamation on the stage.

Just as the Frenchman is preeminent in the taste for conversation, so is the Italian in the *taste for art*. The former prefers *private* amusements; the [317] latter, *public*: pompous pageantries, processions, great spectacles, carnivals, masquerades, the splendor of public buildings, pictures drawn with the brush or in mosaic, Roman antiquities in the grand style, in order to *see* and be seen in high society. However, along with these (let us not forget self-interest) the invention of *exchange, banks*, and the *lottery*. – – This is his good side; and it also extends to the liberty that the *gondolieri* and *lazzaroni*[11] can take toward those of high rank.

The worse side is: they converse, as Rousseau says,[12] in halls of splendor and sleep in rats' nests. Their *conversazioni* are like a stock exchange, where the lady of the house offers something tasty to a large social gathering, so that in wandering about they can share with each other the news of the day without even the necessity of friendship, and has supper with a chosen few from the group. – However, the *evil* side is knifings, bandits, assassins taking refuge in hallowed sanctuaries, neglect of duty by the police, and so forth; all of which is not so much to be blamed on the Romans as on their two-headed form of government. – However, these are accusations that I can by no means justify and which the English generally circulate, who approve of no constitution but their own.

5. The *Germans* are reputed to have a good character, that is to say, one of honesty and domesticity: qualities that are not suited to splendor. – Of all civilized peoples, the German submits most easily and permanently to the government under which he lives, and is most distant from the rage for innovation and opposition to the established order. His character is phlegm combined with understanding; he neither rationalizes about the

---

[11] Trans.: Neapolitan street loungers, lazybones.
[12] In Bk. II, Ch. 8 of *The Social Contract*, Rousseau writes: "In Madrid, they have superb reception rooms, but no windows that close and their bedrooms are like rat holes" (trans. Maurice Cranston [New York: Penguin, 1968], p. 128). Rousseau makes these remarks with reference to the Spaniards, but Kant applies them to the Italians. See also *Mrongovius* 25: 1405.

already established order nor thinks one up himself. At the same time, he is nevertheless the man of all countries and climates; he emigrates easily and is not passionately bound to his fatherland. But when he goes to a foreign country as a colonist, he soon contracts with his compatriots a kind of civil union that, by unity of language and, in part, also religion, settles him as part of a little clan, which under the higher authority distinguishes itself in a peaceful, moral condition, through industry, [318] cleanliness, and thrift, from settlements of all other peoples. – So goes the praise that even the English give the Germans in North America.

Since phlegm (taken in its good sense) is the temperament of cool reflection and perseverance in the pursuit of one's ends, together with endurance of the difficulties connected with the pursuit, one can expect as much from the talent of the German's correct understanding and profoundly reflective reason as from any other people capable of the highest culture; except in the department of wit and artistic taste, where he perhaps may not be equal to the French, English, and Italians. – – Now this is his good side, in what can be accomplished through continuous *industry*, and for which *genius*[h] is just not[13] required; the latter of which is also far less useful than German industriousness combined with the talent for sound understanding. – In his dealings with others, the German's character is modesty. More than any other people, he learns foreign languages, he is (as Robertson puts it)[14] a *wholesale dealer* in learning, and in the field of the sciences he is the first to get to the bottom of many things that are later utilized by others with much ado; he has no

---

[h] *Genius* is the talent for *discovering* that which cannot be taught or learned. One can certainly be taught by others how one should make good verses, but not how to make a good poem; for this must spring by itself from the author's nature. Therefore one cannot expect that a poem be made to order and procured as a product for a good price; rather it must be expected just like an inspiration of which the poet himself cannot say how he came by it, that is, from an occasional disposition, whose source is unknown to him (*scit genius, natale comes qui temperat astrum*). [Horace, *Epistles* 2.2.187. Trans.: The genius knows, that companion who rules our birth star – Ed.] – Genius, therefore flashes as a momentary phenomenon, appearing at intervals and then disappearing again; it is not a light that can be kindled at will and kept burning for as long as one pleases, but an explosive flash that a happy impulse of the spirit lures from the productive power of imagination.

[13] *Crossed out in H*: not [Genius is required as a talent for producing that which cannot be <demanded> acquired through learning from another, but which can only be acquired through one's own inventiveness, such things are the works of genuine poets xx].

[14] William Robertson (1721–1793), Scottish churchman and historian, author of the *History of Scotland during the Reigns of Queen Mary and King James VI* (1759) and other works. The exact source of Kant's citation is uncertain.

national pride, and is also too cosmopolitan to be deeply attached to his homeland. However, in his own country he is more hospitable to foreigners than any other nation (as Boswell admits);[15] he strictly disciplines his children toward propriety, just as, in accordance with his propensity to order and rule, he would rather submit to despotism than get mixed up in innovations (especially unauthorized reforms in government). – – This is his good side.

His unflattering side is his tendency to imitation and his low opinion of his own ability to be original (which is exactly the opposite of the defiant [319] Englishman's); however, in particular there is a certain mania for method that allows him to punctiliously classify other citizens not, for example, according to a principle of approximation to equality, but rather according to degrees of superiority and order of rank; and in this schema of rank he is inexhaustible in the invention of titles (*Edlen* and *Hochedlen*, *Wohl-* and *Hochwohl-* and *Hochgeboren*),[16] and thus servile out of mere pedantry. To be sure, all of this may be attributable to the form of the German constitution, but one should not overlook the fact that the origin of this pedantic form itself comes from the spirit of the nation and the natural propensity of the German to lay out a ladder between the one who is to rule down to the one who is to be ruled, each rung of which is marked with the degree of reputation proper to it. For he who has no occupation, and hence also no *title*, is, as they say, nothing. The state, which confers these titles, certainly yields a profit, but also, without paying attention to side effects, it stirs up demands of a different significance among the subjects, which must appear ridiculous to other peoples. In fact, this mania for punctiliousness and this need for methodical division, in order for a whole to be grasped under one concept, reveals the limitation of the German's innate talent.

***

Since *Russia* has *not yet* developed what is necessary for a definite concept of natural predispositions which lie ready in it; since *Poland* is

---

[15] James Boswell (1740–1795), Scottish writer, author of *The Life of Samuel Johnson* (1791). See p. 290 of the 1769 German translation of Boswell's *Account of Corsica, the Journal of a Tour to that Island, and Memoirs of Pascal Paoli* (Glasgow and London, 1768). See also *Parow* 25: 431, *Mrongovius* 25: 1408.

[16] The approximate English translations of these titles would be: Noble, Most Noble, The Honorable, The Most Honorable, The Right Honorable. *Marginal note in H*: Germans no originality in matters of spirit, rather imitation.

no longer at this stage; and since the nationals of European *Turkey never have* attained and *never will* attain what is necessary for the acquisition of a definite national character,[17] the sketch of them may rightly be passed over here.

Anyway, since the question here is about innate, natural character which, so to speak, lies in the blood mixture of the human being, not characteristics of nations that are acquired and *artificial* (or spoiled by too much artifice), one must therefore be very cautious in sketching them. In the character of the *Greeks* under the harsh oppression of the *Turks* and the not much lighter oppression of their own *Caloyers*,[18] their temperament (vivacity and thoughtlessness) has no more disappeared than has the structure of their bodies, their shape, and facial features. This character-[320] istic would, presumably, in fact reestablish itself if, by a happy turn of events, their form of religion and government would provide them the freedom to reestablish themselves. – Among another Christian people, the *Armenians*, a certain commercial spirit of a special kind prevails; they wander on foot from the borders of *China* all the way to *Cape Corso* on the coast of Guinea to carry on commerce. This indicates a separate origin of this reasonable and industrious people who, in a line from North-East to South-West, travel through almost the whole extent of the ancient continent and who know how to secure a peaceful reception by all the peoples they encounter. And it proves that their character is superior to the fickle and groveling character of the modern Greek, the first form of which we can no longer examine. – This much we can judge with probability: that the mixture of tribes (by extensive conquests), which gradually extinguishes their characters, is not beneficial to the human race – all so-called philanthropy notwithstanding.

---

[17] *ein bestimmter Volkscharakter.*

[18] The Caloyers are Greek Catholic monks belonging to the Order of St. Basil. Külpe lists the following remark from Jacob Friedrich von Bielfeld, *Erste Grundlinien der allgemeinen Gelehrsamkeit III* (1767), as Kant's source: "In this church [i.e., the Greek] there are ... monks (of the Order of St. Basil) who are called Caloyers, and who wear a black dress almost like the Benedictines" (p. 252).

D The character of the races

With regard to this subject I can refer to what Herr Privy Councilor *Girtanner*[1] has presented so beautifully and thoroughly in explanation and further development in his work (in accordance with my principles); I want only to make a further remark about *family kind*[2] and the varieties or modifications that can be observed in one and the same race.

Instead of *assimilation*, which nature intended in the melting together of different races, she has here made a law of exactly the opposite: namely in a people of the same race (for example, the white race), instead of allowing the formation of their characters constantly and progressively to approach one another in likeness – where ultimately only one and the same portrait would result, as in prints taken from the same copperplate – rather to diversify to infinity the characters of the same tribe and even of the same family in physical and mental traits. – It is true that nurses, in order to flatter one of the parents, say: "The child has this from the father, and that from the mother"; but if this were true, all forms of human generation would have been exhausted long ago, and since *fertility* [321] in matings is regenerated through the heterogeneity of individuals, reproduction would have been brought to a standstill. – So, for example, ash-colored hair (*cendrée*) does not come from the mixture of a brunette with a blond, but rather signifies a particular family kind. And nature has sufficient supply on hand so that she does not have to send, for want of

[1] Christoph Girtanner (1760–1800), *Über das Kantische Prinzip für Naturgeschichte* (Göttingen, 1796). In his Preface, Girtanner notes that his book is an explanation of Kant's ideas and a commentary on them. Girtanner was named Privy Councilor of Saxe-Meiningen (a duchy in Thuringia) in 1793.

[2] *Familienschlag.*

forms in reserve, a human being into the world who has already been there. Also, proximity of kinship notoriously results in infertility.[3]

---

[3] *Marginal note in H*: 1st Stage
  The human being is an animal created not merely for nature and instinct but also for fine art (*die freie Kunst*).
  2nd Stage
    Judgment of the Spaniards in Mexico.

E The character of the species

In order to indicate a character of a certain being's species, it is necessary that it be grasped under one concept with other species known to us. But also, the characteristic property (*proprietas*) by which they differ from each other has to be stated and used as a basis for distinguishing them. – But if we are comparing a kind of being that we know (**A**) with another kind of being that we do not know (**non-A**), then how can one expect or demand to indicate a character of the former when the middle term of the comparison (*tertium comparationis*) is missing to us? – The highest species concept may be that of a *terrestrial* rational being; however, we shall not be able to name its character because we have no knowledge of *non-terrestrial* rational beings that would enable us to indicate their characteristic property and so to characterize this terrestrial being among rational beings in general. – It seems, therefore, that the problem of indicating the character of the human species is absolutely insoluble, because the solution would have to be made through experience by means of the comparison of two *species* of rational being, but experience does not offer us this.[1]

---

[1] *Crossed out in H*: this. [The human being is conscious of himself not merely as an animal that can reason (*animal rationabile*), but he is also conscious, irrespective of his animality, of being a rational being (*animal rationale*); and in this quality he does not cognize himself through experience, for it <would> can never teach him the <objective> unconditional necessity <of the determination of his will> of what he is supposed to be. Rather, experience can only teach him empirically what he is or should be under empirical conditions, but with respect to himself the human being cognizes from pure reason (*a priori*) <the humanity also as a>; namely the ideal of humanity which, in comparison to him <with which he> as a human being through the frailties of his nature as limitations of this archetype, makes the character of his species recognizable and describable <and

Therefore, in order to assign the human being his class in the system of animate nature, nothing remains for us than to say that he has a character, which he himself creates, in so far as he is capable of perfecting himself according to ends that he himself adopts. By means of this the human being, as an animal endowed with the *capacity of reason* (*animal rationabile*), can make out of himself a *rational animal* (*animal rationale*) – [322] whereby he first *preserves* himself and his species; second, trains, instructs, and *educates* his species for domestic society; third, *governs* it as a systematic whole (arranged according to principles of reason) appropriate for society. But in comparison with the idea of possible rational beings on earth in general, the characteristic of the human species is this: that nature has planted in it the seed of *discord*, and has willed that its own reason bring *concord* out of this, or at least the constant approximation to it. It is true that in the *idea* concord is the **end**, but in *actuality* the former (discord) is the **means**, in nature's plan, of a supreme and, to us, inscrutable wisdom: to bring about the perfection of the human being through progressive culture, although with some sacrifice of his pleasures of life.

Among the living *inhabitants of the earth* the human being is markedly distinguished from all other living beings by his *technical* predisposition for manipulating things (mechanically joined with consciousness), by his *pragmatic* predisposition (to use other human beings skillfully for his purposes), and by the *moral* predisposition in his being (to treat himself and others according to the principle of freedom under laws). And any one of these three levels can by itself alone already distinguish the human being characteristically as opposed to the other inhabitants of the earth.

I The technical predisposition The questions whether the human being was originally destined to walk on four feet (as Moscati[2] proposed, perhaps merely as a thesis for a dissertation), or on two feet; – whether the gibbon, the orang-utan, the chimpanzee, and so on are destined

---

thus can show the pure character of his species>. However, in order to appreciate this character of his species, the comparison with a standard that can<not> be found anywhere else but in perfect humanity is necessary.]

[2] Pietro Moscati (1739–1824), Italian physician and natural scientist. See also Kant, *Review of Moscati's Work: On the Essential Physical Differences between the Structure of Animals and Human Beings* 2: 421–425.

[for this][3] (wherein Linné and Camper disagree with each other); – whether the human being is a herbivorous or (since he has a membranous stomach) a carnivorous animal; – whether, since he has neither claws nor fangs, consequently (without reason) no weapons, he is by nature a predator or a peaceable animal – – the answer to these questions is of no consequence. At any rate, this question could still be raised: whether the human being by nature is a *sociable* animal or a solitary one who shies away from his neighbors? The latter is the most probable.

A first human couple, already fully developed, put there by nature in the midst of food supplies, if not at the same time given a natural instinct that is nevertheless not present in us in our present natural state, is difficult to reconcile with nature's provision for the preservation of the species. The first human being would drown in the first pond he saw [323] before him, for swimming is already an art that one must learn; or he would eat poisonous roots and fruits and thus be in constant danger of dying. But if *nature* had *implanted* this instinct into the first human couple, how was it possible that they did not transmit it to their children; something that after all never happens now?

It is true that songbirds teach their young certain songs and pass them on by tradition, so that a bird taken from the nest while still blind and reared in isolation has no song after it is grown up. But where did the first song come from;[a] for it was not learned, and if it had arisen instinctively, why did the young not inherit it?

The characterization of the human being as a rational animal is already present in the form and organization of his *hand*, his *fingers*, and *fingertips*;

---

[3] The text is unclear here. Külpe suggests that "to walk on two feet" be added after "destined." Gregor inserts "to walk upright or on all fours" after "destined." Vorländer and Brandt, whom I have followed, suggest that "for this" (*dazu*) seems to be missing after "destined." Külpe also refers readers here to Christian Friedrich Ludwig, *Grundriss der Naturgeschichte der Menschenspecies* (Leipzig, 1796). In Sec. 2 ("Von den besonderen Unterschieden zwischen dem Menschen und den menschennähnlichsten Affen"), Ludwig discusses the views of Linné (Linnaeus), Camper, and Moscati as well.

[a] One can assume with Sir *Linné* the hypothesis for the archaeology of nature that from the universal ocean that covered the entire earth there first emerged an island below the equator, like a mountain, on which gradually developed all climatic degrees of warmth, from the heat on its lower shores to the arctic cold on its summit, together with the plants and animals appropriate to them. Concerning birds of all kinds, it is assumed that songbirds imitated the innate organic sounds of all different sorts of voices, and that each, so far as its throat permitted, banded together with others, whereby each species made its own particular song, which one bird later imparted through instruction to another (like a tradition). And one also observes that finches and nightingales in different countries also introduce some variety in their songs.

partly through their structure, partly through their sensitive feeling. By this means nature has made the human being not suited for one way of manipulating things but undetermined for every way, consequently suited for the use of reason; and thereby has indicated the technical predisposition, or the predisposition of skill, of his species as a *rational* animal.

II The pragmatic predisposition to become civilized through culture, particularly through the cultivation of social qualities, and the natural tendency of his species in social relations to come out of the crudity of mere personal force and to become a well-mannered (if not yet moral) being destined for concord, is now a higher step. – The human being is capable of, and in need of, an education in both instruction and training [324] (discipline). Now the question here is (with or against Rousseau)[4] whether the character of the human species, with respect to its natural predisposition, fares better in the *crudity* of its nature than with the *arts of culture*, where there is no end in sight? – First of all, it must be noted that with all other animals left to themselves, each individual reaches its complete vocation; however, with the human being only the *species*, at best,[5] reaches it; so that the human race can work its way up to its vocation only through *progress* in a series of innumerably many generations. To be sure, the goal always remains in prospect for him, but while the *tendency* to this final end can often be hindered, it can never be completely reversed.[6]

III The moral predisposition The question here is: whether the human being is *good* by nature, or *evil* by nature, or whether he is by nature equally susceptible to one or the other, depending on whether this or

---

[4] See Rousseau's *Discourse on the Arts and Sciences* (1750).   [5] *aber allenfalls nur die Gattung.*

[6] *Crossed out in H*: reversed [Now because the transition from the crude to the civilized condition is <unstoppable but also at the same time> not a leap but an imperceptible, progressive achievement of civilization, it is <although one can certainly point out epochs which> <first of all> as futile to warn against it as to stem the tide under the pretext that natural <evil and misfortune> as well as injustice will fall with violence directly out of Pandora's box with force on the unlucky world. <On the other hand> The quiet simplicity and contentedness (of the shepherd's life), which does not require much art <and> or applied skill, remains free. But this calculation of advantage with disadvantage is incorrect. For the growth of the number of human beings in the civilized condition constricts the scope of human intentions through war. And this <is> gives the progressive culture of the human race such a rich surplus over the loss, that the sum of virtues as well as joys of life always outweigh their opposites on the whole, and over the course of centuries they must promise a constantly growing advantage, since prudence seasoned by means of experience naturally knows how always to lead progress onto a better track.]

that formative hand falls on him (*cereus in vitium flecti etc.*).[7] In the latter case the *species* itself would have no character. – But this case is self-contradictory; for a being endowed with the power of practical reason and consciousness of freedom of his power of choice (a person) sees himself in this consciousness, even in the midst of the darkest representations, subject to a law of duty and to the feeling (which is then called moral feeling) that justice or injustice is done to him or, by him, to others.[8] Now this in itself is already the *intelligible* character of humanity as such, and in this respect the human being is *good* according to his innate predispositions (good by nature). But experience nevertheless also shows that in him there is a tendency actively to desire what is unlawful, even though he knows that it is unlawful; that is, a tendency to *evil*, which stirs as inevitably and as soon as he begins to make use of his freedom, and which can therefore be considered innate. Thus, according to his *sensible* character the human being must also be judged as evil (by nature). This is not self-contradictory if one is talking about the character of the *species*; for one can assume that its natural vocation consists in continual progress toward the better.

The sum total of pragmatic anthropology, in respect to the vocation of the human being and the Characteristic of his formation, is the following. The human being is destined by his reason to live in a society with human beings and in it to *cultivate* himself, to *civilize* himself, and to *moralize*

---

[7] Trans.: like wax to be molded toward evil.

[8] *Crossed out in H*: others. [Therefore one can also raise the question whether the human being *by nature* (that is, before he can think about the determining grounds of his free doing and forbearing, consequently before he can <represent> think of a law) could be called *good or evil*, which is to ask whether the human being is inclined to act according to principles, to give preference to the impulses of sensual stimulus, in contrast to the motives of the moral law, or whether there is in him an innate propensity, for which he must then be declared evil by nature. However, the human being inclined primarily toward evil cannot immediately be <made> declared to be an *evil human being*, for this same freedom of choice also makes it possible for reason to outweigh this propensity habitually through its maxims, though admittedly only through a <new> particular resolution for each act, <but not> without as it were making a persistent propensity toward the good take root.

In other words, whether he in the crudity of his condition has a greater propensity toward that which he realizes is evil than toward that which he realizes is good and therefore also, because it is good, recognizes: consequently <which also> here would be the character of the human species.

The stages of emerging from this crudity are: that the human being is cultivated, civilized, and eventually also moralized.]

Marginal note in H: The question of whether human nature is good or evil depends on the concept of what one calls evil. It is the propensity to desire what is impermissible, although one knows very well that it is wrong. The crying of a child, when one does not fulfill his wish, although it would be fulfilled just as little by anyone else, is malicious, and the same holds true with every craving to dominate others. – Why does a child cry at birth without shedding tears.

[325] himself by means of the arts and sciences. No matter how great his animal tendency may be to give himself over *passively* to the impulses of comfort and good living, which he calls happiness, he is still destined to make himself worthy of humanity by *actively* struggling with the obstacles that cling to him because of the crudity of his nature.

The human being must therefore be *educated* to the good; but he who is to educate him is on the other hand a human being who still lies in the crudity of nature and who is now supposed to bring about what he himself needs. Hence the continuous deviation from his vocation with the always-repeated returns to it. – Let us state the difficulties in the solution of this problem and the obstacles to solving it.

A

The first physical determination of this problem consists in the human being's impulse to preserve his species as an animal species. – But here already the natural phases of his development refuse to coincide with the civil phases. According to the *first*, the human being in his natural state, at least by his fifteenth year, is *driven* by the *sexual instinct*, and he is also *capable* of procreating and preserving his kind. According to the *second*, he can (on average) hardly venture upon it before his twentieth year. For even if, as a citizen of the world, the young man has the capacity early enough to satisfy his own inclination and his wife's; nevertheless, as a citizen of the state, he will not have the capacity for a long time to support his wife and children. – He must learn a trade, to bring in customers, in order to set up a household with his wife; but in the more refined classes of people his twenty-fifth year may well have passed before he is mature for his vocation. – Now with what does he fill up this interval of a forced and unnatural abstinence? Scarcely with anything else but vices.

B

The drive to acquire science, as a form of culture that ennobles humanity, has altogether no proportion to the life span of the species. The scholar, when he has advanced in culture to the point where he himself can broaden the field, is called away by death, and his place is taken by the mere beginner who, shortly before the end of his life, after he too has just taken one step forward, in turn relinquishes his place to another. – What [326] a mass of knowledge, what discoveries of new methods would now be on hand if an Archimedes, a Newton, or a Lavoisier[9] with their diligence and talent had been favored by nature with a hundred years of continuous life without decrease of vitality! But the progress of the species is always only fragmentary (according to time) and offers no guarantee against regression, with which it is always threatened by intervening revolutionary barbarism.[10]

C

The species seems to fare no better in achieving its vocation with respect to *happiness*, which man's nature constantly impels him to strive for; however, reason limits the condition of worthiness to be happy; that is, morality. – One certainly need not accept as his real opinion the hypochondriac (ill-humored) portrayal which *Rousseau* paints of the human species, when it ventures out of the state of nature, for a recommendation to reenter that state and return to the woods. By means of this picture he expressed our species' difficulty in walking the path of continuous approximation to its vocation. The portrayal is not a fabrication: – the experience of ancient and modern times must disconcert every thinking person and make him doubt whether our species will ever fare better.[11]

Rousseau wrote three works on the damage done to our species by 1) leaving nature for *culture*, which weakened our strength, 2) *civilization*, which caused inequality and mutual oppression, 3) presumed *moralization*, which brought about unnatural education and the deformation of our way of thinking. – These three works,[12] I maintain, which present the state of nature as a state of *innocence* (a paradise guarded against our return by the gatekeeper with a fiery sword), should serve his *Social Contract*, *Emile*, and

---

[9] Archimedes (287–212 BC), Greek mathematician, physicist, and inventor; Isaac Newton (1642–1727), English natural philosopher and mathematician; Antoine Laurent Lavoisier (1743–1794), French chemist and physicist, guillotined during the Reign of Terror.

[10] *durch dazwischen tretende staatsumwälzende Barbarei.*

[11] *Marginal notes in H*: [The prosecutor – lawyer and judge. The intermediary is he who is instructed to defend any matter, be it illusion or truth to him]

That there is a cosmopolitan disposition in the human species, even with all the wars, which gradually in the course of political matters wins the upper hand over the selfish predispositions of peoples.

[12] Presumably, the *Discourse on the Arts and Sciences* (1750), the *Discourse on the Origin of Inequality* (1754), and *Julie, ou la Nouvelle Héloïse* (1761).

Savoyard Vicar only as a guiding thread for finding our way out of the labyrinth of evil with which our species has surrounded itself by its own fault. – Rousseau did not really want the human being to *go* back to the state of nature, but rather to *look* back at it from the stage where he now [327] stands. He assumed that the human being is good *by nature* (as far as nature allows good to be transmitted), but good in a negative way; that is, he is not evil of his own accord and on purpose, but only in danger of being infected and ruined by evil or inept leaders and examples. Since, however, *good* human beings, who must themselves have been educated for this purpose, are necessary for moral education, and since there is probably not one among them who has no (innate or acquired) corruption in himself, the problem of moral education for our *species* remains unsolved even in the quality of the principle, not merely in degree, because an innate evil tendency in our species may be censured by common human reason, and perhaps also restrained, but it will thereby still not have been eradicated.

***

In a civil constitution, which is the highest degree of artificial improvement[13] of the human species' good predisposition to the final end of its vocation, *animality* still manifests itself earlier and, at bottom, more powerfully than pure *humanity*. Domestic animals are more useful to the human being than wild animals only because of *weakening*. The human being's self-will is always ready to break out in aversion toward his neighbor, and he always presses his claim to unconditional freedom; freedom not merely to be independent of others, but even to be master over other beings who by nature are equal to him – which one even notices already in the smallest child.[b] This is because nature within

---

[13] *der höchste Grad der künstlichen Steigerung.*

[b] The cry of a newborn child is not the sound of distress but rather of indignation and furious anger; not because something hurts him, but because something annoys him: presumably because he wants to move and his inability to do so feels like a fetter through which his freedom is taken away from him. – What could nature's intention be here in letting the child come into the world with loud cries which, *in the crude state of nature*, are extremely dangerous for himself and his mother? For a wolf or even a pig would thereby be lured to eat the child, if the mother is absent or exhausted from childbirth. However, no animal except the human being (as he is now) will *loudly announce* his existence at the moment of birth; which seems to have been so arranged by the wisdom of nature in order to preserve the species. One must therefore assume that in the first epoch of nature with respect to this class of animals (namely in the time of crudity), this crying of [328] the child at birth did not yet exist; and then only later a second epoch set in, when both parents had already reached the level of culture necessary for *domestic* life; without our knowing how, or through what contributing causes, nature brought about such a development. This remark leads

the human being strives to lead him from culture to morality, and not [328] (as reason prescribes) beginning with morality and its law, to lead him to a culture designed to be appropriate to morality. This inevitably establishes a perverted, inappropriate tendency: for example, when religious instruction, which necessarily should be a *moral culture*, begins with *historical* culture, which is merely the culture of memory, and tries in vain to deduce morality from it.

The education of the human race, taking its species as a *whole*, that is, *collectively* (*universorum*), not all of the individuals (*singulorum*), where the multitude does not yield a system but only an aggregate gathered together; and the tendency toward an envisaged civil constitution, which is to be based on the principle of freedom but at the same time on the principle of constraint in accordance with law: the human being expects these only from *Providence*; that is, from a wisdom that is not *his*, but which is still (through his own fault) an impotent *idea* of his own reason. – This education from above, I maintain, is salutary but harsh and stern in the cultivation of nature, which extends through great hardship and almost to the extinction of the entire race. It consists in bringing forth the *good* which the human being has not intended, but which continues to maintain itself once it is there, from *evil*, which is always internally at odds with itself. Providence signifies precisely the same wisdom that we observe with admiration in the preservation of a species of organized natural beings, constantly working toward its destruction and yet always being protected, without therefore assuming a higher principle in such provisions than we assume to be in use already in the preservation of plants and animals. – As for the rest, the human species should and *can* itself be the creator of its good fortune; however, that it *will* do so cannot be inferred *a priori* from what is known to us about its natural [329] predispositions, but only from experience and history, with expectation as well grounded as is necessary for us not to despair of its progress toward the better, but to promote its approach to this goal with all prudence and moral illumination (each to the best of his ability).

us far – for example, to the thought that upon major upheavals in nature this second epoch might be followed by a third, when an orang-utan or a chimpanzee developed the organs used for walking, handling objects, and speaking into the structure of a human being, whose innermost part contained an organ for the use of the understanding and which developed gradually through social culture.

One can therefore say that the first character of the human being is the capacity as a rational being to obtain a character as such for his own person as well as for the society in which nature has placed him. This capacity, however, presupposes an already favorable natural predisposition and a tendency to the good in him; for evil is really without character (since it carries within itself conflict with itself and permits no lasting principle in itself).[14]

The character of a living being is that which allows its vocation to be cognized in advance. – However, for the ends of nature one can assume as a principle that nature wants every creature to reach its vocation through the appropriate development of all predispositions of its nature, so that at least the species, if not every *individual*, fulfills nature's purpose. – With irrational animals this actually happens and is the wisdom of nature; however, with human beings only the species reaches it. We know of only one species of rational beings on earth; namely the human species, in which we also know only one natural tendency to this end; namely some day to bring about, by its own activity, the development of good out of evil. This is a prospect that can be expected with moral *certainty* (sufficient certainty for the duty of working toward this end), unless upheavals in nature suddenly cut it short. – For human beings are rational beings, to be sure malicious beings, but nevertheless ingenious beings who are also endowed with a moral predisposition. With the advance of culture they feel ever more strongly the ill which they selfishly inflict on one another; and since they see no other remedy for it than to subjugate the private interest (of the individual) to the public interest (of all united), they subjugate themselves, though reluctantly, to a discipline (of civil constraint). But in doing so they subjugate themselves only according to laws they themselves have given, and they feel themselves ennobled by this consciousness; namely of belonging to a species that is suited to the [330] vocation of the human being, as reason represents it to him in the ideal.[15]

---

[14] *Marginal note in H*: Quite different is the question, what one should do in order to furnish *conviction* for the moral law rather than just *entry*.

[15] *Marginal note in H*: The character of the species can only be drawn from history.

That the human species taken *collectively* possesses in itself a striving toward artistic skill through which the selfishness of all individuals (*singulorum*) works toward the happiness of all (*universorum*) by means of the moral predisposition.

Main features of the description of the human species' character

I The human being was not meant to belong to a herd, like cattle, but to a hive, like the bee. – *Necessity* to be a member of some civil society or other.

The simplest, least artificial way to establish such a society is to have one leader in this hive (monarchy). – But many such hives next to each other will soon attack each other like robber bees (war); not, however, as human beings do, in order to strengthen their own group by uniting with others – for here the comparison ends – but only to use by cunning or force *others'* industry *for themselves*. Each people seeks to strengthen itself through the subjugation of neighboring peoples, either from the desire to expand or the fear of being swallowed up by the other unless one beats him to it. Therefore civil or foreign war in our species, as great an evil as it may be, is yet at the same time the incentive to pass from the crude state of nature to the *civil* state. War is like a mechanical device of Providence, where to be sure the struggling forces injure each other through collision, but are nevertheless still regularly kept going for a long time through the push and pull of other incentives.

II *Freedom* and *law* (by which freedom is limited) are the two pivots around which civil legislation turns. – But in order for law to be effective and not an empty recommendation, a middle term[c] must be added; namely *force*, which, when connected with freedom, secures success for these principles. – Now one can conceive of four combinations of force with freedom and law:

A. Law and freedom without force (anarchy).
B. Law and force without freedom (despotism).
C. Force without freedom and law (barbarism). [331]
D. Force with freedom and law (republic).

The character of the species is that the human race as a whole has a natural tendency always to become better.

The species can be considered collectively as a whole or distributively as the logical unity of the concept of the human being.

The character of the species cannot be constituted historically through history alone. This is to be understood only of the human species as animal species. – It can be inferred from reason, provided that reason subjectively knows and modifies itself individually and in relation to others.

[c] By analogy with the *medius terminus* in a syllogism which, when connected with the subject and predicate of the judgment, yields the four syllogistic figures.

235

One sees that only the last combination deserves to be called a true civil constitution; by which, however, one does not have in view one of the three forms of state (democracy), but understands by *republic* only a state as such. And the old Brocardian dictum: *Salus civitatis* (not *civium*) *suprema lex esto*[16] does not mean that the physical well-being of the community (the *happiness* of the citizens) should serve as the supreme principle of the state constitution; for this well-being, which each individual depicts to himself according to his personal inclination in this way or that, is no good at all for an objective principle, which requires universality. The dictum says only that the *rational well-being*, the preservation of the *state constitution* once it exists, is the highest law of a civil society as such; for society endures only as a result of that constitution.[17]

The character of the species, as it is known from the experience of all ages and by all peoples, is this: that, taken collectively (the human race as one whole), it is a multitude of persons, existing successively and side by side, who cannot *do without* being together peacefully and yet cannot *avoid* constantly being objectionable to one another.[18] Consequently, they feel destined by nature to [develop], through mutual compulsion under laws that come from themselves, into a *cosmopolitan society* (*cosmopolitismus*) that is constantly threatened by disunion but generally progresses toward a coalition. In itself it is an unattainable idea, but not a constitutive principle (the principle of anticipating lasting peace amid the

---

[16] Trans.: The well-being of the state (not of the citizens) is the highest law. Compare Cicero, *De Legibus* 3.3: "Salus populi suprema lex esto" (the well-being of the people shall be the highest law). The version of the dictum cited by Kant can be traced to the collection of church laws compiled by Bishop Burchard ("Brocard" in French and Italian) of Worms (d. 1025). Most of the laws were formulated as proverbs.

[17] *Crossed out in H*: constitution. [Now regarding what belongs to a character of the human species, this is not gathered from history in the way that it shows other human beings in different times and in different lands. For with the mixture of good and evil, which they <themselves> display according to different occasional causes, sometimes the result would turn out favorably for them and sometimes unfavorably. Therefore the most extensive and most careful interpretation <according to> of history can give no safe teaching here. But to attempt the inner examination of how one is held together, and how one will be judged by <other> one's fellow human beings, *reveals* his character, which consists precisely in not *revealing* himself. And at least in the case of a negative semblance, he will deceive others to his advantage in their judgment concerning him. Therefore his character consists in the propensity to lie, which not only proves a lack of frankness, but also a lack of sincerity, which is the hereditary cancer of the human species. – And so the character of the species consists in the attempt not to allow character to be visible and to take each of these searching looks or investigations for affronts.]

[18] *die das friedliche Beisammensein nicht entbehren und dabei dennoch einander beständig widerwärtig zu sein nicht vermeiden können.*

most vigorous actions and reactions of human beings). Rather, it is only a regulative principle: to pursue this diligently as the vocation of the human race, not without grounded supposition[19] of a natural tendency toward it.

If one now asks whether the human species (which, when one thinks of it as a species of rational *beings on earth* in comparison with rational beings on other planets, as a multitude of creatures arising from one demiurge, can also be called a *race*) – whether, I say, it is to be regarded as a good or bad race, then I must confess that there is not much to boast about in it. Nevertheless, anyone who takes a look at human behavior not only in [332] ancient history but also in recent history will often be tempted to take the part of *Timon* the misanthropist in his judgment; but far more often, and more to the point, that of *Momus*,[20] and find foolishness rather than malice the most striking characteristic mark of our species. But since foolishness combined with a lineament of malice (which is then called folly) is not to be underestimated in the moral physiognomy of our species, it is already clear enough from the concealment of a good part of one's thoughts, which every prudent human being finds necessary,[21] that in our race everyone finds it advisable to be on his guard and not to allow others to view *completely* how he is. This already betrays the propensity of our species to be evil-minded toward one another.

It could well be that on some other planet there might be rational beings who could not think in any other way but aloud; that is, they could not have any thoughts that they did not at the same time *utter*, whether awake or dreaming, in the company of others or alone. What kind of behavior toward others would this produce, and how would it differ from that of our human species? Unless they were all *pure as angels*, it is inconceivable how they could live in peace together, how anyone could have any respect at all for anyone else, and how they could get on well together. – So it already belongs to the original composition of a human creature and to the concept of his species to explore the thoughts of others but to withhold one's own; a neat quality[22] which then does not fail

---

[19] *nicht ohne gegründete Vermuthung.*
[20] Timon of Athens, a famous misanthrope, was a semi-legendary character. Momus is the god of blame or censure. See, e.g., Plato, *Republic* 487a, Hesiod, *Theogony* 214.
[21] *Marginal note in H*: There could be beings who would not be able to think without at the same time speaking, therefore they could only think aloud. These beings would have an entirely different character than the human species.
[22] *saubere Eigenschaft.*

to progress gradually from *dissimulation* to *intentional deception* and finally to *lying*. This would then result in a caricature of our species that would warrant[d] not mere good-natured *laughter* at it but *contempt* for what constitutes its character, and the admission that this race of terrestrial rational beings deserves no honorable place among the (to us unknown)

[333] other rational beings – except that precisely this condemning judgment reveals a moral predisposition in us, an innate demand of reason, also to work against this propensity. So it presents the human species not as evil, but as a species of rational beings that strives among obstacles to rise out of evil in constant progress toward the good. In this its volition is generally good, but achievement is difficult because one cannot expect to reach the goal by the free agreement of *individuals*, but only by a progressive organization of citizens of the earth into and toward the species as a system that is cosmopolitically united.[23]

---

[d] Frederick II once asked the excellent *Sulzer*, whom he valued according to his merits and whom he had entrusted with the administration of the schools in Silesia, how things were going there. Sulzer replied, "They're beginning to go better, now that we have built on the principle (of Rousseau's) that the human being is good by nature." "Ah (said the king), *mon cher Sulzer, vous ne connaissez pas assez cette maudite race à laquelle nous appartenons.*" [Trans.: my dear Sulzer, you don't really know this wretched race to which we belong – Ed.] – It also belongs to the character of

[333] our species that, in striving toward a civil constitution, it also needs a discipline by religion, so that what cannot be achieved by *external* constraint can be brought about by *internal* constraint (the constraint of conscience). For the moral predisposition of the human being is used politically by legislators, a tendency that belongs to the character of the species. However, if morals do not precede religion in this discipline of the people, then religion makes itself lord over morals, and statutory religion becomes an instrument of state authority (politics) under *religious despots*: an evil that inevitably upsets and misguides character by governing it with *deception* (called statecraft). While *publicly* professing to be merely the first servant of the state, that great monarch could not conceal the contrary in his agonizing private confession, but he excused himself by attributing this corruption to the evil *race* called the human species. [Johann Georg Sulzer (1720–1779), aesthetician, member of the Berlin Academy of Sciences, translator of Hume's *Enquiry Concerning Human Understanding* (1756). See also Kant's reply to "a letter from the late excellent Sulzer" in the *Groundwork of the Metaphysics of Morals* 4: 410n. However, according to Külpe, Sulzer was never appointed administrator of the schools in Silesia, and only spoke personally with the King on one occasion. Kant's report of this alleged discussion perhaps comes from Christoph Friedrich Nicolai, *Anekdoten von König Friedrich II. Von Preussen*, 2nd ed. (1790) – Ed.]

[23] *in und zu der Gattung als einem System, das kosmopolitisch verbunden ist.*

Index

Index

Cambridge Texts in the History of Philosophy

Leibniz *New Essays on Human Understanding* (edited by Peter Remnant and Jonathan Bennett)

Lessing *Philosophical and Theological Writings* (edited by H. B. Nisbet)

Malebranche *Dialogues on Metaphysics and on Religion* (edited by Nicholas Jolley and David Scott)

Malebranche *The Search after Truth* (edited by Thomas M. Lennon and Paul J. Olscamp)

Medieval Islamic Philosophical Writings (edited by Muhammad Ali Khalidi)

Melanchthon *Orations on Philosophy and Education* (edited by Sachiko Kusukawa, translated by Christine Salazar)

Mendelssohn *Philosophical Writings* (edited by Daniel O. Dahlstrom)

Newton *Philosophical Writings* (edited by Andrew Janiak)

Nietzsche *The Antichrist, Ecce Homo, Twilight of the Idols and Other Writings* (edited by Aaron Ridley and Judith Norman)

Nietzsche *Beyond Good and Evil* (edited by Rolf-Peter Horstmann and Judith Norman)

Nietzsche *The Birth of Tragedy and Other Writings* (edited by Raymond Geuss and Ronald Speirs)

Nietzsche *Daybreak* (edited by Maudemarie Clark and Brian Leiter, translated by R. J. Hollingdale)

Nietzsche *The Gay Science* (edited by Bernard Williams, translated by Josefine Nauckhoff)

Nietzsche *Human, All Too Human* (translated by R. J. Hollingdale with an introduction by Richard Schacht)

Nietzsche *Untimely Meditations* (edited by Daniel Breazeale, translated by R. J. Hollingdale)

Nietzsche *Writings from the Late Notebooks* (edited by Rüdiger Bittner, translated by Kate Sturge)

Novalis *Fichte Studies* (edited by Jane Kneller)

Reinhold *Letters on the Kantian Philosophy* (edited by Karl Ameriks)

Schleiermacher *Hermeneutics and Criticism* (edited by Andrew Bowie)

Schleiermacher *Lectures on Philosophical Ethics* (edited by Robert Louden, translated by Louise Adey Huish)

Schleiermacher *On Religion: Speeches to its Cultured Despisers* (edited by Richard Crouter)

Schopenhauer *Prize Essay on the Freedom of the Will* (edited by Günter Zöller)

Sextus Empiricus *Against the Logicians* (edited by Richard Bett)

Sextus Empiricus *Outlines of Scepticism* (edited by Julia Annas and Jonathan Barnes)

Shaftesbury, *Characteristics of Men, Manners, Opinions, Times* (edited by Lawrence Klein)

Adam Smith, *The Theory of Moral Sentiments* (edited by Knud Haakonssen)

Voltaire *Treatise on Tolerance and Other Writings* (edited by Simon Harvey)